WAR BRIDES OF WORLD WAR II

Ellie Shukert is a veteran of the Army (1976–79), who served in Germany. She has a Master's degree in English and Creative Writing from San Francisco State University and lives in San Francisco, where she is busily raising a family.

Barbara Scibetta, the daughter of a career soldier who met and married her mother during the occupation in Germany, was reared in army camps in Germany and Italy before coming to the United States in 1963. She studied English literature at San Francisco University and lives in Pacifica, California, with her family. The women met while attending a course in "Problems of American Identity" and joined forces to write this book.

War Brides
OF WORLD WAR II

Elfrieda Berthiaume Shukert
Barbara Smith Scibetta

PENGUIN BOOKS

PENGUIN BOOKS
Published by the Penguin Group
Viking Penguin Inc., 40 West 23rd Street,
New York, New York 10010, U.S.A.
Penguin Books Ltd, 27 Wrights Lane,
London W8 5TZ, England
Penguin Books Australia Ltd, Ringwood,
Victoria, Australia
Penguin Books Canada Ltd, 2801 John Street,
Markham, Ontario, Canada L3R 1B4
Penguin Books (N.Z.) Ltd, 182–190 Wairau Road,
Auckland 10, New Zealand

Penguin Books Ltd, Registered Offices:
Harmondsworth, Middlesex, England

First published in the United States of America
by Presidio Press 1988
Published in Penguin Books 1989

1 3 5 7 9 10 8 6 4 2

LIBRARY OF CONGRESS CATALOGING IN PUBLICATION DATA
Shukert, Elfrieda Berthiaume.
War brides of World War II/ Elfrieda Berthiaume Shukert, Barbara Smith Scibetta.
p. cm.
Bibliography: p.
Includes index.
ISBN 0 14 01.1679 6 (pbk.)
1. World War, 1939–1945—Women.   2. Wives—United States—
History—20th century.   3. United States—Emigration and
immigration—History—20th century.   4. Women immigrants—United
States—History—20th century.   I. Scibetta, Barbara Smith.
II. Title.
[D810.W7S525   1989]
306.8'45'0973—dc19   88–28981

Printed in the United States of America
Set in Bembo

For all the war brides, especially our mothers,
Mary Grill Berthiaume and Else Dickel Smith.

In a war one has to love, if only to reassert that he's very much alive in the face of destruction. Whoever has loved in wartime takes part in a passionate reaffirmation of his life.

John Horne Burns, *The Gallery*

Contents

Acknowledgments

Heartfelt thanks to our husbands and families for their encouragement, for taking over the "Mommy" duties, and for generally going without to make it possible for us to work on this book. We also appreciate the early encouragement given by Dr. Judith Breen, Susan Harper, and Michael Rubin at San Francisco State University. Thanks also to Dr. David Reynolds of Christ's College, Cambridge, England, for leading us to the British Foreign Office Files; to James Mays for sharing his collection of newsclippings about the war bride transports from England; and to Fred Stindt for records of the *Lurline* voyages from Australia. Donald Zboray was an ardent correspondent who gave us valuable insight into the lives of wartime couples and military life. And thanks to Judy Yung and Jane Wilson for information regarding Chinese war brides.

Col. William Strobridge, Fort Point and Army Museum Association, showed an ongoing interest in the project, which reminded us of the role war brides played in shaping the character of today's military family. Mrs. Helen Thompson Colony of the American Red Cross, who accompanied numerous war brides on their journeys to the U.S. aboard the *Queen Mary*, gave generously of her time, memory, and energy. Peggy O'Hara of Canada kindly shared her research on American war brides. More thanks to Eva Moseley, Curator of Manuscripts at Radcliffe College, for recognizing the significance of the arrival and assimilation of the war brides and the need to record and preserve their histories.

We are also grateful to the many spouses of war brides and grooms, and to the children and parents who wrote and called to tell us about the experiences of war brides they loved, many of whom are now deceased. Among the many children of war brides whom we have befriended, with whom we enjoy a special camaraderie as the daughters of war brides, and whom we wish to thank, are Lois Battle, Velina Hasu Houston, Marilyn Hall, Elena Creef, Johanna Della Valle, and war bride niece Inga Dóra Björnsdóttir.

Introduction

Little attention has been paid to the unprecedented immigration of nearly one million foreign brides of U.S. servicemen, who came to the United States during and after World War II. Nearly every other facet of the war and its aftermath has been covered in thousands of volumes, but the experiences of these women and their impact on American society have been largely ignored. Historians generally place a higher importance on strategic and political events, and since this immigration was spread over a period of years, its impact was more cumulative than immediate.

Not since the last great wave of immigration in the 1920s had so many people, so many women in particular, come to America. Unlike their immigrant predecessors, they came, not to escape religious or political persecution or to improve their economic life, but primarily for the love of an American soldier.

It is not really surprising that so many women came to the U.S. from foreign countries as the brides of Americans, since sixteen million Americans were mobilized between 1939 and 1946 to take part in a world war which involved fifty-seven countries. Americans called to duty were primarily single men between the ages of eighteen and thirty. Although demobilization began shortly after hostilities ended, the postwar occupation lasted for many years.

Our estimate of one million World War II war brides, perhaps

75 percent of whom eventually entered the U.S., was arrived at by studying military documents, immigration tables, newspaper reports of arriving transports, and regional and local statistics. This figure is much higher than the usual estimate for war brides, since the American public is used to thinking of war brides as the 70,000 British women whose military-sponsored arrival in the U.S. during 1946 was highly publicized. War brides actually came from over fifty countries (see Appendix A), many through private sponsorship. During the war, 30,000 British war brides alone were transported secretly to the U.S. on a standby basis with POWs and wounded American soldiers. Between 1944 and 1950, 150,000 to 200,000 continental European women were known to have married American military personnel, and 50,000 to 100,000 couples were married in the Far East. Restrictive U.S. immigration and marriage laws often delayed marriages indefinitely, so some wartime brides did not travel to America for many years. Many thousands were deserted, others were widowed and remained in their own countries. Several thousand GIs decided to immigrate to their wives' homelands. All things considered, the estimate of one million overseas marriages between 1942 and 1952 is quite probable, although ultimately unverifiable.

For the purposes of our study, a war bride or groom is any foreign national who married an American member of the armed forces or an American civilian who was in a foreign country as a result of U.S. mobilization for World War II or as a result of the subsequent military occupation. Our study begins in 1942, when the first marriages took place in Great Britain and Australia, and continues through 1952, when Japanese war brides were allowed to enter the U.S. after the repeal of the Oriental Exclusion Act. Subjects are included whether or not they entered the U.S. during that time and whether or not they entered under the provisions of the War Brides Act or the Fiancées Act.

More than 2000 war brides from all fifty states contacted us over a five-year period after reading about our project in newspaper editorials and articles. These women, who come from all walks of life, represent the Allied and enemy countries from which war brides came in significant numbers.

As the daughters of war brides, we are intimately aware of the joy and pain so many of them experienced. As children we listened quietly when the neighborhood war brides congregated for a "kaf-feeklatsch" in the living room and shared their painful, funny, and revealing stories. Sometimes we eavesdropped on the tearful private conversations in the kitchen, too. We cried with our mothers when the airmail letters arrived, not often enough, from "home" across the sea, bringing happiness and a fresh wave of homesickness.

As adults we wanted to know more about the collective history of World War II war brides: Who were these women? What were the conditions of their courtships and marriages? How were they transported to the U.S., and what type of reception awaited them? What effect did this mass immigration have on American society?

We have not set out to write an academic history or a sociological study, but to document the history of the war brides, using their personal recollections along with archival material. Because circum-stances differed depending on whether the woman was from an Allied or enemy country, and on her race, we divided the book into four parts: I) English-speaking Allies—Great Britain, Australia, New Zealand; II) Europe—Liberators and Conquerors; III) The Far East—Victors and Vanquished; and IV) Into the Melting Pot, which covers the war brides' collective accomplishments.

When we began our research, we found that very little documen-tation exists on World War II war brides. What we did find were romantic novels and Hollywood films depicting stereotyped war brides: the spy, the opportunist, the naif, the femme fatale, the prostitute; or the dauntless partisan, allied agent, the loyal and submis-sive beauty. Magazines displayed provocative photos of foreign women and sensational newspaper articles of the postwar period depicted disappointed and abandoned brides. Eighty percent of over-seas marriages were projected to fail.

Instead, we found that 86 percent of the war brides who filled out our questionnaire have remained married. It would be difficult, however, to conclude that this is the success rate of these marriages in general, since war brides whose marriages failed may have been reluctant to contact us. Women who had a successful marriage were more likely to complete our questionnaire or agree to an interview. Some marriages, although they endured, were not necessarily happy, but it is our belief, based on this study, that by far the majority of these couples had no regrets. Reports that overseas marriages had a higher success rate than American marriages during the same war-time period would appear to be substantiated. The reasons, however, could vary; divorce was a more acceptable and accessible alternative for American women than for most foreign women during that time.

Because we believe that our country is strong due to its cultural diversity, we want to acknowledge these women who are often unaware themselves of their significant contributions to the social, economic, and cultural life of America. We hope that future researchers will be interested in continuing the study of war brides on a country-by-country basis, including those smaller nations underrepresented in this book due to lack of time and space and funds.

The Arthur and Elizabeth Schlesinger Library on the History of Women in America at Radcliffe College, Cambridge, Massachusetts, is the official repository for this project.

English-speaking Allies
Great Britain, Australia, New Zealand

Part One

Allies who needed permission to date: Lt. Theodore Wurm, U.S. 8th Air Force, carried his "Permission to Escort a Female Noncommissioned Member of Her Majesty's Forces" when he dated Betty Taylor, British WAAF. Ted's brother, Dick, on left. 1944.

BETTY TAYLOR WURM

Chapter 1

Hey Honey, How About a Date Tonight?

A few of us said we would wait for our lads to come home . . .
the wait was just too long, so one by one we started dating the
GIs.
—*Wynn Hill, Bocking, Essex, England*

Of the 2,000,000 GIs stationed in Great Britain or passing through to other destinations, more than 100,000 married British women during and just after World War II. In the Pacific, 16,000 of the 1,000,000 American servicemen married Australian and New Zealand women.[1]

Americans were welcomed by the British, Australians, and New Zealanders as allies who were desperately needed to help win the war against the Axis nations. A common language also bound the nations together. Few impediments presented themselves to the American soldier who wished to fraternize with the natives. Young women were eager to meet men their age, since so many of their own countrymen were fighting on foreign soil.

Beverley Schoonmaker, a war bride from Edinburgh, Scotland, attributes the attraction of the GIs to the fact that "they were *there*—all young Scottish men were gone into service. I worked in a city office with 92 girls, several elderly men, and one young man who was a conscientious objector!" "A few of us said we would wait for our lads to come home," said Wynn Hill of Bocking, Essex, England, but "the wait was just too long, so one by one we started dating the GIs."

Mrs. Elsie Curtin, wife of the Australian prime minister, stated that Australia looked favorably upon relationships between American men and Australian women. On a visit to the United States in April 1944, Mrs. Curtin told a *New York Times* reporter "there has been a larger proportion of females in the Australian population ever since the last war. Of a 7,000,000 population, only 2,800,000 are adult males." [2]

In May 1944, *Newsweek* reported that Australian war brides who had arrived in the U.S. felt no guilt regarding Australian men, charging that "the Aussies were far from lonely—they were marrying English and Canadian girls and in fact had populated their country with English girls after the last war." [3] British soldiers were busy marrying other nationals as well.

The happy-go-lucky attitude of so many of the GIs attracted war-weary women. After Joan Cater had lost her British air force boyfriend and her home in London had been bombed, requiring her evacuation to Baldock, Hertfordshire, she felt "any bright promise for future days had gone." The new GI presence raised her spirits:

I spied two Yanks in the churchyard sitting astride the old wooden tomb embellished with the gloomy words:

> Remember me as you pass by,
> As you are now so once was I,
> As I am now so you will be,
> Prepare thyself to follow me.

Its prophecy meant nothing to them. They had a gathering of children around them and were happily handing out the inevitable chewing gum and candy. I smiled at them, I couldn't help it.

Although attracted to GI nonchalance, at the same time Joan was repelled by their cocksure brashness:

Walking home from the office at 5:30 P.M., we would have to pass Americans leaning against the wall of their favorite pub, waiting for it to open, chewing gum, offering gum, and calling out such endearments as, "Hey Honey, how about a date tonight?" We passed on, noses in the air. The Americans were just too smart for words. I almost lost my equilibrium when one tall GI drawled, "Hey, see that tall brunette with the lovely legs? She's for me." My fingers holding my pocketbook itched to smash it in his face, as I walked on and past the owner of the voice.

Other young women enjoyed the attention and encouraged their flatterers, welcoming the possibility for adventure. Sheila Ochocki, another evacuee who returned to London alone at fourteen, said, "All I wanted by the time I was sixteen was to have fun and live. My emotions controlled my life, not good common sense. I was caught up in the hysteria of war."

Parents were especially concerned about youthful and reckless exuberance. Although American servicemen were welcomed as political allies, they weren't entirely accepted socially, especially by parents of marriageable women who feared that a romantic escapade might result in an unwanted pregnancy. Norman Longmate, author of *The G.I.'s: The Americans in Britain 1942–1945,* counts the number of unwanted wartime pregnancies in Great Britain in the tens of thousands.[4] If a daughter married a GI, parents feared they might never see her again or be able to come to her aid if she needed them. As one war bride put it, "Going to America then was like going to the moon!"

Molly Purse's mother warned her not to have anything to do with the Americans who were camped at Barnstaple, Devon. But one day Molly had trouble turning her horse to go into a side street, and a motorcycle screeched to a stop behind her. She "turned to see a handsome Tyrone Power-looking American grinning up at me and he said, 'Hi.' We saw each other often after that, and we continued to exchange smiles, Hi's and Hello's until a friend of my sister's introduced us and we started dating." Her mother's attitude changed after meeting Ken Ingersoll; she liked the young soldier and decided to rely on Molly's good judgment.

Although Wynn Hill knew her stepfather didn't ever want "Yanks" in his house, one day she and her mother found themselves unexpectedly entertaining two soldiers who had followed them home.

On Saturday my mother and I went to Braintree shopping. Mum bought a new tea kettle. (It was not wrapped, you had to take your own paper if you wanted something wrapped up in those war days.) We were on the bus going home and as usual it was crowded with GIs. One said to Mum, "Oh, you are going to make tea, Ma'am. May we have some?" Mum didn't know what to say but she smiled and said, "Of course you may." When we got off the bus we found two Americans following us across the road, through the garden gate and into the house for tea.

The Yanks were everywhere, often making a nuisance of themselves. Wynn remembers how they disrupted life in Bocking:

Our little village was surrounded by about a dozen airfields as the American GIs took over. They crowded our buses, bought up our bicycles, bought out our bakeries and anything they could that wasn't rationed. They mobbed our pubs, movies and dance halls. Many of them were loud and pushy; they called all the women "Ma'am" and yelled and whistled at the girls.

Attempts to ostracize American soldiers were not only futile, they could have a deleterious effect on community life. As the numbers of lonely and homesick GIs grew, so did the venereal disease rate. According to Longmate, "By December 1942, the number of cases in the United Kingdom had already risen by 70 percent since the start of the war," and the percentage continued to rise.[5] Joan Cater described what happened in Baldock, near London:

We were beginning to see an influx of women the like we had never seen before. We called them "camp followers," and "ladies of the night," and other more descriptive names. Most were far better dressed than the female population of Baldock.

We were in really short supply, thanks to rationing of clothes and material. Our stockings were terrible, the glorious silk hose of prewar days had vanished completely. We wore utility stockings of a cotton blend. Nylons were something read about in news from America. Makeup was nonexistent, unless you happened on a black market brand, and it was affordable. These strange girls had everything. Where they came from and where they lived was a mystery, and all of them had an American escort. The rise of venereal disease on the four air bases was alarming.

We were beginning to realize that under the brashness and puppy-like friendliness of the Americans were very homesick young men, put into a strange country with a deplorable climate that rained unexpectedly with cold dampness that penetrated to the marrow in the winter. They had left behind so much, the love of their families, the comforts of their homes, to face death as the war progressed into its third year.

The camp followers offered solace at a price. The American Red Cross in Hertfordshire decided something had to be done. Once a week the American Red Cross recreation centers on an airbase would hold a dance for the enlisted men but before the girls could attend they were to be handpicked by the leaders of the local Women's Volunteer Service. They had to be local girls of good standing and their identity known to the W.V.S. leader. The churches also cooperated. This way they felt the Americans would meet the less dubious types of English womanhood, and perhaps get a chance to sample English family life by being invited out to tea. The experiment worked superbly and slowly the camp followers disappeared to new pastures. I was one of the twenty girls from Baldock who went to the 8th Air Force base at Steeple Morden for the first Anglo-American dance held at the Red Cross Club.

We were transported to the base in a large GI truck escorted by two chaperones. We arrived at 8 P.M. and departed at 11 P.M. Our chaperones made sure that no one left the dance and everyone was on the truck before it took us back home.

That first dance was unforgettable. It was as though we had entered another world. Everything was sparkling new, not like our old Town Hall where we usually went, and the "Flying Eagles" band—such a collection of brass and drums, unlike our Town Hall five-piece band. The music blared loudly and the dancers were doing the Jitterbug with its collections of strange steps and athletic contortions.

I couldn't believe the diversity of the American men. Englishmen were more or less stamped in the same mold: blue eyes, brown hair, ruddy complexion. But the Americans! A

GI wearing a flower tucked behind his ear went by singing as he danced. His face with its dark eyes and curly hair made him look as if he had come from a painting of Renaissance Italy. There were Nordic types with broad cheekbones. The artist in me was fascinated by these young men whose ancestors were from all parts of Europe. I danced the slow dances and enjoyed asking, "Where are you from?" I loved the Boston accent, so similar to my own. I fell for the Southerner's broad "ah" for "a."

But for Joan, the refreshments made an even greater impression than the GIs.

It was the food—Food with a capital F. That was the crowning glory of that first Red Cross dance. Such food we had never seen before and some we had missed for three years. With one accord we ran across the floor to the buffet, leaving our partners, who couldn't understand why, and then after we had eaten and explained our partners piled our plates with extra food, macaroni salad, potato salad, cold meats, rolls, butter pickles, olives and chocolate cake.

Soon the Americans were invited into English homes for tea and they appeared brash no longer. They were like our brothers, sons, and the boys down the street. They loved their homeland and worshiped their families. They went to church with their English hosts and shared letters and photographs from home around their hosts' tiny living room fire. Noting the appalling shortages we were suffering, they brought nylons as gifts for the ladies, cigarettes or tobacco for the men, and sometimes food sent to them from their homes in America.

The presence of American servicemen in Great Britain, Australia, and New Zealand was so overwhelming that it became nearly impossible for local men to compete with them; GI affluence contrasted sharply with native austerity. Many war brides described the attractive American uniforms, which fit better and were of softer, better quality material. An English war bride thought:

British army uniforms were coarse and rough and had that British army material odor. Americans used after shave lotion which was unheard of for men—99 percent of the Americans had charming manners, with their "Yes Ma'am" and "Yes

Sir," helping little old ladies run to the bomb shelters (and also young ladies, too), very generous with their cigarettes, candy, etc., especially to the Moms and Pops.

The image of the GI grew to mythical proportions. A war bride from Southampton, England, described GIs as "all good looking, had fantastic sense of humor, seemed to have unlimited spending money, could obtain items that were rationed or unavailable, most were gentlemen at least to the second date, and they all had perfect teeth."

Yvonne Indelicato of Australia described the GIs as "well dressed, sent a girl flowers, candy, etc., were very family oriented and treated you like you were really someone special. The Aussies at a party like to go off with the other fellers in another room and leave the girls to themselves."

Many women also appreciated the fact that GIs were oblivious to the subtleties of speech denoting social class. Quicker to size up a woman by the shape of her ankles than by the lilt of her speech, they treated any woman they liked as someone special. But it soon became apparent that although they weren't class conscious, many were color conscious.

Mona Janise was seventeen years old when the first contingent of Americans, a company of black soldiers, arrived in Porthcawl, Wales.

We had dancing in the Pavilion five nights a week and when the black Americans arrived we girls danced with them and socialized with them just as we would if they had been white. We all had fun, but when the white Americans arrived, they were so appalled at us it was unbelievable, and the coloured were stopped from participating in many things, including not visiting certain hotels. Talk about sin in the Garden of Eden, we thought we had done something wrong but didn't know what. Those were the first and last blacks to be in our town.

Some white GIs kept a list of the names of women who'd danced with blacks and encouraged other whites not to dance with them. The army, still segregated at that time, instituted a "Blacks Tuesday–Whites Wednesday" policy for social events in Britain.[6]

In Australia, women who went to functions at Sydney's Booker T. Washington Leave Center for black GIs were sometimes beaten up as they left the dance hall. Other black servicemen's clubs in Townsville, Sydney, and Brisbane were subjected to harassment by Australians and Americans.[7]

Although racial incidents sometimes marred social gatherings, service clubs were tremendously popular during the war. Aside from being convenient places to meet other young people, to dance, and to enjoy refreshments, the music brought many visitors in. The presence of celebrities on American bases and in service clubs created a lot of excitement. Doris Hutchinson met her GI at a rhythm club in London:

> Jazz was very popular in England, more so I think than in America. We were purists who discussed every aspect of the music with the musicians. My husband once brought some of the musicians from "This is the Army" to the Club, and we had a great jam session. They loved the "Big Bands" and dancing.

Service clubs were opened all over Great Britain and Australia. Some of the smaller village halls and shops that served as clubs were called "doughnut dugouts," named after the ubiquitous doughnut served by the American Red Cross. By D-Day there were 265 American Red Cross clubs in operation in Britain. Rainbow Corner in London, where 300 couples could dance at one time, and hamburgers and sandwiches were offered all night, was the largest and best known of them all.[8] To keep out the camp followers, the Red Cross screened British women volunteers and issued photo ID cards to those found suitable. In Australia, admittance to social events planned by the U.S. military was by invitation only.

Comdr. Roy Stratton, who later married Monica Dickens, writer and great-granddaughter of Charles Dickens, recalled the dances held at the Drymen Arms for servicemen of the 20,000-man base near Glasgow, Scotland, when forces were building up for the assault in North Africa. "Women were invited from the city through the Red Cross. The servicemen would meet them at the gate. Some of the men hadn't seen a woman in three months."

Lalli Coppinger of London met her husband-to-be when she worked as a hostess at the American Red Cross's Washington Club, Mayfair, London, just off Piccadilly. "We were screened quite thoroughly . . . and supposed to circulate but not fraternize or leave the club together. Of course we broke this rule."

In Australia, most soldiers enjoyed the parties arranged for them in local homes even more than the entertainment in clubs. Many were already boarding with Australian families due to lack of barracks to house them. The pleasure park of Ballarat, Australia, was transformed into a camp for the U.S. Marines returned from Guadalcanal, and two Americans were billeted in every home in the city. Maj. Dale Heely met Isobel Boustead at a tea party in Ballarat. He asked her to play *Clair de Lune* by Debussy, which his mother liked to play. Isobel required the music for this, so he accompanied her to her home and became a frequent visitor from then on.

Couples who didn't meet at the clubs or parties met any number of ways. Hundreds of women literally bumped into American soldiers during the blackouts. Sybil Roberts of Ipswich, Suffolk, recalled that "during the blackouts, some GIs would use a flashlight (torch in English) to look at our legs. One night my slip fell down at that moment. I scooped it up and my girlfriend and I ran like mad to our bus stop." Although she didn't make a date with the mysterious torch bearer, she did meet a GI on a blind date. Frequent air raids forced them to spend much of their courtship in the family's air raid shelter in the backyard.

Betty McIntire of Melbourne, Australia, was walking in the streets of Sydney with her girlfriend during a blackout when they collided with their future husbands. "They were newly commissioned officers, just out of officer's school, on their first night in town." However, she suspects that they may have planned the whole thing, since "they had the advantage because there was a light behind us from an open doorway."

"The place that we met was Piccadilly, which was the hangout at that time for all the hookers," said Londoner Nita Blashaw. "It's been the joke in the family all these years that we're not sure if Dad got exactly what he was expecting that night, but he was certainly too much of a gentleman to show it!"

The train stations were also meeting places. Gloria Richards of Hull, England, met her GI while they were each on their way to visit a nearby city on different trains, when it was discovered that "there was a bomb on the tracks from the previous night's raids. The passengers all had to get out at a small depot to wait for a way to be cleared." Lillian Blanchard of Dartford, Kent, met her future husband at a railroad station. "My sister had a blind date," she explained. "I went along just for the ride. Paul also went along for the ride with his friend who was my sister's date. Paul and I dated from then on."

An army air corps major went to Auckland, New Zealand, on rest leave, intending to look up relatives. He found himself dating his attractive third cousin, Marjorie Miller. Before long, he proposed.

Common interest brought Marjorie Popple of Melbourne and Tony Schiappa together. Tony, an artist in civilian life, and some of the men in his outfit rented a studio where they could print and draw. When he met Marjorie, who lived just around the corner, and learned that she, too, was a commercial artist, he invited her to use the studio to paint whenever she wished.

While the discovery of a common interest could start up a romance, working side by side in the war effort brought others together. About half of the GI brides from Great Britain served in the armed forces of their country, often working alongside American troops. Comdr. Roy Stratton's office employed four members of the British WRENs who "had their own quarters and did bookkeeping for us."

When an officer wanted to date a noncommissioned officer, some red tape had to be dealt with, as in the case of Betty Taylor, WAAF, and Lt. Theodore Wurm, U.S. Air Corps. After signing a request for "Permission to Escort a Female Noncommissioned Member of Her Majesty's Forces" and acknowledging Betty as his fiancée, Lieutenant Wurm had to have his commanding officer give him permission in writing to be seen with her socially.

GIs often pitched in with the harvest during their off-duty hours and worked on farms with the Women's Land Army. Eighth Air Force Staff Sgt. Santo DiNaro came to Lily Vicky Blackmore's aid when she was trying to milk a temperamental cow on a farm in Eye, Suffolk. "The cow kicked when I tried to milk her. Santo came along and offered to hold her down." Lily Vicky says, "It was love at first sight."

Some couples met through the mail. Pen pals were popular during the war. A correspondence with a soldier could blossom into romance and even marriage, sight unseen. A woman from New South Wales, Australia, had a romance by mail with an American sailor and never saw him until she arrived in the U.S. as his fiancée:

My girlfriend was dating my husband's friend and they introduced us by mail. We tried many times to meet, but my being in the army and he being in the navy, we just didn't make it. We almost did once, missed each other by about ten minutes because the man on board ship thought he was Don Juan and never gave him the correct message.

A British sailor was destined to become a war groom as a result of his letters to an American girl in Atlanta, Georgia. Her girlfriend, who had been writing to a young man from New Zealand for a year, started the whole thing:

She let me read one of his letters one day and I just remarked how nice it was. I *did not* know she had sent my name to him and asked that he get someone to write me. She told me later that she told him I would be a good pen pal. He and some other sailor both wanted it so the New Zealander made them draw straws. You know who got the short one!! When I came home from my last year in school one day, I found this strange looking letter for me. Until this day, I remember how it started . . . "I have always wanted to write to an American girl. . . ."

A number of British soldiers stationed, training, and on leave in the U.S. fell in love with American women. Donald Rayner, a British sailor in the Royal Navy was sent to Baltimore, Maryland, in 1942 in connection with the Lend-Lease program. "I met my American wife in Baltimore on New Year's Eve 1942/43. We were married three weeks later and I sailed away to the invasions of Sicily and Italy as soon as the wedding was over."

Roy Ellis, a Royal Air Force pilot from Kent, England, who'd trained in Moose Jaw, Saskatchewan, Canada, met Rae Romano on the last day of a September 1944 leave at California's Hollywood Guild Canteen, where many stars had turned out to raise money for the armed forces entertainment:

My friend, Alan, and I had been talking to two girls, but they thought I was drunk (it was my British sense of humor), so we wandered off and as we stopped for something I heard these girls giggling and one girl say, "How are we going to get through?" and "Let's push." I turned round and said, "It's rude to push you know." More giggles and off they went. I thought to myself, I would like to know that girl. Luckily they came our way again and I stopped Rae, started a conversation and spent the rest of the evening with her. Alan and I were supposed to leave for Canada next morning, so I asked Rae for her address and phone number, but she didn't want to give it to me, as she said I wouldn't write. But I insisted.

Well, came the next day and we decided to stay over and see Rae and her friend that evening if we could. We were in luck, and we went to see Ken Murray's *Blackouts of 1944*. The next day we were off to Moose Jaw.

When the time came for a soldier to depart, sometimes quite abruptly, absence either ended the romance or simply made the heart grow fonder. Just how many hearts were yearning was reflected in the numerous romantic wartime songs about "meeting again," "remembering when," and "waiting." Radio requests for sentimental love songs outnumbered requests for the Big Band orchestral hits of the day. Time was precious for lovers who made the most of every minute that remained to them before one or both had to return to their ships or planes or stations to fight the war again. As one war bride told the authors, "I feel sorry for your generation; we knew what *romance* really *was!*"

Chapter 2

I Love You Truly

My parents offered John £3,000—now about $12,000—to go away.
—Peggy Klaren, Boonah, Queensland, Australia

Although there were many whirlwind romances, most GI brides overseas had been courted by or engaged to American servicemen for about a year, which was longer than the average courtship and engagement of American women who married during the war. This was due largely to restrictions imposed after many unfortunate British and Australian women, who married early in 1942, learned that their marriages were illegal because their GI husbands already had wives. Before military restrictions were imposed, some GIs used assumed names, intending to desert foreign wives.[1]

In April 1942, *Newsweek* reported "lightning marriages" in Australia as American troops arrived by the thousands. Just how many marriages had taken place by then was not revealed, since the figures might have indicated the distribution of forces to enemy intelligence. Australian bishops argued about the advisability of hasty alliances:

Church leaders, urging girls to think twice or oftener before wedding, have two fears—first, of a mutual matrimonial hangover when the troops are transferred, perhaps a few days after marriage; second, American citizenship and immigration laws, leading to a long postwar separation, with the wives unable to enter America.

Roman Catholic Archbishop Duhig of Brisbane finds no supporters for his proposal to ban such marriages. Sentiment alone is sufficient to kill any such plan. The Protestant clergy feel the government might as well pass a law against biology.[2]

Although the Australian government was concerned about the advisability of American-Australian marriages, members of Prime Minister Curtin's party generally had a favorable attitude. Thomas O. W. Brevner, New Zealand Consul in New York, told a *New York Times* reporter, "It's a jolly good thing. It brings us all closer together. There's nothing like a baby or two to break down international barriers."[3]

In June 1942, the U.S. War Department issued a regulation requiring personnel on duty in any foreign country or possession of the U.S. and in the Canal Zone to notify their commanding officers of their intention to marry at least two months in advance. In some cases, usually where the woman was pregnant, the waiting period was waived. The commanding officer, who had to approve the marriage application, was required to write a letter to the civil or ecclesiastical authority who was to conduct the marriage and to interview the potential bride. Any member of the U.S. armed forces who married in violation of these regulations was subject to court-martial.[4]

On the whole, the U.S. government discouraged servicemen from marrying, believing the single soldier, who was not distracted by family responsibilities, to be more valuable to the war effort.[5] It was believed that wartime marriages were unlikely to succeed, although an estimated 80 percent of the 8,000 marriages overseas during World War I were said to have worked out.[6] The complaints about the bureaucratic red tape one had to shuffle through to obtain permission to marry were endless and universal, although requirements varied in different locations. Policies were set by the headquarters commander in each theater of operations.[7]

The waiting period for the required interview varied greatly. Beverley Schoonmaker of Edinburgh, Scotland, was summoned to her fiancé's camp in Peterborough, England, one year after filing an application. Permission granted, she and her fiancé were finally married in November 1944.

On the other hand, a fiancée could also be given very short notice by a GI's commanding officer. Lily Vicky Blackmore was working in the fields wearing her Women's Land Army jodhpurs when she was told to report for her interview. "Here I was walking into his office smelling of manure!" Vicky apologized, only to have the officer reply, "It's much easier for me to recommend you as you are than if you'd walked in here smelling of cheap perfume."

Some war brides were subjected to a series of interviews. "I went to American Navy Headquarters in Sydney for many interviews," said Joyce Stone of Port Kembla, New South Wales, Australia, "and finally was told that I would be notified. Well, I never was, but when Woodie was discharged from the navy he was handed a stack of papers that indicated that the navy did approve and gave us permission to marry. Woodie laughed at them and said, 'I don't need your permission. I'm a civilian.'"

Papers could also be deliberately pigeonholed. Connie Baker of Kidderminster, Worcestershire, England, and Peter Hettinga applied to marry in 1942 but were not granted permission until December 1943. Connie recalls their difficulty:

> They tried to discourage us at first, because so many servicemen were marrying girls. They thought that they would later regret it, so they decided to put us to the test by transferring Peter to Ireland for 3 months. But then he got transferred back to England and when he asked if they ever sent the papers in for us to get married, they hadn't sent them but said, "So you still want to marry this girl. Well, I guess we'll just have to go ahead and send them in."

"One of my husband's officers remarked that he should wait until he was back in the U.S. and marry an American girl," remembered Peggy Harrah of Leicester, England. "My husband replied that it was a matter of opinion. He was then demoted in rank!"

The waiting period was often extended by a commander who was personally against marriage overseas. Marjorie Schiappa of Melbourne, Victoria, explained why she and her fiancé waited to submit their marriage application:

> The Commandant of American Forces [Melbourne] disapproved, and any Americans who got engaged or married with-

out permission were sent immediately to the war zone, New Guinea, etc. After two years this colonel was transferred—in two weeks all permissions were granted by the new colonel.

We had many obstacles placed in our path. The Red Cross personnel were supposed to investigate the girl's family until they refused to do this any longer. The men had to get letters from home stating that they had jobs to return to and how much savings they had in the bank and so on. Each requirement would be met, only to have another one imposed, and in war-time letters sometimes took months.

American Red Cross representatives were sent to interview prospective brides and bridegrooms and sometimes attempted to discourage marriages they thought inadvisable.[8] The Australian Red Cross refused to investigate the backgrounds of Australian women, saying that there was no means of reciprocation, since it wasn't possible to investigate an American serviceman's situation in the U.S.[9] In Isobel Boustead Heely's case, her minister wrote to the Episcopal bishop in her husband's hometown: "He made a full check of my husband's family, morals, status, etc., before my family gave their consent to our marriage, so I knew pretty well what I was coming to in America."

In November 1943, Senator Dorothy Tangney, the only woman in the Australian Senate, introduced a bill to extend the waiting period before marriage to six months. This bill, passed by the Australian Parliament in January 1944, required character references along with a doctor's certificate and a letter from the bride's parents. An American serviceman had to have the recommendation of his commanding officer and a "certificate of singleness."[10] Doreen Battle of Subiaco, Western Australia, married under the new provisions after having been courted for eleven months by a sailor who had been boarding in her parents' home:

After the new bill had been passed you waited for six months and if the papers were cleared and everything was OK then you could marry. I talked to the lawyer when we went back and he told me that since they had introduced this bill that only a third of the people ever came back to get married, so I guess it was a good bill because it stopped all these hasty marriages. They had time to think things over and then decided not to get married. It did save a lot of heartache.

Marriage application papers from 1944 belonging to Beryl Lynch of Perth, Western Australia, and a U.S. Navy torpedoman illustrate their long trail of red tape to the altar:

April 20	TM1c., USN, Colvin submitted application to marry 16 ½ year-old Beryl Lynch.
May 5	Commissioner of Police reported no record against Beryl Lynch.
May 29	Medical officer reported Colvin free of disease.
June 9	Chaplain reported he had investigated the couple and recommended approval. (Application had 11 attachments by then.)
June 11	Commanding Officer of Submarine Repair Unit recommended approval.
June 12	Commanding Officer of Task Group recommended approval.
June 16	P. G. Nichols, Commander of U.S. Naval Forces Western Australia, rejected application at that time with further consideration to be given if application was resubmitted after October 20.
October 16	Second request submitted. Same Unit Commander recommended approval.
October 21	R. W. Christie, Commander of U.S. Naval Forces, Western Australia, granted permission.
November 11	Married.

Soldiers who married without permission not only faced court-martial, they risked a quick transfer to a war zone. Those who couldn't obtain permission before the serviceman was shipped out would have to plan on getting married in the U.S. after the war, if and when transport could be obtained for fiancées.

Parental approval could be as difficult to obtain as military permission to marry. "My father tried to prevent my marriage by appealing to the British and American Embassies," recalled Dilys Lewis of

Newcastle-on-Tyne. "He was a retired British Naval Officer who had traveled the world many times and had seen some of the disastrous marriages of World War I. He never forgave me."

"Father thought it terrible to go to the colonies!" remembered Ann Brown of Weymouth, Dorset, whose father served in the British army. Another war bride's father "had visited in Chicago during the depression years, primarily to see if he wanted to immigrate with my mother and his seven children. He warned me I would not like it in America as it was nothing but hoodlums with guns or cowboys and Indians."

In Brisbane, Norma Jean Gardner could not even talk about her wedding plans with her father who "would not discuss it. He was too upset. He was very bitter. He would not attend my wedding, neither did any of my relatives. I gave up a very important career as a news reporter. It was very 'romantic' and made news because of my position." Peggy Gnech, of Boonah, Queensland, learned that her fiancé had been offered a bribe to break off their engagement. "My parents offered John £3,000—now about $12,000—to go away. Being one of only three girls in the whole family in the past three generations, and over thirty boys, my parents didn't mind my being married, it was moving to the U.S. that bothered them, and maybe never seeing me again." John Klaren didn't accept the money and they were married on July 19, 1943.

Some parents hoped that their American sons-in-law would settle in Australia and New Zealand rather than take their daughters away. Stella Frey of Sydney had parents who "loved Don but didn't want me to leave Australia. My mother felt that if I would wait till after the war that he would come back and settle there . . . I know he would not have returned for me. Home was pulling too strong for those boys."

If a GI said he was seeking a divorce from an American wife, it made the decision to pursue a relationship even more difficult. When Joan Cater of England said good-bye to her Eighth Air Force boyfriend, they promised to keep in touch, but Joan had reservations:

Marriage was in our minds, but there were obstacles. He said he was enduring an incompatible marriage. At that piece of news I said, "Oh no, not another one of those." We girls were always listening to tales of "My wife doesn't understand me, etc." As for marriage, I refused to give a definite answer. The U.S. was a long way from home. So we parted with promises to wait until he could settle things. I didn't tell my parents he was a married man contemplating divorce, as it would have been unthinkable.

A few GI brides had the wholehearted support of their families, some of whom wished to immigrate with them to the U.S. Maureen Roth, who met her GI at Rainbow Corner while she was an American Red Cross hostess, had her father's approval to marry: "I got a lot of support from my father who felt there was no future for young people in England—that I would have a much better life in America."

Monica Dickens, who was thirty-six when she married U.S. Navy Comdr. Roy Stratton, said her family "loved Roy—had been worried because I was 'on the shelf.' The Dickens family had many naval officers and looked forward to visits to America."

Parental acceptance was a great relief, but GI brides and fiancées also had to face the negative opinions of their colleagues and the press. In Potter's Bar, Middlesex, Jean Dahler found that "many women I worked with started horrible rumors about my relationship." Beverley Schoonmaker of Edinburgh recalled that "the local papers in Edinburg did not write articles in favour of the local girls marrying GIs. On the contrary, we were made to feel like traitors!"

Although the path to the altar was an obstacle course for many, it did not prevent record numbers of marriages from taking place in Great Britain during the spring of 1944, just before the invasion of Europe.[11] Sylvia Beaver and her GI made it to the altar just eight days before D-Day. She was an ambulance driver and had met her husband at a nearby American hospital which invited members of the Civil Defense to monthly parties. "His commanding officer informed me that we would have to wait at least three months for permission to marry, except in certain circumstances 'which of course do not apply to you???' Upon being assured I was not pregnant, he gave us his blessing." They were married on May 29, 1944, without her father's blessing, however. "My father was in the British Army and could not imagine his little girl dating one of those 'Damn Yanks,' let alone marrying one. However, once he met my fiancé, he was partly agreeable but not really enthusiastic. To make matters worse, all troops were confined to barracks because it was so close to D-Day . . . Franklin had to go AWOL for 24 hours for our wedding (with instructions from his CO not to get caught)." But he was caught, and Sylvia spent the rest of her wedding day with him in an army jail.

Marion Capek of Dartmouth, Devonshire, who also married shortly before D-Day, noted that the spring of 1944 was a time of particularly severe rationing:

Maids at the hospital where I worked saved teaspoonsful of flour and shortening every week until they had enough to bake us a small sponge cake. Cook at headquarters where Jim was gave me some icing for it—I bicycled 13 miles to mother's with it. Patients at the hospital gave pieces of ham and chicken from their farms. A cook stationed with Jim was transferred shortly before the wedding but he baked us a cake and drove 200 miles in a jeep to deliver it to us. The members of the church gathered with flowers and decorated the church—the nurses at the hospital gave up their days off so I could have three days of honeymoon. My parents gave me their coupons so I could buy a dress, stockings and shoes. We weren't allowed out of town so had to spend our honeymoon in a local hotel.

In view of the severe rationing, Catherine Roberts-Swauger's wedding a year earlier, in February 1943, was particularly opulent for the times. Catherine, although American born, had been adopted by a Welsh couple. Anxious to serve during the war, she became the only American in the British WAAF. Stationed in the south of England, near Tidworth, she met her GI at the ancestral home of the Duchess of Marlboro, which had been loaned to the American Red Cross for the duration of the war. Catherine related the events leading to her courtship and her spectacular wedding:

Mrs. Theodore Roosevelt, cousin of F.D.R., President of the United States, and wife of General Theodore Roosevelt, was Director of the American Red Cross in England and lived temporarily at Tidworth House. Five nights of the week, the ARC would invite the neighboring camps, both British and American, to enjoy a dance and coffee and good old American doughnuts. One night it would be the GIs and WAAFs. Another night it would be the GIs and the WRENs and another night the ATS. We all looked forward to this as we would be taken by lorry to Tidworth House and for a few carefree hours, forget the bloody war. It was at one of these dances in August 1942 that I met my future husband who had befriended Mrs. Roosevelt and the Duchess of Marlboro. In his spare time he used to help with various organizations of the ARC. So of course, when Mrs. Roosevelt heard of our engagement, she insisted on giving us a party at our next dance. Again, Mrs. Roosevelt and the Duchess insisted on giving us our wedding reception to be held at Tidworth House.

My bridesmaids were buddies stationed with me at Old Sarum. My family in Wales was kind in trying to collect enough coupons for me to have a traditional white wedding gown. We were married in the little church of St. Mary's on the grounds of Tidworth House. The uniforms of the United States on one side and the Air Force Blue of the Royal Air Force on the other. A young GI sang *Oh, Promise Me* and *I Love You Truly*.

After the ceremony, the Duchess and Mrs. Roosevelt led the way across the old oak-lined driveway to Tidworth House and there they had the most magnificent reception. I didn't think there was that much food left in the world. Dear, kind Mrs. Roosevelt had it all flown from the U.S.A. via M.A.T.S. and compliments of F.D.R. The traditional doughnut was right there on the head table. My three-tiered chocolate wedding cake was also flown in, compliments of my husband's unit. As we were ready to leave the "Boys from over there" and the girls in blue formed an arch and sang, *For He's a Jolly Good Fellow* and with a huge cry of "hip, hip, hooray!" we got into our ARC car and were taken to the nearby railroad station for a three-day honeymoon. Of course, the GIs, always full of fun and life, decided to precede in the jeeps with signs of "Just Married" trailing behind.

Others who didn't have as splendid a wedding and honeymoon as Catherine's surely thought theirs just as romantic. Wynn and Bill Hill found themselves without a roof over their heads on their honeymoon. Wynn explained:

When we arrived at our hotel we found it had suffered bomb damage; from our bathroom you could see the sky. We didn't care though, we were so much in love and we enjoyed every minute of our four days, sightseeing, going to the theatre and looking around the shops. The air raids were infrequent at that time, there was an occasional V-1 (doodlebug). Few of them got as far as London.

Although a record number of couples were honeymooning shortly before D-Day, a great many more weddings would have taken place if all the applications had been processed in time. A woman from Southall, Middlesex, said her fiancé's "commanding officer withheld our papers until he was in France after D-Day. It was a year before he could get back to England and we were able to get married."

Another English fiancée, who was separated from her GI for fifteen months after his departure on D-Day, recalled the torment she went through because her family disapproved of her decision to wait for him:

I wrote to him every day and didn't date. My mother told me I was a stupid young girl, that he was never coming back for me. He had been lonely and enjoyed my company while he was in England but when the war was over he would go back to America and marry "one of his own." She insisted he would never come back for me.

Around April 1945 I sent him pictures and in the return mail was an application for marriage. Mum was furious, said he had not even asked my father for permission and I was too young. However, I filled out the application and returned it. My aunt worked as a sorter in the post office at the time and she "sorted" my letter. Years later she told me that she had wanted to "lose" the letter, but her conscience wouldn't let her do it. We were married in August 1945.

One group of marriage applicants learned that weddings and honeymoons might forever be pipe dreams for them: interracial couples were almost always denied permission to marry. Donald Zboray, a former nurse with the Thirtieth General Hospital (who would later be assigned to process GI brides at Tidworth), recalled the case of Allen, a Chinese-American soldier who worked with

English-speaking Allies   29

him when he was a first sergeant with the Thirtieth in Manchester during 1943:

Allen started seeing Betty, a beautiful red-haired girl, and they fell in love. He was Chinese-American and came from Texas, where his father had a restaurant. Allen put his application in to be married to Betty. He ran into a lot of trouble. The CO and the Protestant chaplain were in agreement and presented a strong objection, based on racial lines, to any marriage between Allen and a "white" girl. They tried to influence Betty's family to put a stop to their wedding plans. They tried to enlist me, as Allen's boss and First Sergeant of the organization, to put pressure on Allen to give up his plans to marry Betty.

There were four of us who worked in the detachment office: Allen was a clerk, Jim a Sears Roebuck executive, and Mike was a newspaper man and my assistant. We all sat down and had a serious conference concerning what to do about Allen and his marriage plans.

I grilled Allen closely and asked him to level with us. My question was, "Are you in love with this girl really, truly and seriously?" Allen swore that he was and we all believed him. We decided we would help Allen marry Betty, regardless of what the army policies were, so we covered up for him when he wasn't on the base or literally snuck off base to be with Betty.

Betty's mother sided with Betty and Allen in their marriage plans, but her father took the same position as the chaplain and commanding officer. They did everything they could to sabotage the marriage, and Betty's mother and the guys in the detachment office did everything they could to offset the attempts by those who disapproved.

The date of the invasion of Europe was getting closer and closer. Large numbers of Americans were arriving all over England every day as part of the build-up. Our CO maneuvered Allen into the situation where he was transferred to a different base. This was a way of breaking up Allen and Betty's marriage plans. It didn't work, though, because even though all transfers were classified as secret, we told Betty where Allen was and she went there and they were eventually married in spite of all the efforts of the U.S. Army and prejudiced individuals at the time.

Black U.S. servicemen encountered extreme difficulty in obtaining permission to marry their fiancées. The results were dramatically publicized in an article entitled "U.S. Race Prejudice Dooms 1,000 British Babies," which appeared in Britain's *Reynold's News* in February 1947. The article was written by Ormus Davenport, an ex-GI who'd served in Britain with the Education Division:

> Scattered throughout Britain, in ones and twos, never more than a score in any one place, are somewhere between 700 and 1,000 children who are the helpless victims of racial intolerance and governmental red tape. They are the illegitimate half-caste babies born of the U.S. Negro servicemen and British girls. . . .
>
> Scores of young couples to whom these children were born were genuinely and legitimately in love. Some had acquired parental permission to wed—*but could not get the permission of the U.S. Army authorities!*
>
> There were a few couples who were able to marry secretly, but it was not easy for a coloured man to adopt an assumed name and get a birth certificate in order to marry. . . . When it was discovered that a particular Negro's social life had brought him to a request for marriage, or a pregnancy claim, the man was usually transferred to some other country or to a distant part of Britain.[12]

When this problem was brought to the attention of Prime Minister C. R. Attlee, concerned British government officials raised the matter with the U.S. Embassy. The embassy denied awareness "of any rule invoked by United States Army authorities that discriminated against officers or enlisted men by reason of their race, creed, or color."[13]

Meanwhile, overseas marriages in general were causing storms of protest as newspapers in the U.S. printed more and more articles about them. Marriageable American women were especially concerned. GIs were constantly quizzed by their families, friends, and former sweethearts about why they had chosen to marry women from foreign countries. One of the standard GI jokes was the one about the girl back home who wrote to her boyfriend overseas and asked him what those foreign women had that she didn't have. His answer: "Nothin', honey, but they got it over here!"

Some GIs said that foreign women catered more to them and wouldn't think of challenging them the way American women did. An article entitled "Not for this GI," by Victor Dallaire, a former correspondent for *The Stars and Stripes,* who had married an English woman, described American women as competitors, while women overseas

> seemed to be there for the sole purpose of being pleasant to the men. . . . While American women insist on a big share in the running of things, few European women want to be engineers, architects or bank presidents. They are mainly interested in the fundamental business of getting married, having children and making the best homes their means or conditions will allow. They feel that they can attain their goals by being easy on the nerves of their menfolk.[14]

This article prompted hundreds of angry replies from men and women, both American and foreign; 85 percent of the people who responded attacked Dallaire's views. A British woman was insulted by Dallaire's attempt to categorize foreign women as docile and subservient and held that the most respected women overseas were "the ones who fought fascism wherever they saw it." She was equally appalled by his negative attitude toward American women, as was a British man who'd married an American. He wrote that he admired American women who

> acted on their own initiative. They waited for no man to breathe the breath of life into them, to tell them what to do and what to say. . . . You never could grow bored with an American wife. Vexed, frantic, furious possibly, but never bored.[15]

Although a great many Americans resented the prospect of American soldiers returning to the U.S. with foreign brides, some citizens spoke up for the serviceman's right to marry. In a letter to the War Department, dated June 28, 1942, a woman from Vallejo, California, questioned

> the right of the War Department to deny any sound-bodied American his right to mate. Is not self-determination in marriage

one of the basic American liberties we uphold? Surely if our young men are prepared to offer their lives as shields for the protection of the rest of us, we should be equally prepared to care for their offspring when the need arises. America is made up of "foreigners," isn't it? [16]

Other American citizens argued that foreign women wanted to marry GIs simply to procure a better economic lifestyle than they had in their own countries. Some resented the expenditure of government funds to transport the GI brides. A woman from Cranston, Rhode Island, expressed her objection to overseas marriages in a letter to Senator Green in February 1946:

Why should the taxpayers of America be burdened with the expense of bringing all these foreigners here, to the detriment of our own girls, and *who* is responsible for appropriating funds for this project?

I worked in the local USO as a volunteer and heard the stories of hundreds of returnees, and know the unfortunate circumstances under which most of these foreign marriages took place, also that it was a slogan in Britain to "Nab a Yank, and go to America free." I talk to hundreds of people a week and have yet to hear anyone who is not thoroughly disgusted at the idea of we taxpayers being penalized to the tune of approximately $1,500 per bride when the government is staggering under such a heavy load as it is. All seem to agree that if the boys want to marry these girls they should finance their passage. Are our boys on duty overseas to become a prey to the women of all the nations where our troops are stationed, for the sole purpose of getting into this country and given an extra bonus of an ocean trip and spending money as well? [17]

Although many of the women who married GIs expected to have more opportunities in the U.S., they also hated to leave their own beloved families and countries realizing that they might never have an opportunity to return. "Someone asked me if I married an American just so I could get to America," recalled Doris Hutchinson. "My mind filled with thoughts of the sobbing when my parents and I said our good-byes!"

Elizabeth Roberts wrote about some of her feelings prior to

her departure to the U.S. in an article entitled "Diary of an Oxford G.I. Bride," for *The Oxford Mail,* in March 1946:

> Most of us are Englishwomen who love our country as much as anyone, are proud of all she stands for in the world, and are certainly not rushing off without so much as a backward glance.

> We married Americans I suppose for the same reason Englishmen have married girls from South Africa and Belgium, and Canadians have married Dutch girls, and Scotswomen have married soldiers from Poland. People just seem to be made like that, and maybe it's a good thing they are when you consider the international acrimony that goes on at high political levels.[18]

Looking back to that time, Elizabeth added:

> Other than my love for my husband, my primary motivation, above all others, in coming to the U.S. was a desire to have children and to bring them up in a land free from the constant threat of war.

> All my life I had heard of the horrors of World War I from my father (who was in the medical corps) and how we must never let that happen again. Then it did happen again, and it seemed to me that Europe had always been beset by war, and that if I had a chance to go to a more peaceful land, I should take it, no matter what it cost to tear up my roots and leave my homeland.

Reluctant to leave home, but anxious to join their husbands in the U.S., war brides gathered together for emotional support. Elizabeth joined the Forty-Eight Club, formed by war brides and fiancées in Oxford for sharing support and information about their prospective new country. "Forty-Eight" referred to the forty-eight states of the union at that time. Eleanor Roosevelt wrote the foreword to the club brochure, which included thumbnail biographies of its members.

On a visit to London, Mrs. Roosevelt was asked to speak to GI brides at the Rainbow Club. Thelma Gailey remembers:

> She was unbelievably gracious and really held our attention as she spoke. One of the brides asked her whether we would be allowed to participate in politics. She replied "yes" most

enthusiastically. I couldn't help wondering whether she would have been quite as encouraging had she known the person belonged to the Communist Party. However, I'm certain it would have been a gracious reply.

Jean Cornwell, also in the audience, remembers that Mrs. Roosevelt

gave us an insight into American life. At the close of the meeting we were handed the text of the song, *America*. She hoped that before too long we would be able to sing the song without the aid of the written word.

In 1953 my husband, children and I were returning from a trip to England and at the train station in New York I spied Mrs. Roosevelt walking toward the same train that we were to board. I wanted to run up and tell her that I learned the words of *America*—but naturally I didn't.

Hundreds of GI bride and fiancée clubs were formed all over Great Britain and also in Australia and New Zealand in an effort to prepare war brides for their new homeland. In Sydney, the Australian News and Information Service organized a club for wives and fiancées of American servicemen. Stella Frey recalled with pleasure the weekends spent learning what to expect in the U.S., and what it was hoped these war brides would remember about Australia:

Several weekends were spent in a large cottage sleeping on cots dormitory style on the verandas surrounding the house, up to thirty girls mostly in their teens, all alive with the spirit of adventure. Several different speakers spent time with us, giving us information and lessons on the country we planned to settle in and reviewing what we should be proud of as Australians. We were told that we were to be ambassadors for our homeland, something that I have never forgotten.

We had a botanist who took us for walks and told us what we had forgotten about the flora of the country. We had cooking lessons, lots of tests on our lessons. A black American army officer spoke to us about the racial problems in America.

The New Zealand Eagles Club was formed by Mrs. W. R. Nye, who advertised in the Wellington papers in September 1944, hoping to get a dozen or so wives and fiancées to meet at the YWCA. The fact that 250 women showed up is not surprising, since 637

New Zealanders had already married Americans by December 1943. The club soon had a membership of 400 wives and fiancées, ranging in age from seventeen to thirty-five. The original idea was for a combined club and mutual education society, with study groups on American history, literature, art, music, child psychology and education, cooking, dressmaking, and arts and crafts, but with the unexpected turnout, a more feasible plan of general lectures was adopted.[19]

With only a hundred immigrants from New Zealand allowed to enter the U.S. per year, for most of the women, joining their husbands and fiancés seemed a long way off. While waiting, they met for mutual support and information, sharing letters, books, and magazines from husbands, fiancés, and in-laws in the U.S. Earlier immigrants from New Zealand sent information from America, too. Those who were to travel to the U.S. early were to keep up correspondence with those still waiting. The wives and fiancées compared maps to see how far apart from each other they would be in America. Most of them agreed: "It sure is a big place!"

Chapter 3

We Want Ships!

Asked if they wished to travel like animals, the brides said anything would do.
—Life, *November 19, 1945*

"We want our husbands! We want ships!" shouted British wives of American servicemen as they picketed in front of the American embassy in Grosvenor Square in October 1945. Many of the women carried a baby under one arm and held a banner in the other which read "We demand transport" and "Forgotten GI Wives" or "Who will feed GI babies?" [1]

More GI brides demonstrated in Hyde Park for an hour and a half until uniformed and civilian crowds drowned them out. One heckler laughed and shouted: "Are you sure you're going to find him when you get out there?" [2]

Organized into a group called "The Married Women's Association," over 3,000 of these women got a hearing from Ambassador Winant's assistant at Caxton Hall on October 11, but they received little sympathy. They insisted that transport was available, since zoo animals had been transported to the U.S. When asked if they would like to be shipped like animals, the women replied that anything would do. [3] They were then reminded that shipment home of American troops took precedence over their transport, and the American War Department had promised that by the end of October troops would be released at the rate of a million a month.[4] After V-E Day, transportation had been virtually suspended in order to leave all available shipping space for redeployment of troops.

For women in Australia, the problem was more acute because of the great distances many had to travel to departure points. In December 1944, 1,200 war brides and children of U.S. Army and Navy personnel were stranded in Sydney when they were told it would take one to twelve months to get passage to the U.S. Some had travelled nearly 3,000 miles to reach Sydney and were without funds. Even with the necessary funds to return home, women would be detained in Sydney indefinitely, since railroad bookings were filled for months ahead.[5]

Members of the Australian Wives' Club were busy demonstrating for transport to the U.S. at MacArthur's headquarters in Brisbane, and others pursued Sir Thomas Gordon, the Australian representative of the British War Transport Ministry. In reply to the women pounding on his door, Sir Thomas said politely that he would do all he could for them. Their spokeswoman, Mrs. E. Hightower, said, "We will pester everyone who can help us." [6]

An ex-U.S. Navy man from Portland, Oregon, impatient to have his wife with him, wrote to Senator Morse accusing Matson shipping administrators (Matson was under the control of the War Department at this time) of delaying the arrival of Australian brides by giving precedence to businessmen requesting transport on the U.S.S. *Monterey* and the U.S.S. *Mariposa*.

I feel it is my duty to inform you of some of the repugnant conditions which are occurring (in the shelter of our State Department) at Brisbane, Australia, where thousands of American citizens, and their mothers, namely wives of ex-GIs, are becoming desperate due to unfulfilled promises and lack of financial assistance.

By what right have the Matson people, or anyone else for that matter, the power to take these businessmen in preference to the wives of we ex-GIs who gave everything we had for our country.

Marriage is a fragile thing, even when conditions are at their best. Faced with months of separation, it becomes delicate indeed. I believe I speak for every man when I say that we should have our wives and children with us as soon as it is humanly possible. Many of the brides have been waiting over two years for transport. Many have had their allowances cut off since their husbands were discharged and are in dire circumstances.[7]

Senator William R. Thom of Ohio, representing frustrated husbands demanding transport for overseas wives and American wives demanding the return of their husbands, wrote to the Honorable Robert P. Patterson, Secretary of War, on November 9, 1945, for clarification of U.S. policy:

I have called your Department on several occasions to inquire in behalf of soldiers of World War II as to whether they could bring their brides to the United States from foreign countries. Each time I was told specifically that the Army will not transport any brides until after the evacuation from Europe of all veterans entitled to discharge and of persons who were collected in concentration camps.

Despite this stated policy the newspapers are carrying pictures showing brides disembarking from troop transports.

I am receiving numerous letters protesting the use of shipping accommodations for wives when soldiers are awaiting transportation. The wives of these men residing in my District are up in arms about the matter.

Furthermore, I shall begin to receive letters from soldiers whom I advised that their wives were not eligible for accommodations on transports at this time.

Is the War Department in peacetime incapable of enforcing its orders and what right have the area commanders to disobey the policy issued in Washington?[8]

Newspaper stories depicting the arrival of war brides were appearing all over the country, even though a formal plan to transport them had not yet been approved by Congress. News reporters, no longer hampered by government restrictions on reporting ship movements once the war was over, were right at the docks when a new group of brides arrived.

Had it been known in 1945 that as many as 30,000 British and Australian women had already travelled to the U.S. on a standby basis on troop and hospital ships, the outrage of servicemen still waiting for their wives would have been even greater.[9] Wartime transports of GI brides were confidential, and passage was paid for by the bride or a sponsor, usually her husband or his family.

Molly Ingersoll of Barnstaple, North Devon, England, arrived on the *Queen Elizabeth* in October 1944. She was seven months pregnant.

The telegram came that I had waited a month for with orders to report to London prepared to sail for the U.S.A. On arrival at the Embassy I was handed the instructions below:

CONFIDENTIAL

Report to the United States Army Regional Transportation Office at EUSTON Station at 8:00 P.M. TUESDAY October 3. Baggage should be marked ONLY with the individual's NAME and CODE which is L 83. Proceed to the Station ALONE and tell NO ONE of the prospective journey. The approximate rail fare, first class, is 5.10.0. Destination will be given by the R.T.O. at EUSTON.

On arriving at Euston I was told that my port of embarkation was to be Greenock, Scotland. I left London on the night of the worst buzz bomb raid of the war and I was praying to get out alive as incendiary bombs were dropping everywhere.

On arrival in Glasgow and changing trains I lost my handbag with my passport, money and all my documents. It wasn't until the train arrived in Greenock that I discovered this, and I don't think I had ever felt so alone and upset in my life.

While everyone was hurrying through customs I was at this little Scotch railway station trying to get a very old and slow station master to put down his pipe and help me try to locate my purse. I can hear him to this day cranking an old telephone on the wall and shouting "kin you no hear me Jock?" Thank God for honest people, my handbag was located but it was doubtful it could be forwarded before the departure of the last tender to the boat that I was to sail on.

I went through customs with my luggage and was standing undecided what to do as the ropes were being cast off when a 6-foot American MP came running down the dock waving my handbag, so as I left my home shores, my tears were of joy instead of sorrow.

Wynn Hill's husband also insisted on her applying for early passage, saying she would be safer in the U.S. with his parents in New Jersey, since at that time the Germans were attacking England with V-2 rockets. Wynn was told at the American embassy to report to London at 10:00 A.M.:

They said there at Euston Station I would see a man wearing a black overcoat carrying a briefcase; he would tell me what to do.

I rushed home quickly and had to rinse out a few pieces of clothing. My mother helped me to dry them by the fire so we could press them and pack. I had bought a steamer trunk and had started putting things in ready. My mother and family were so sad to see me leave and were worried about me crossing the Atlantic during the war. I was on my way when the train stopped and we all had to get out and were taken in buses for a few miles before we could get on another train for London. A V-2 rocket had fallen on the railway line just ahead of us. A close call!

At Euston Station I saw the man in the black overcoat talking to some women. I could tell they were war brides, too. Quite a few of them had babies. I showed the man my papers; he took them, stamped my passport and gave me a boarding pass for a train to Liverpool.

We thought we would be sailing right away on the H.M.S. *Mauretania* but days kept going by and we were still in port. We kept busy by playing cards with the boys in the ship's hospital; there were many wounded on board.

Sunday morning, January 28, 1945, one week after boarding, the tugs were attached and we were being pulled out. I remember it was a bright sunny morning and Handel's *Largo* was being played over the loudspeakers. We were escorted out to sea and then we were on our own to zig-zag across the Atlantic. I hoped my parents had remembered to send a cable to Bill's parents saying, "Happy Birthday Dad." This was the way we planned to let them know I was on my way.

"I was told by American authorities that there would be a long waiting list after the war so that it would be best to go while the war was still in progress and not wait," recalled Marion Capek of

Dartmouth, Devonshire, England, who traveled to the U.S. aboard the *Mauretania* in February 1945:

There were 1,500 Canadian and U.S. wounded on board and 500 brides with 200 babies. Our cabin was crowded. We nurses helped with the wounded. There was also a USO troup on board, Mary Martin amongst them. Some days the babies were put on a big tarpaulin and left to crawl where they pleased, much to the delight of American soldiers. As there was still a U-boat threat at that time I wasn't allowed to notify anyone that I was on my way. All our written material had been censored in Bristol—even my Bible—and was put into sealed packages which we weren't allowed to open until we got to the U.S. There were no pressmen on the dock; it was all hush-hush because the war was still on. If I remember correctly, my fare was $600 one way.

"Only the officers aboard the *Queen Mary* were informed as to who we thirteen war brides were and why we were crossing," told Beryl Allen of Port Talbot, Wales, who arrived in the U.S. in December 1945. "We took our meals in the officers' dining room and had use of the officers' lounge. The second day out the rumors began: 'the girls on board were there for the entertainment of the officers.' Next day a printed news sheet explained who we were really."

One Australian war bride preferred to risk a voyage across the Pacific during wartime to the possibility of being left behind after the war. She took up residence with her GI's parents to remind him that she was part of the family now.

Isobel Heely, another Australian bride from Ballarat, got passage on the *Mariposa* in April 1944, shortly before the D-Day invasion:

We had to carry our life jackets everywhere we went and participate in drill each morning. The ship had to zig-zag across the Pacific to avoid being bombed from the air. We were to arrive in San Francisco in fifteen days, but when almost there orders were received to turn south and go through the Panama Canal and land in Boston. On board were German prisoners, Australian troops, air force. No one could leave the deck on which their cabin was. It was almost 6 weeks before we landed in Boston. The reason for the change, we later found, was to have the *Mariposa* and all other available ships ready to go to England and load up with troops for the June 6, 1944, invasion of Europe.

In September 1945, Marjorie Schiappa was given one week's notice in which to say all good-byes before boarding a train filled with war brides and babies from Western Australia:

We left Melbourne on gales of tears. Sat up two days and nights. Army trucks took us to the *Lurline* in Brisbane. It was filled with GIs. They were a little touchy at first, because some GIs and some Queensland brides had to be off-loaded.

We had ten women in a cabin for two. We were under military rule and not allowed on deck at night, etc. The GIs pulled our legs unmercifully, told us the captain had died and was in the freezer. Told us we had to have coupons for drinking water and so on. I believed all of it.

The *Lurline* arrived in San Francisco on September 24, and husbands waiting for brides who had been "bumped" in Brisbane were sorely disappointed. One had come all the way from Montana.

The number of passengers, both war brides and military, far exceeded the estimates given to the officers of the *Lurline* and exceeded its capacity as well. The chief purser's records gave an account of the calamity that occurred when 236 Brisbane war brides were off-loaded to make room for veterans:

150 of the cancelled war brides had stormed the Matson office and were creating a riot. A Capt. Buckley, who had the duty of contacting the cancelled Brisbane war brides and informing them that they could not sail, evidently had lost control of the situation. As they started to "close in" on him with screaming questions he passed the word to have Lt. Col. Jacobs come there at once and take over the situation. When Lt. Col. Jacobs arrived he gathered the 150 war brides in an assembly room in the building and explained the facts to them. Although they were very bitter, no further commotion resulted.

To further complicate matters, that day a message was received from General Headquarters in Manila by the U.S. Army in Brisbane stating that all Military personnel had first priority and to please amend. This message was also somehow received by a Mr. Mintern, Chargé d'Affaires of the American Legation at Canberra. He phoned the State Dept. in Washington. Evidently the Legation at Canberra took the stand that the war brides were all aboard and to remove them now and place Military personnel aboard would be close to complete chaos. He further stated that if the war brides were off-loaded by the U.S. Army he would not permit the vessel to sail until ordered to do so by the State Dept. in Washington. The situation was evidently clarified with the War Dept., as the brides remained aboard and the vessel was set to sail at 11:00 A.M. the next morning.[10]

Some resentment lingered aboard ship during the voyage. Army nurses asked to volunteer to help care for sick war brides and infants did so very reluctantly. The nurses were opposed to the transportation of war brides when there were so many enlisted men on various Pacific islands waiting to come home; they felt an allegiance to the ninety-seven enlisted men they saw off-loaded in Brisbane.

In October 1945, there were 60,000 known British war brides still awaiting transport, and roughly 6,000 Australians and New Zealanders anxious to be reunited with their American husbands.[11] Some couples had been separated for as long as two or three years. Many of the women were in financial distress and some were ill or had a husband who was hospitalized in the U.S. The long separations threatened marital ties, and many women had received the shocking news that they were being divorced.[12]

In the U.S., some former GIs applied for visas to enter Britain to be with their wives—many of whom were expecting babies—or to marry their fiancées. The British government refused, reasoning that allowing them to enter would only hinder the transportation program, requiring passage back to the U.S. for two rather than one. It was also feared that former American servicemen might seek employment in Britain and add to the returning British servicemen's difficulties in finding work.[13]

One fiancée from London remembers her disappointment when her American flyer experienced difficulty in obtaining a visa to return to England to marry her:

He was in one of the original Eagle Squadrons. He'd been with the RAF flying spitfires in the Battle of Britain and then transferred to the U.S. 8th Air Force when America came into the war. He was shot down over Berlin and taken prisoner in April 1944. After the war, while he was on survival leave in the U.S., he started trying to get back to London. Being on survival leave, he could not leave the States until it was over.

They would not issue him a passport. England was suffering an unemployment problem with the servicemen returning and wanting work so they would not let him have an entry visa until he deposited enough money in a British bank to cover his living there without needing to work. I thought this was rather stinky of them since he had spent three years fighting for them, however, this he did. It was $500 which at that time was quite a sum. After this was done he started trying to get a passage. Most of the liners were being dry docked for remodeling into luxury liners from troop ships and the waiting list was very long. Eventually he had every paper document and passage in order, only to find after driving to New York that there was a tug strike on and he could not get out to the ship awaiting in the harbour. At home I had been planning this wedding and had to postpone it twice before I finally had a cable saying that he was coming and would arrive on February 14, 1946, Valentine's Day, quite appropriate I felt.

Roy Ellis, RAF pilot, also encountered difficulty when he applied for a visa to visit Rae Romano in California, whom he had met on the last day of his leave at the Hollywood Canteen. They'd corresponded and wanted to see each other again. "The [U.S.] Consul wouldn't give me a visa, as he said I was going there to get married and it was against the law," Roy explained. "He was wrong at the time, but right in the end." Rae got passage to England and they were married there and eventually returned to California together.

As early as January 1945, a joint resolution had been introduced to Congress which authorized and directed the secretary of war to assign shipping space for GI brides. When passage of the resolution was sought in August, the secretary of war stated that he already had authority to move such traffic, but the priority was still to move troops and military patients home. He also noted that most of the ships had been converted for war service and were not suitable for transporting women and children. The secretary objected to the resolution and Congress did not pass it.[14]

Public and congressional pressure mounted as letters from American servicemen, their wives and fiancées, and foreign governments flooded the Capitol, demanding government-sponsored transport for these passengers by government or commercial means. The army published rules stating that dependents were to be subordinated to military requirements and to be controlled by overseas commanders. Army and navy, war shipping administration, and other American and foreign vessels were to be used in that order of preference. War brides were also to receive inland transportation to their future homes.[15]

On December 28, 1945, Public Law 271, known as the War Brides Act, was passed by Congress. The act facilitated the entry of alien spouses of U.S. servicemen by granting them nonquota status. This act remained in effect for three years, until December 28, 1948. Prior to its enactment, selective U.S. immigration laws limited the entry of immigrant aliens to a total of 150,000 a year. (See Appendix B.)

Public Law 271 did not apply to foreign spouses of civilian employees of the War and Navy Departments, nor did it cover members of the Merchant Marine. This law facilitated admission to the U.S. only for alien wives (or husbands) and minor children of U.S. citizens in active service or honorably discharged from service during World War II. Alien widows of American servicemen could not enter the U.S. free of the quota. If a petition had been filed before the serviceman's death, it was revoked.

The chief of transportation made a careful study of transportation needs and problems and by January 1946, the War Department announced that vessels would be made available to transport more than 60,000 war brides (and grooms) and children from Great Britain to America by the end of June 1946. Subsequent plans were also made to transport the brides waiting in Australia and New Zealand.[16]

About thirty vessels, mostly army troopships and hospital ships, were designated for this unprecedented movement. This "family fleet" included the *Queen Elizabeth,* the *Argentina,* the *Santa Paula,* the *John Ericsson,* and the *Alexander.* The *Queen Mary* was also designated to carry GI brides to America and, because of her capacity to carry up to 2,500 passengers and her quick turnaround time, she played an important role in the undertaking. Each ship carried from two to four army doctors, five or more nurses, and a detachment of WACs, Red Cross personnel, enlisted men, stewardesses, and matrons. Among the ships used to transport brides from Australia were the *Mariposa*, the *Monterey*, the *Fred C. Ainsworth*, the *Lurline*, and the *Marine Phoenix*.

A priority system was established to decide who would have precedence when the bookings were made. No limitations of grade were to be imposed on those eligible to claim transportation for dependents. The Military Appropriations Act of 1945 provided that dependents of military and civilian personnel outside the continental limits of the U.S. could be transported prior to relief of such personnel from their overseas stations. Dependents included wives, husbands, and children of military personnel, Red Cross personnel, and full-time civilian employees of the War Department or army. This directive covered all personnel who had been or were on duty outside the continental U.S. since September 1939. Personnel who had been separated from service were eligible for dependent transportation if discharged honorably. Fiancées who had obtained a quota number were to be granted a priority, although not a very high one.

Top priorities were granted to dependents of personnel above the fourth enlisted grade; to dependents of personnel who had already been placed on orders to the U.S.; and to wives of men who had been POWs, men who had been wounded in action, or men who were hospitalized in the U.S. Applications for transportation were processed in the order received, once all other requirements for entry into the U.S. had been met.[17]

A GI bride required a visa for admission to the U.S. along with her husband's sworn affidavit of support, indicating the amount of his salary, bank deposits, insurance, and other financial resources. British women were only allowed to take £10 in British money. A statement from her husband's commanding officer confirming the information in the affidavit was also necessary. If she was travelling ahead of her husband, she needed documentary evidence from his relatives stating that they were willing and able to receive her into their home. The GI bride also had to present her passport and two copies of her birth certificate, two copies of her police record if she had one, her original marriage certificate, her discharge papers if she'd served in the military, and evidence showing that on arrival in the U.S. she would have a railroad ticket or enough money to buy one. She also needed $10.00 to cover her visa fee.

War brides and fiancées who attempted to reach America without military sponsorship risked being turned back by immigration authorities. On arrival at LaGuardia Airport in New York, one English woman was detained and eventually sent back to Britain. She had obtained a visa to enter the U.S. after a prolonged medical examination by American authorities in England who had declared themselves satisfied with her health, although she had formerly suffered from tuberculosis, which had been arrested. A letter to the parliamentary under secretary of state at Downing Street, London, described her plight:

> On arrival at LaGuardia airport, New York, she admitted in reply to questioning that she had had tuberculosis and was sent to Ellis Island. Here she again was medically examined and treated in the main as a prisoner. Her fiancé took legal advice and appealed to his Veteran Society but to no effect.
>
> When Miss W. was informed that she would not be admitted to the United States she asked to be sent home but still further delays occurred owing to the loss of some of her papers. Finally, after 2½ months on Ellis Island, she was sent back to this country, having been told that her fare would be refunded.
>
> She reached this country on September 12, 1946, and has been to see the American Consul. She is now told, however, that the refund of her fare should have been made on Ellis Island.[18]

Brides and fiancées of nonwhite American servicemen soon learned that their applications for visas and transport to the U.S. were not being handled according to the usual priority rules. They were discouraged from applying for visas because the laws in a majority of states did not recognize marriages contracted between persons of different races as valid, regardless of whether the marriage was valid where contracted.[19] If their existing marriage or intentions to marry were not going to be recognized in the U.S., then they had to apply individually for entrance on a quota basis, which could have extended their wait up to ten years.

U.S. immigration laws prohibited the admission of aliens who were ineligible for citizenship or who might become public charges. Employees of the visa section of the U.S. Immigration Department warned women married to or planning to marry Americans of another race that they could be refused visas, since their intention to marry or cohabit with colored men could result in their becoming public charges as a result of conviction and imprisonment under the miscegenation laws of some states.

A public complaint was made declaring that 2,000 British wives of black American servicemen had been prevented from leaving Britain to join their husbands in America. Russian newspapers quickly picked up on this when they were cited for refusal to allow the Russian wives of British and American ex-servicemen to join their husbands.[20] A reply from the American Foreign Office stated:

> To exonerate ourselves entirely we should have to quote the U.S. regulations, but these can hardly be considered consonant with the rights of man and human liberties, and it would obviously be unwise to embarrass the U.S. by bringing them into the limelight more than necessary.[21]

Regulations did not always prevent determined wives and fiancées from joining their husbands and intended husbands, as in the case of Miss G. of Britain, who "obtained an immigration visa, reached the States and, despite repeated warnings, persisted in cohabitating with her fiancé and was subsequently jailed." [22]

Those who were fortunate enough to be going to the U.S. under what became known as "Operation Diaper Run" found that the transportation program in Britain was threatened by a manpower shortage just as it was getting underway in January 1946. American military personnel who were operating staging areas were slated for redeployment, and they protested the delay that would be caused by the processing of war brides and their babies. Another 4,000 American soldiers sent cables to President Truman and to American senators and congressmen as well as to newspaper columnists, such as Walter Winchell and Drew Pearson, protesting the shipment of brides ahead of them when they'd served their obligatory thirty months overseas.[23]

A large military area at Tidworth, Southampton, England, with a capacity of 3,600 persons, was developed as an assembly point where the war brides and babies could be processed and then shipped to the U.S. Early manpower estimates to oversee the operation were reduced from 1,500 soldiers to 70 officers and 850 to 900 enlisted men. Arrangements were made to replace some American military personnel with British service personnel and clerical workers, and also with Italian and German prisoners of war.

Hundreds of women from all over Britain began a procession to Tidworth. They boarded railcars, one dubbed "War Brides Express," or were herded onto army trucks. Over and over they said their good-byes and wrenched themselves from their families and friends.

Lily Vicky DiNaro, now married to Santo, picked up her twin sons and sensed her father's apprehension that he would never see her or them again, while her mother, cheerfully optimistic, said, "You'll be back." Her brother left for work earlier than usual that day because he couldn't bear to say good-bye. A neighbor offered to take her to Waterloo Station in a taxi since no one in the family had any petrol to drive her there. On the way, Vicky panicked and kept saying, "Stop, I'm going back!" but the neighbor urged the driver on. "I wouldn't have made it without her."

"Since I have matured I have come to realize what a tremendous amount of courage it took for my father to embrace me on the Bristol Railway platform for possibly the last time in his life," recalled Mary Coffman of Bristol. "People did not fly back and forth between America and Europe like they do today."

In London, Maureen Roth's father "broke down and cried— I'd never seen him cry—and said if I were unhappy he'd send me a ticket to return, quite a promise since he was making £8.00 a week at the time."

"My parents, relatives, and friends came to Charing Cross Station to see me aboard the boat train," recalled Joan Cater:

> The moment is a blur in my memory of thankfulness for a bouquet of yellow roses handed me by a friend, of a gentle hug and kiss from my father and my eyes filling with tears and my voice faltering as the familiar faces faded from view as the train moved out of the station. I shed loads of tears behind a magazine, but someone as they passed my seat gave my shoulder a gentle squeeze.

War brides journeyed to Tidworth camp with a mixture of excitement and apprehension. Mary Coffman's trip started out on an optimistic note, which lasted only until her arrival at Tidworth:

There I was bag, baggage, and baby starting on the most important journey of my life. At the nearest railway station to Tidworth we were met by U.S. soldiers who were very helpful carrying babies and baggage aboard the waiting buses which transported us to the camp. Unfortunately, the reception committee at Tidworth was not quite as friendly. The cadre consisted mostly of officers and men who had been held over in England to handle the war brides. I have never forgotten assembling in an auditorium to hear our "Welcome to the U.S.A." speech. It was delivered by an American captain. He opened with, "You may not like conditions here, but remember no one asked you to come." I truly feel we were deeply resented by the men who were naturally anxious to return home themselves.

"My God what have I done!" cried Doris Hutchinson of London as she stepped into the camp:

It was a horribly bleak place, miserably cold, with dustings of snow all over. I think a lot of us were in mild shock anyway at leaving home and family. We were told that we had a hot meal waiting for us and that it was chicken. That was a delicacy in wartime London. We filed into the mess hall, held trays that had little indentations for each food, and had lumps of chicken splashed in one section, peaches slopping over it, and sauerkraut reeking over all. Sauerkraut? What was it?

We had to have a physical exam while we were there, even though I had already had one in the American Embassy in London. I put it off as long as I could, because stories from the women already examined were horrible. By the last day I had no choice, and taking a deep breath, I went. We walked to the theatre, undressed in any of the seats we chose—completely undressed, even if you were menstruating—put a robe on if there was one available, and walked onto stage. We waited in line to go to the doctor who was seated center stage. There he examined us, but the only thing I remember is him shining a flashlight between my legs, evidently to check for venereal disease. The back of the theatre was filled with American army officers who were watching the proceedings.

The medical exam was almost always reported as the most mortifying experience at Tidworth. After three army doctors told Mary Coffman to remove her clothing and raise her arms above her head and then turn around, she was told she had "passed." The next in line was summoned after her. Mary felt "it was nothing more than a 'Peep Show.'" Joyce Peattie from Coulsdon, Surrey, remembered being "bundled into the Garrison Theatre, told to strip naked and then line up for ages with crying and fidgety babies in our arms."

Brides who arrived with babies found that there were no cribs in the barracks, until an inventive colonel from Texas came to the rescue with army footlockers and file drawers and lined them with pillows and rubber mattresses. Numerous complaints were made about the lack of proper washing facilities, especially by the mothers with babies in diapers.

"Little had been done to accommodate hundreds of women and children versus GIs that had been waiting there to be sent to France during the war," observed Mary Coffman:

Confronted with the situation I had my first doubts about what I was doing. I was assigned to a barracks room with about forty other girls and babies who were as dismayed as I. I laid my three-week-old son on my bed, immediately a flea jumped on him. I could have died. Here was my little antiseptic newborn with a flea!

As the days passed I realized my breast fed baby was becoming more and more fretful. It was apparent my milk was drying up. I had one four-ounce baby bottle with me for water and that was the limit of my resources. I was young, inexperienced and frantic. At no time in my life had I been around babies, I didn't know what to do. Fortunately working in the kitchens was a very cheerful motherly British woman (God Bless her). I turned to her for help, and she promised to get me a supply of dried milk after work that day, which she did. I mixed it with tap water for him and fed him. At no time did it occur to me to ask one of the U.S. personnel for help. I have since rationalized it was because they were so unfriendly to us. I'm guessing there were about 800-1000 war brides there, all British, and do you know there was not one cup of tea in the whole camp!

Molly Brown of Malvern, Worcestershire, found solace at a canteen at Tidworth run by the local Church Army: "If not for them, more girls would have gone home."

Doris Hutchinson remembered that the rooms at Tidworth were heated with

little coal stoves that must have been designed by some devious mind, just to try one's patience. No matter how I tried, the fire always went out during the night, and I had to hunt around to find an Italian prisoner of war to light it again for me. The prisoners of war were all around and being very young, we thought it was strange to see these men we had been fighting for so long.

Various problems were encountered with the German and Italian POWs working at Tidworth. Gwendolen Dieckerhoff of Hunton Bridge, Hertfordshire, described two embarrassing incidents:

In our particular group, we were fairly young with the exception of P. who was about thirty. She decided that we must stay busy and have some sort of routine to follow. She had us doing exercises two or three times a day, letter writing, and then walking around the camp perimeter. We had one problem with P. though and we took turns watching her like a hawk. Due to the fact that her parents had died at the hands of the Germans, she despised the POWs, and we all had the hardest time keeping her from picking fights with them. Nothing would have pleased her more than to have gotten them into trouble.

The main topic on our minds was when would we embark. It was during this waiting period that a few of the girls set up a different type of routine, and as a consequence, were sent home for entertaining the POWs in the neighboring fields.

Conditions at Tidworth deteriorated until authorities had received numerous complaints and newspapers began reporting on the inadequacies of the camp. A Los Angeles newspaper ran an article on May 27, 1946, in which Robert Porter charged authorities at Tidworth with running a "concentration-type camp" after his six-month-old son, Allen, became critically ill on the subsequent journey to the U.S.[24] Nine other babies died after arrival in New York. Because many infants became ill during their voyage to the U.S., particularly with infantile diarrhea, a new ruling was passed requiring that babies be at least six months old before they were allowed to travel. Women in advanced stages of pregnancy were also required to postpone their voyage.

By May 1946, some improvements were becoming apparent. A May issue of the *Tidworth Tattle,* a newsletter for war brides at the camp, introduced four members of the American Red Cross staff with a cheerful welcome. The notice from these Red Cross women told war brides "If there are any questions we can answer for you, any way we can help to make your stay here at Tidworth more enjoyable, please let us know. . . ." The Red Cross club was open from 10 A.M. to 10 P.M. and served tea and biscuits at 10:15 A.M., 3:30 P.M., and 8:30 P.M. The club offered easychairs, a phonograph, a radio, a piano, games, magazines, books, and the like. Messing hours at the consolidated mess hall were organized for brides with children, and formula for babies could be secured at stated hours. Movies were scheduled each night at the Garrison Theatre.

The American Red Cross was officially requested by the War Department to assist war brides and children during the long and often difficult journey to their new homeland.[25] Red Cross volunteers were assigned certain responsibilities at the assembly areas abroad, on board ship, at ports of entry, and along the way, as dependents of both army and navy personnel proceeded from ports of entry to their destinations in the United States.

Red Cross chapters at entry ports provided canteen service and a nurse's aid service to care for children while the mothers passed through customs. Chapters at intermediate points between the port of entry and the final destination met groups of dependents and provided whatever assistance was needed to make the journey more comfortable.

At the port of entry, Red Cross workers would receive a list of dependents due to arrive on the next ship. The workers would wire the Red Cross chapter in the community where American relatives of the service member resided, asking that a chapter worker make sure that the relatives were prepared to receive the newly arrived dependents.

Red Cross workers involved with transporting the thousands of dependents soon adopted the slogan "Be alert, adjustable and ready for change." [26]

Chapter 4

You'll Be Sorry!

---

*As we sailed from Southampton after ten days in camp, we ran
into a British troopship of these returning souls who booed us out
of sight.*
—*Mona Janise, Porthcawl, Wales*

On January 26, 1946, the first official war bride contingent boarded
the S.S. *Argentina*, a 20,600-ton Moore-McCormack liner which
had transported over 200,000 troops during wartime.[1] There were
452 brides, thirty of them pregnant, 173 children and one war groom
whose wife, a WAC, and their two-month-old daughter awaited
him in New York. The women had husbands in forty-five of the
forty-eight states. Mrs. Edna Butler, bound for Roanoke Rapids,
North Carolina, was the youngest at sixteen and was accompanied
by her eighteen-month-old daughter. At forty-four, Mrs. Harold
Cooper was the oldest bride, with a seventeen-year-old daughter
by a previous marriage and a fifteen-month-old son by her GI husband
from Manhattan Beach, California. The majority of the women
represented Britain's middle and upper middle classes. Their applica-

tions had taken precedence over 27,000 others already filed. Most had been given a priority because their husbands had been wounded in action, were hospitalized in the U.S., or had been redeployed to the U.S.

Transport Commander Col. Floyd Lyle gave them a hearty greeting aboard ship:

> Welcome to the United States, for even now on the decks of an American liner you are on American soil. We are cousins, not in blood and language alone, but in a heritage of freedom and democracy which goes back to Magna Carta. May you find warm hearts and kindness, peace and happiness even in a far country.

Newspapers on both sides of the Atlantic called the brides "Pilgrim Mothers." The transport plan was nicknamed the "Diaper Run" (the army was said to have cornered the market on diapers), "Operation Mother-in-Law," and "The War Bride Special."

Stormy seas whipped the *Argentina* shortly after her departure from Southampton. Four out of five passengers suffered from "mal de mer."

Betty Newton of Bristol, bound for Meridian, Mississippi, felt well enough on January 27, despite inclement weather, to inspect the ship with her thirteen-month-old daughter, Valerie. She wrote in her diary that things were beautifully organized:

> On "A" deck there is a room full of play pens. Wonderful toys for small children, which gives one a bit of free time and very welcome. They also opened a canteen today where we can buy all those luxuries that had disappeared in England during six years of war. All kinds of cosmetics, lipsticks and sweets, nail varnish, cigarette lighters and fountain pens. Protestant and Catholic services in the lounge this morning. Tonight there is a film. We eat our meals in two sittings. Women with children have a separate mess hall with small chairs for infants that fit on the arms of the dining chairs where children can sit and not hinder the mothers. The food is excellent, chicken, beef, celery, ice cream, etc. There is an exceptionally good medical staff on board to help us all, and during these last two days they certainly have been kept busy.

Not long after, it was the storms that captured her attention:

Ship seems to be spending most of its time out of the water. Almost impossible to do anything but hang on to something steady. Ship foghorn keeps going all the time.

Margaret Gerdus, on her way to Binghamton, New York, from Accrington, England, was one of the luckier brides. Her father had handed her a precious flask of prewar Scotch for "medicinal" purposes before she boarded ship:

I drank half of it the first night on board—never having drunk Scotch or liquor like that before, I passed out and had sweet dreams whilst the majority were deathly ill. The next morning, Aileen, who had crossed the North Sea many times, took me in tow and insisted I eat breakfast—"better sick on a full stomach than an empty one" she advised. Her strategy worked and we were two of the survivors on a ship full of sick women.

On the third day, with winds blowing across the decks at 65 MPH, the dining saloon ceased to be filled to capacity as on the first day out. Meal attendance was down to 20 percent.

By Wednesday, January 30, winds reached a velocity of 70 MPH as the *Argentina* collided with a full gale. Rain and hail whipped across the decks so fast it took paint off the masts. The ship groaned and creaked at no more than 5 knots.

Women collapsed on the decks, fell in passageways, and sat miserably on staircases. The doctors, nurses, WACs, Red Cross personnel, and ship's crew worked frantically to bring the ailing women and children to their cabins. Screaming children had been separated from their mothers, who became too sick and weak to care for them. One horrified mother lost hold of her little boy, who climbed the deck rail and almost fell overboard as she struggled to crawl toward him while the ship pitched and tossed. Some women lost their balance and fell down staircases. A child was thrown from his crib and suffered a head injury requiring twelve stitches.

Crewmen were kept busy swabbing the decks and corridors. At one point the ship had been so soiled with vomit that an outbreak of disease was feared, and an emergency inspection of the entire ship was ordered by the transport commander. The ship's doctors attributed the high incidence of seasickness to the combination of bad weather, the rich food to which the women were unaccustomed after rationing, the women's fears, apprehensions, and homesickness, and the excitement over the approaching reunions with their husbands and meetings with their new families.

Margaret, who slept through her first night on board with the help of her father's prized Scotch, continued to be a good sailor and decided to rescue some of the wives with children. Trained as a preschool teacher, she put her skills to use by setting up a nursery with the help of Mary Black, a Red Cross nurse, Aileen, and Rosie, a Portuguese attendant on board. Margaret recalls:

> Mary decided to have a birthday party for all the children, balloons and toys, but there was a catch—the ship's doctor wouldn't allow food in the nursery area, for health reasons. Aileen and Mary and I were determined they would have a cake so we concocted one out of cardboard and frosted it with flour and salt paste. The icing rosettes were crepe paper roses and we stuck some candles in it and voila! A pretty "cake" which the children loved.

Margaret and Aileen spent many hours at the piano entertaining the children. Rosie insisted that no one could arrive in America without learning a patriotic song and made Margaret sing *East Side, West Side, All Around the Town* until she had it letter perfect.

A large map of the United States on the lounge wall became a focal point for all the wives. They traced paths with their index fingers through the multicolored state borders beyond New York to their final destinations.

During brief spells of calm weather, the women did their laundry in specially equipped quarters with metal frames which had been designed to support hammock beds when the *Argentina* served as a troop transport. The need for some laundry was eliminated by the 18,000 disposable diapers on board. Mary helped the mothers all she could by distributing layettes, bottles, and clothing.

The ship's newsletter, *Wives' Whispers,* gave them information about their homeland and world events. Margaret found time to brighten up the paper with her jolly drawings of women and children.

The last issue of *Whispers,* on Saturday, February 2, included a map of New York Harbor with points of interest. The women gave their heartfelt thanks to the crew, especially Lt. Col. Lyle and Lt. Hepburn, who worked hard and long to provide them with amusement, information, film shows, games, and lectures. They gave special thanks to the Red Cross women, who helped them solve problems and soothed them with understanding.

The national news that February told of the steel shortage and the Ford motor plant employees' fears of an impending layoff of 1,000 workers. Leaders of the mine workers in Connecticut were predicting a 20,000-worker layoff. In Chicago, 2,000 employees of a packing company threatened to strike.

The radiant but tired GI brides from England, Scotland, Northern Ireland, Wales, and Malta crowded the decks of the *Argentina* during the early morning hours of February 4, 1946, in thirteen-degrees-above-zero cold to see the Statue of Liberty, specially floodlighted and glowing an unexpected green above the dark icy waters of New York Harbor, which was strangely quiet due to a tugboat strike. The artificial lights faded as the dawn brightened over the shoreline.

Mary Burkett of Tewkesbury recalled that most of the women were ill until they docked at New York:

We got up about 3:30 that morning to see the Statue of Liberty and then waited for the boat to move into the harbor. But a miracle must have happened because suddenly all the women who were so ill were able to be up and about again. Not one of those brides wanted to greet her husband from a stretcher.

The GI wives struck up an uneven chorus of *The Star Spangled Banner* which they'd practiced all the way across, only to be drowned out as they approached the shore by a band playing hot tunes, as cameras rolled and Mayor William O'Dwyer of New York City awaited them along with 200 newsmen. Not since the days when sailing ships brought wives to colonial New England had such "bride ships" reached American shores. Eager husbands, many of whom had arrived a day early, unaware that the ship had been delayed by stormy seas, broke lines and waved frantically as they cheered their wives.

The women struggled to keep their hair in place in the wind and their hats from flying into the Hudson, and they wished they could remove the flapping identity cards that made them feel like refugees, each tag a distinctive color to indicate their destination.

Some found that their clothes were baggy after prolonged bouts of seasickness.

If the brides who had missed the *Argentina* felt disappointed, they were soon appeased on learning that they would be passengers aboard the *Queen Mary*. "Finally all was ready for the final step of the journey to America," said one bride:

We boarded yet another train that took us to the docks at Southampton. There she was in all her glory: the liner R.M.S. *Queen Mary*. For years I had heard of this magnificent ship, never dreaming that one day I would be going aboard her. Though she was still outfitted as a gray troopship, she was beautiful.

The *Queen Mary* left on February 5. Aboard were 1,666 brides, 688 children, and one groom, Lt. Comdr. Robert H. Burrows of Bermuda, on terminal leave from the Royal Navy and on his way to join his wife, former WAC Sgt. Nancy Naylor, whom he had married while he was a liaison officer with the Navy Department in Washington.

Peggy Jauncey Johnson of Bedford remembered their departure on that cold morning in the rain, with the bands playing *Sentimental Journey* and *There'll Always Be an England:*

I didn't really know what I was coming to or even why I was coming. I remember vividly the family was there to see me off and I pretended it was a happy occasion for me. I couldn't tell them I hadn't heard from my husband for many months. But I knew he had been discharged from the air force. I didn't know where he was.

"It's all worry, worry, worry, wash, wash, wash, and sick, sick, sick, since I left home," wrote Joyce Peattie in her journal aboard the *Queen Mary*. She was in a cabin with eight bunks but "fortunately only five occupied, with three babies in cots made of fish net attached to our bunks."

On one of her rare excursions from the stateroom, Mary Coffman encountered her first case of "culture shock":

There was a small P.X. on board where we could buy necessities as well as many luxuries that we had not seen for years, so understandably there was always a line waiting to be served. I was standing there when a WAC came along. She took one look at the long line and yelled to the man serving, "Hey Joe, throw out a box of Kotex!" Sanitary napkins were something that in England were sold "under the counter" in chemist shops (drug stores). And by law a chemist shop had to employ a woman for just such an occasion. We would enter and ask for the lady assistant to wait on us!

Disposable diapers were issued and then soon withdrawn after they'd been flushed down toilets, causing a back-up which overflowed into the passageways. "One of the stewards who'd been with the *Queen* from the start was so disgusted," recalled a war bride from Chelmsford, Essex, on a subsequent voyage:

"Never thought I'd live to see the day on the *Queen Mary* with nappies drying in the large indoor pool. What is the world coming to?" he said. Poor man, I felt sorry for him. Not for me, just happy we could wash and hang the darn things up to dry. Needless to say, you seldom got your own back. Can you imagine that sight? *Hundreds* of nappies drying!

Lily Vicky DiNaro and her twins were assigned to a cabin marked "Reserved for Mr. Churchill." On seeing her babies, her childless cabinmate requested another cabin, only to be placed with several women with babies, so Vicky had this special suite to herself.

Although she thought she would be assigned to the *Queen Mary*, when Gwen Dieckerhoff got to the dock, she saw a sad-looking grey ship called the *Santa Paula*.

We were herded aboard and assigned our cabins. My cabin was originally intended for *two* people; now there were *eight* packed in it like sardines. As we were heading out to sea, a ship was coming in, loaded with "Tommies," and they were all shouting, "You'll be sorry."

Edna Gordon, from Sunderland, remarked that the *Santa Paula* looked like a tugboat next to the *Queen Mary*. As they were making their way up the gangplank into the narrow confines of the ship, she saw "one girl refuse to go any further in, turn around with her little boy protesting tearfully that he wanted to go to America, but his Mom said 'No. Come on Eugene. I wouldn't go on this ship if you paid me!' "

The first of three shiploads of brides from Northern Ireland and Eire sailed from Belfast aboard the *Henry Gibbins* on March 7, 1946. There were 314 wives (35 from Eire), some of whom had been married since 1942, and 140 children. The greatest number hailed from areas where the largest numbers of troops were stationed: Cookstown, Derry, Coleraine, Kilrea, Portrush, and Belfast. In March 1945, Comdr. T. J. Keane, U.S. naval officer, had disclosed that 25 percent of the men under his command had married women from Northern Ireland.[2]

The women were already feeling homesick, but they brightened when told they would arrive in New York on St. Patrick's Day. A group of workers on the Belfast docks gathered on the quay and sang *When Irish Eyes Are Smiling* and *Come Back to Erin*. The brides sang *Auld Lang Syne* through their tears. A reporter for the *Belfast Telegraph* heard one relative call out, "Keep up your heart, perhaps we'll join you some day." "Don't worry, Mary, I've posted your shamrock," shouted a mother from the shelter of a shed along the dockside.[3]

The flotilla of war bride ships crossing the Atlantic seemed endless. Those slated for later voyages were not much encouraged at the prospect of leaving, after reading some of the negative publicity regarding the type of reception some war brides had experienced in the U.S.[4] One war bride's feelings were decidedly mixed, because "Stories about dissatisfied war brides occasionally appeared in papers such as the tabloid *Daily Mirror:* 'He promised her a mansion and all she found was a shack.'"

There was also the resentment of family and countrymen to deal with. "My mother's parting words to me were, 'You have made your bed, lie in it,'" recalled Mona Janise of Porthcawl, Wales, who set sail on the hospital ship *Bridgeport* in March 1946:

> There was a letter published in a British paper a week before I left, from the editor to the returning British troops—it informed them that the British trash were leaving the country and the best were home waiting for them. As we sailed from Southampton, we ran into a troopship of these returning souls who booed us out of sight!
>
> Reporters on earlier ships had photographed the brides in pretty awful conditions, so no photographers were allowed

on our boat and we had to arrive in New York in decent condition.

Trying to arrive "in decent condition" was no easy task on these voyages. Mona recalled that aboard ship:

We used to say we had six meals a day, three down and three up. We were told to eat and that would help us overcome our "mal de mer," and so we had to go through the dining area whether we ate or not. The first things that met my seasick eyes were boiled eggs, fried eggs, scrambled eggs, and anything else they could do with eggs. Some of our less hardy brides just passed out, and there was a sailor with a stretcher ready and waiting. As for me, I just took one look at those eggs and tore up on deck and threw up, which was usually on the wrong side of the boat and ended up back in my face.

There was no dentist on board and I had an impacted molar which also added to my misery. I always think of my husband telling his sister what a beautiful girl he had married, skin so white, hair so blonde, and what must have been her first impression of me getting off the boat, skin so red, hair so matted from the wind, and my cheap fur coat shedding like a dog from the salt air.

A traveler aboard the June 1946 voyage of the *Bridgeport,* Gwen Chushcoff of Rhyader, Wales, was told by a Red Cross woman that "all American wives arrived at the breakfast table with hair and make up and dress impeccable!" Gwen described the dress code aboard ship:

Shorts, halters and, heaven forbid, swimsuits were forbidden on deck. Anyone caught wearing them was threatened to be put aboard the next ship returning to England never to see their husband again. Seems this was threatening to the crew's libido. This seemed rather silly to many and there were those who braved the deck in shorts only to be escorted below "in disgrace." However, perhaps they had a point. One night we were awakened in our cabin by screams and a voice yelling, "I was clutched!" A shadowy figure was seen beating a hasty retreat through what was supposed to be a locked door. After that episode, an MP was stationed outside the door each night. And he was no help at all when a squabble broke out between two girls who became quite raucous. A lieutenant yelled at the sergeant, whose chest was ablaze with medals, "For heaven's sake, Sarge, keep those women quiet!" To which the sergeant replied, "Not me, sir, I ain't going in there *noways*."

Anxiety, sea sickness, and crowded conditions created unbearable tensions. Harmony aboard ship was further threatened by close confinement with soldiers and crew members who occasionally made overtures—sometimes with the compliance of female passengers. Sheila Ochocki of London wrote to her mother about her voyage aboard the *Holbrook,* which arrived in New York on April 8, 1946; however, she left out the more lurid details which she included in her private journal:

April 1, 1946 [letter to mother]. The crew isn't allowed to mix with the girls, so they put a rope right down the center of the deck. It was lovely moonlight, and the men sat on one side of the rope and the girls the other. They had banjos and mouth organs and we all had a lovely sing song.

April 16, 1946 [journal]. During the night one of the crew came in our room and tried to make love to one of the girls. This morning she reported him and he's now in the brig. There is lots of things going on this ship that's disgusting. The girls are fratting with the men, going to all lengths. Two girls are not being allowed to land. They are classed as undesirable people. The crew are a rotten lot and half of them are being fired when we get to New York. Thank God these things don't go any further than the ship or else I don't know what people would think of GI brides. Two girls had a fight last night. One of the crew went to part them, and one of the girls hit him over the head and cut his head open with a bottle, then she hit the other girl and cut all her face. I think she is one that isn't going to land.

Another traveler aboard the *Holbrook* in June 1946, Betty Bachman from Burton-on-Trent, had a miserable crossing. "Some babies got sick, some died. Food was terrible. We felt like prisoners, hit all storms in the ocean. Red Cross told us no one would like us. In-laws would tolerate us. They made us leery."

Crossing with a baby was especially difficult. Cecilia Joan Selhorst of Oxford, who boarded the *E. B. Alexander* with her son on March 27, 1947, described her preparations for the voyage and her accommodations:

The only baggage we were allowed to bring was two suitcases and one trunk which would go in the hold of the ship until our arrival. Since it was requested that we bring with us enough baby formula (canned) to last us three weeks and six baby bottles, most of the precious space in one case was taken up with this. I can remember spending two days in the pouring rain in England going from drug store (or chemist shop as they were known to us) to drug store trying to buy the bottles. Every store, if they had any, would only let me have one bottle as they, like everything else, were in short supply during the war years. At home we had one bottle at a time which was used until it got broken, then we would hope to be able to find another one.

Our accommodations were not those of any pleasure cruise. All brides with babies under a year of age were put in several large cabins with about 50 bunks in tiers of three each. The babies were assigned to several large nurseries with about 50 bassinets and cribs in each. Brides that were pregnant or with toddlers were assigned cabins with cribs for their children. We were told that we would each be responsible for our own child between the hours of 6 A.M. and 10 P.M. We were to be at the nursery at 6 A.M. to give the babies their first feedings and bathe them. After breakfast, if we could eat, we had to do the laundry. We could not retire until the final formula was given at 10 P.M. At no time were we allowed to take the babies down to our cabins which were four flights down just above the engine room. We were allowed to use the nursery during the day for the infants to take their naps but the supervision during the day was entirely up to us. It was decided that individual formula making was completely out of the question, so all of the babies were put on the same formulas which were made up and dispensed to us in bottles supplied by the authorities. Imagine my frustration as I remembered those rainy days when I trudged from store to store in search of bottles and the space that they took in my limited baggage. Needless to say, the formula did not agree with many of the babies, neither did the strange bottles with the hard new nipples. Many of the mothers, concerned that the babies would not eat, surreptitiously poured the formulas from these very sterilized bottles into their own unsterilized ones with the familiar nipples and for this we were severely reprimanded if caught.

On an earlier voyage of the *Alexander* in March 1946, June Romano of Plumstead, London, "was initially placed down on E deck where one could see the rats running along the rafters. Terrified by this, I went up on B deck and squeezed in with some other girls I knew and never went below decks again!!!"

In Australia, the American Red Cross assisted war brides on trains to the ports of embarkation and helped them procure accommodations while they awaited passage. The first official brideships left Sydney Harbor in February 1946. The U.S.S. *Monterey* arrived in San Francisco on March 3 with 562 women and 253 babies from Australia and New Zealand. Army welcome boats escorted the ship to the dock where a WAC army band played *Sentimental Journey.* The U.S.S. *Mariposa* followed on March 6.[5]

Fred Stindt, the chief purser aboard the *Lurline,* which followed on March 22, gave a sense of the particular problems encountered in transporting dependents from Australia:

On March 21, 1946, at 8:30 A.M. the loading of war brides at Sydney started. The train from Brisbane came in first and was followed by the train from Western Australia and Melbourne. From observation the loading was very smooth and well handled. The army loading authorities stated that they had only one complaint and that was cancellations. Some one hundred war brides had cancelled their passage in the last four days, thirty on the last day. This made it very difficult in trying to "round up" other war brides to take their place in the last minute. At 4:00 P.M., one dependent went insane, causes unknown, so she and her infant child were removed from the ship. All war brides, but one, were on board by 5:00 P.M. The "one" came aboard at 10:00 P.M., only being notified six hours before that she could travel.[6]

To keep spirits up aboard the *Lurline,* the Red Cross staff arranged various entertainments in which the war brides participated. A beauty contest packed the lounge with spectators. The Red Cross gave prizes for winners in seven categories: most engaging smile; best looking legs; snappiest costume; best suntan; most freckles; most representative blonde, redhead, and brunette; silliest.

Shipboard entertainment distracted brides and helped them recover from the shock of separating from home and family. One bride on an earlier voyage of the *Lurline* described her emotional farewell from Brisbane:

We arose bright and early this morning and sat on the deck and laughed and joked about our future, but each girl's face belied her real feeling—each was very sad at leaving her country, but still not one of us would turn back. Australian women are brave and amongst this bunch that courage was showing. The American band came on the dock and many of our army and navy friends were there. Evie Hayes, President of the Wives and Husbands Association, was standing on the dock waving each and all of us a real American farewell. She pinned her American pin on me—the "U.S. and Us" one—and said, "You are now the U.S. and I am the Us."

The band had struck up *California, Here I Come,* everyone laughed and said, "I'll say—just let me see that Golden Gate." *Waltzing Matilda* was played—none of us dared look at the other. The Aussie men sang out, "You'll be sorry." Before the lines were released the band played *Aloha.* It was too much for us, no dry eyes then. A couple of American soldiers standing near me developed, within a few minutes, a bad cold in the head and for comfort's sake blew their noses very hard. I wonder if they felt for us leaving our native country, or, were they sorry to leave our sunny land. But, she was not sunny that day . . . she was grey as if in sorrow at losing us.

The lines were released and we were being towed out as *Auld Lang Syne* was played. No need to ask us, will we ever forget. All the decks available to us were lined by the girls as we proceeded down our beautiful river. Someone appropriately played, *I'll See You Again.* My cabin pal and I shook hands and vowed we would even if we had to hitchhike the Pacific.[7]

Three war brides aboard the *Mariposa* voyage in April 1946 couldn't bear to leave and disembarked the night before the ship was to sail. The remaining passengers got an enthusiastic send-off when the ship left the next morning. The ship's lounge, filled with flowers sent by family and friends of the departing war brides, looked like a garden. The passengers enjoyed stopovers in Fiji and Honolulu. Joy Baase recalled their departure on April 10:

> We sailed at dawn and high tide. I'll never forget the feeling of the ship starting to move, and watching the water widening from the dock edge. I went up to the very top deck to watch for my relatives and friends on the riverbank. Just before we reached the ocean entrance, there they were—about twenty of them—some on the bank and others out on a boat jetty waving white sheets, calling out good-bye to me. I had a large white towel in my hand, too, and I was waving back. And we could hear very plainly as we called to each other and waved till out of sight.
>
> We arrived at Suba in the Island of Fiji four days after departure. Everyone received five hours shore leave and my dear cabin mates decided being on land would help my seasickness so up they came and got me, helped me dress, and we went ashore. We walked towards the main section of town and I felt just great on the land. Our group went looking for fresh fruit, especially lemon, as we were told they were good for seasickness. Next morning we sailed for Honolulu. We had a wonderful welcome dockside at Honolulu. There were Hawaiian dancers, bands, and lei makers and sellers. We were allowed to mingle with them for a few hours.

Shore leave was restricted on later voyages as some of the brides unintentionally hampered debarking passengers. Also, war brides who left the ship often missed friends and relatives who came to see them while they were in port. Some got lost sightseeing in the city. Doreen Battle, who travelled on the *Fred. C. Ainsworth* in May 1946, recalled:

> We stopped in Hawaii but we were not allowed ashore. The two previous ships that came from the eastern states stopped

in Hawaii and I guess they had so much trouble with a lot of the girls. When it was time for the ship to leave some of them were missing and some had to be brought back to the ship—they had been drinking—so it ruined it for any other ship that came over.

There was one girl went ashore there. She found out on her way over that her husband had been transferred to Hawaii and he came out in a launch to meet her and she went down over the side of the ship on the rope ladder. We all cheered her and sang to them and wished them good luck. It was kind of a sad feeling because we felt that that was the first one to leave us and we were breaking up. And, I don't know—it just did something to you because you thought here's someone you'd been very friendly with on the ship all the way, and all of a sudden they're gone, and you may never see them again. I never did see her again. I became very friendly with her because we had a measles epidemic on board the ship and then they were trying to double up people. Seeing I had a cabin all to myself and I had plenty of room, I offered to take her into the cabin with me, so we really were quite close.

Others did not enjoy such camaraderie on their voyage. "It was boring, nothing to do but knit and we all got lice," recalled Madge Kiefer of New South Wales who came over on the S.S. *Knox Victory* in October 1945.

U.S. immigration agents were aboard some of the brideships in order to expedite customs and immigration procedures. Down Under accents occasionally caused considerable trouble. A customs agent aboard the *Monterey* in March 1946 had difficulty locating an American town allegedly named "Hotfoot." Shown a map, the bride pointed to her destination: Hartford, Connecticut.[8]

Fiancées became increasingly restive as they watched brides depart for America. Due to their low priority, when they applied for passage the waiting period was estimated in years. Proxy marriages over transatlantic telephone lines became increasingly popular during the spring of 1946 as fiancées tried to circumvent the priority rules. In an effort to discourage such marriages, Joseph F. Barr of the Veteran's Administration solicitor's office announced that no state would recognize the validity of these proxy ceremonies. After careful study, however, the VA decided to recognize proxy weddings as valid common law marriages in the nineteen states which did recognize such unions. Mr. Barr stressed that proxy marriages would not stand up in those states where they were not recognized.[9]

On July 13, 1946, Reverend F. W. White of Salisbury, England, refused to conduct a transatlantic telephone marriage between a seventeen-year-old English girl, Maureen Chamberlain, and a former American serviceman, James Grider of Hot Springs, New Mexico, stating that the ceremony "was not legal in England." Despite his refusal, a newspaper announced their marriage by transatlantic telephone hook-up had taken place three days later and the bride planned to leave soon for the U.S.[10] In London, on November 10, 1946, Doris Press, a twenty-one-year-old movie usher, married Marvin Kite of Atlanta, Georgia, a former U.S. pilot, by telephone. The pub where the couple used to play darts offered its phone and the owner decorated the establishment with chrysanthemums, barring the public for the evening. The family looked on and listened to the ceremony being recorded over a microphone as Doris' father stood by with the wedding ring. With a free hand, Doris and Dad held up Marvin's photo, and the groom on the other side of the Atlantic clung to Doris' portrait as she said, "I do."[11]

Chrystal Hatzinger, a fiancée from Baldock, England, managed an exceptionally early departure in May 1946 by plane:

I got lucky—*really* lucky! The steel foundry where I worked had offices in Pittsburgh and they had business representatives going back and forth on a regular basis. Someone at work suggested I contact the Managing Director to see if he could give me some advice. Shaking like a leaf, I stood at his desk and began to pour out my tale of woe and waited for his wrath to descend on me for bothering him with such trivia. In fatherly fashion he patted my shoulder, told me not to fret anymore and gave me the name of the firm's travel agents and, as an afterthought, handed me his business card "just in case there's any problem."

When I finally found the place I wondered if I had the right one. It didn't look anything like a travel agency. There was a fellow behind the counter who rather languidly inquired if he could help me. I stated I wished to book a flight to the United States. He looked at me as if I'd just crawled out of a piece of cheese and snorted with laughter saying, "Sure, you and a hundred thousand others," and still snickering kind of waved me off like a pesky fly and returned his attention to his newspaper. Then I fished around in my purse for the business card and said, "I was told to present this." If I live to a hundred I'll never forget that guy's reaction. The insolent look disappeared from his face and his whole demeanor turned as deferential as if I'd been royalty. He began apologizing all over the place. "When would you like to go—next week?"

I picked May 23. Thereupon he wrote out my ticket, collected £100 ($403.00 at 1946 exchange rate) and wished me a pleasant trip.

Seats on infrequent commercial flights were difficult to book during the postwar years. In November 1946, when Yvonne Mason Indelicato of Melbourne flew on the "Arkana," an Australian National Airways plane, it was only on its second commercial flight. Australian planes were not allowed to land passengers on American soil at that time, so she landed in Vancouver, Canada. In Vancouver she was able to secure a reservation to Oakland, her destination, via Chicago. But after being fog-bound for two days in Vancouver, she lost her seat on the plane to Chicago. "I was alone, and in tears I retired to the Restroom," she said. "The crew sent someone to find out the problem and did get a reservation for me [a serviceman gave up his seat for her]. I arrived in Chicago—of course at the wrong terminal—a frustrated fiancée, a dozen wilted red roses. I was sick and cold. I left Sydney November 10, arrived in Oakland, California, November 13."

The military provided air transport under some extenuating and exceptional circumstances. In January 1946, Cherylene Robison, the two-month-old daughter of an Australian war bride and an ex-sailor from Kansas, was flown 8,000 miles on army and navy planes to California with her mother. The baby needed a cranial operation to save her life.[12]

The U.S. Army arranged a special surprise Christmas flight in December 1946 on Pan American's "Intrepid" for twenty-four English war brides with twenty-five infants. Their names were chosen at random, and the entire cargo of the plane was listed as "military equipment." Patricia Lewis was one of the lucky passengers. Her husband Arnold, an air force veteran from Canton, Ohio, was waiting for her on arrival at LaGuardia Field on December 25. Arnold was eager to see her and hold their eight-month-old daughter, Diana, for the first time. "It was a wonderful Christmas present the army gave us," Patricia said. "The best I ever had." [13]

Chapter 5

Here Come the Brides

My first impression of America was of a husband (not mine)
walking up the gang plank in a zoot suit. I remember thinking,
"Oh God, I hope mine doesn't look like that."
—Sheila Ochocki, London, England

There was mass confusion at the dock when the *Argentina* arrived
in New York on February 4, 1946. Because it was the first official
war bride ship, the passengers were besieged with newsmen and
photographers. Margaret Jean Tune, from Hounslow, Middlesex,
England, blamed the press for delaying the disembarking war brides.
She finally met her husband at three in the afternoon, nearly twelve
hours after spotting the first lights of Manhattan. "Harold had to
sign for me and then we were free to go on our way."

Brides who were being met in New York were permitted to
leave the ship in groups of fifty. Others remained aboard until transportation to other parts of the United States was arranged. The
Red Cross Home Service was busy answering phone calls from all
over the country regarding their arrival. Margaret Gerdus remembers

how angry she was when her husband failed to show up at the Red Cross center:

I was agitated and determined to go to Binghampton alone, so to take my mind off it, Mary took me over to a radio announcer, either WABC or CBS. When he asked me where my husband was, I angrily replied, "I don't know, but I'd like to break his neck!" Imagine the relatives at Don's home— they couldn't understand what had happened to him. He had been told the wrong time by the Red Cross. When he finally arrived everyone breathed a sigh of relief!

Rosemary Berdo, also on the first official *Argentina* voyage, did find her husband waiting on the pier to meet her. "It was like landing in fairyland. Next, shopping for clothes and other luxuries. Stayed for five days at the Hotel Taft, saw the stage show *Oklahoma* and Sonja Hennie in the Ice Follies at Madison Square Garden."

On February 10, twelve army tugs escorted the *Queen Mary* through the chunks of ice that surrounded Pier 90. The 378th Army Service Forces band from Fort Hamilton welcomed the war brides with *Here Comes the Bride* and a "hot" version of *Rock-a-Bye Baby*. Most husbands were waiting, many since early morning, at the armory on 66th Street. "They came near rioting!" according to Joyce Peattie.

The "near riot" occurred at 6:50 P.M., when the first busload of fifty war brides arrived at the armory and many of the 2500 waiting husbands and relatives crowded the entrance of the building all at once, disrupting the army's carefully devised plans. The place was "*jammed,*" remembered one war bride. "Husbands and in-laws were all over the place and we were quite overwhelmed."

Lily Vicky DiNaro, with twins John and Santo Jr., was embraced warmly by her husband, Santo, who said, "Why it's reverse Lend-Lease. As far as I'm concerned, the British debt is paid off."

Lily Vicky and Irene Roop appeared on the Vox Pop radio program along with several other war brides who had arrived on the *Queen Mary*. They received telegrams and letters from all over America. Irene was also invited to a toy show for her son, who was presented with a large box of toys.

A GI bride who arrived on the *Santa Paula* on February 16,

1946, said that the newsreel men wanted the war brides to act out parts for their cameras. Many photographers seem to have enjoyed posing war brides looking through, sitting in, or even climbing out of the ships' portholes. Some couples were happy to repeat their welcome-to-the-U.S. kiss for photographers, but some women were reticent about such a public display of affection.

Many brides found Americans to be more demonstrative than they were accustomed to. Sometimes a war bride's shyness or reluctance to show affection publicly was misunderstood as coldness or snobbishness. "My in-laws wanted to slobber all over me, but being my polite self I simply extended my hand," said one bride. "That put me on the wrong side right away. They also had a gooey cake, and not being used to such things, I couldn't eat it. Well, they got mad again!"

On the other hand, June Selby, who married her American in Melbourne, Australia, on September 16, 1944, and arrived in New York on the U.S.S. *Orion* in May 1946, was so excited when she saw her husband that she hugged him so hard she broke his glasses.

But some women faced the longed-for reunion with mixed emotions. Would he still feel the same way toward her now that he was back in his own surroundings? Would the months or years of separation have changed him? Sheila Ochocki's "first impression of America was of a husband (not mine) walking up the gang plank in a zoot suit. I remember thinking, 'Oh God, I hope mine doesn't look like that.' He didn't, but still looked very strange in a civilian suit. I felt like I was meeting a stranger."

One couple still laughs over the studio photograph the GI had made after his return to the States to send his wife in England. "He looked like one of Al Capone's gangsters with his wide-brimmed trilby hat." Shortly after her arrival in the United States, she must have thought she really had married a gangster, for her husband was in jail for car theft when she went to join him on the west coast. The car owner did not press charges, though, due to the soldier's wartime service overseas.

Gloria Richards' husband met her in New York with a distant relative who endeared herself to the couple by making herself even more distant. After driving the happily reunited couple to her home in New York, where dinner was prepared, the relative and her husband left for the evening, so the young couple could be alone for their first few hours in America.

Many personal kindnesses were extended to the new immigrants. In New Jersey, a group of workmen presented a busload of war brides with many bags of fruit to welcome them to the U.S., because they knew there had been a shortage of fruit in England during the war. Winifred Stanizzi from St. Helens, Lancashire, was greeted with a massive bunch of bananas from her in-laws in New York because her husband had told them they couldn't get bananas in England.

Elizabeth Roberts related an incident which occurred on a shopping tour arranged by the Red Cross in April 1946 for newly arrived war brides: "A Chicago shop girl insisted on paying for a blouse chosen by one of our girls. 'We just don't realize how lucky we've been in this country,' she said." [1] Doreen Grove, from Dorset, also received an unexpected gift from a stranger: "When I arrived I had a very bad cold. My husband and his brother-in-law went to the local drug store to get something for it. They came home with a huge box of chocolates sent by the druggist as a 'Welcome to America' gift." At the Gramercy Park Hotel, Maisie Oldendorph of Scotland was surprised with "a vase of beautiful red roses, with compliments from the hotel management, welcoming me to America and wishing us a very happy stay with them, and with much success for a happy life in America."

Joan Cater vividly remembers being overwhelmed by New York City and its people:

Everything seemed shiny and new, the buildings reaching into the sky, the shiny cars and yellow cabs. The smell in the air of cigars, gasoline and steam, mingling with restaurant odors. It was all so different and somehow carefree.

Our destination was Grand Central Station, simply unbelievable to me after London's smoky late 19th century terminals. We paused at a snack bar. I was longing for a cup of tea. What I got was a tea bag in a cup of hot water. Was this how Americans drank tea? I also eyed the luscious cakes and pies, missing from England's bakeries even then. I ordered a piece of chocolate cake. The man who waited on us asked where I was from. We chatted for a second and when Al began to pay the bill the man behind the counter said, "No charge for the lady. After all those people went through in London, and still are rationed, it's my pleasure to do this." This was my first taste of the famed American generosity we saw among the men of the 8th Air Force.

Everything was so much larger than ours at home. We had often heard the Americans say things like, "Gee, our trains would make three of yours," and "our cars are much bigger," etc. We put it down to typical American-style bragging, but I was finding out it was true.

Joan Stevens arrived in Charleston, South Carolina, on July 29, 1946, with her husband, who had returned to England as a civilian to marry her. They travelled on the freighter *Andrew Jackson,* the only available ship, which carried twelve passengers, including two honeymoon couples and seven English fiancées. Upon arrival, the two war brides were met by the Department of Immigration and Customs and separated from their husbands.

Mary and I were driven to the Department of Immigration to be fingerprinted and interviewed by an officer who looked and talked like Sidney Greenstreet as he sat in a huge cane chair under a ceiling fan, wearing a white linen suit. He remarked that this country could use some good foreign blood.

Although the majority of Americans were friendly, not all of the war brides received the greeting promised by "A Short Guide to the United States," the talk series given to war brides by the American Red Cross on the *Queen Mary* in early 1946:

You are going to be pleasantly surprised at the great friendliness with which you will be received. For you come, not as strangers as you may have expected, but as the new wives of American soldiers who have returned from war. By their choice of you as wives, these soldiers have drawn even tighter the tremendous bond of friendship which exists between the United States and Great Britain.[2]

When the *Vulcania* docked in New York on February 21, 1946, the war brides were allowed ashore to see a show. Irene Jones recalls, "People watching us knew we were war brides. Many told us to go home, they didn't want us in the USA." Mary Dolleman, from

Scotland, heard women yelling, "Go Back to England!" to war brides who arrived on the *E. B. Alexander* on June 28, 1946. On an earlier *Alexander* voyage, Pearl Patterson from Bury St. Edmunds, England, also received a rude welcome:

> We who had sick babies were taken off first and went by cab with military escort to Ft. Hamilton where the children were hospitalized. The civilian driving the ambulance (or cab?) was very rude—told us we were *not wanted over here*—that the American women hated us. I told him if all Americans were like him I didn't want to stay here anyway.

Isolationists (who blamed foreigners for getting the U.S. into World War II) and jilted American women were not limited to New York. Doreen Battle, who travelled from Australia on the *Fred C. Ainsworth,* described her experience in San Francisco:

> They said that there would be a band to meet us and they gave us flags to wave when we got there. It was a rainy, foggy sort of a day and there wasn't any band; it didn't arrive til long after we had been there. There were a lot of girls yelling out "You stole our husbands. You stole our boyfriends."

Brenda Hasty, from Liverpool, said that "Even middle-aged married women seemed resentful that I had 'caught' one of their boys. 'Pity they didn't wait to marry a nice, clean, American girl,' I was told by a professor's wife."

The hated name tags that war brides had to wear aboard ship accompanied many of them ashore in the U.S. Those who were not met by their husbands or family members in New York had to wear the tags on their railway journeys to their destination. In St. Louis, Gwen Chushcoff of Wales was met by a woman from Traveller's Aid who

> . . . scolded us soundly because we all refused to wear our large label which proclaimed to the world who we were. This label struck us as unnecessary and totally insensitive—who wants to be a package?

> Our dedicated Traveller's Aid woman irritated all six of us. We had the dubious distinction of being placed on the train ahead of the natives and she led the way through a huge crowd calling officiously, "Make way for the War Brides." It was like the parting of the Red Sea; Moses could not have done

better. The crowd was large because it had been a 4th of July weekend. Needless to say we felt like freaks. This was the first time as I sat alone on the train that if it had been possible to have been zapped back to Britain, I would not have hesitated for one moment.

The conductor on the train, a very nice man who was also only doing his best by us, strolled through asking if there were any war brides in each coach. I sat and never uttered a sound. I would have to be put on the rack before they'd get a peep out of me. As he wearily returned on his third trip through, he was very frustrated. "I found five of them—but there's one missing," he kept repeating. On the fourth trip he met my eye and said, "Honey it's got to be you. I've questioned everyone else on this train." I admitted I was indeed the sixth and told him how horrible it was to be stared at. He understood and brought a young college girl to sit across from me.

I shall always be appreciative of the kind railway man who gave me my tickets and said "Welcome to America, young lady. You will be a great addition to our country, I'm sure!"

To a group of war brides who arrived in New York at 2 A.M. without an escort, Grand Central Station, bustling with activity, seemed immense and frightening. The terminal was filled with soldiers returning from a night out in the Big Apple, and employees at the information desk were too busy to answer questions. Even the ladies room offered no refuge from the commotion, for there were "girls in fancy dresses being sick" as an attendant stood by swearing at them. Retreating to the din of the busy terminal, the five war brides encountered an American officer who looked as though he'd really had a night on the town and was still feeling the effects. Apprehensively, they accepted his help. After he worked out the details of train times and routes to each of their destinations, June Rogers discovered he was going her way, she to Trenton and he to Princeton:

By this time all that was available was the 5:00 A.M. milk train. It was full to the brim with soldiers on their way back to Fort Dix after a night in New York. They were sprawled all over the train. We stood outside the compartment with two MPs. When he got off at Princeton he told the MPs to watch over me—he would know who they were. He gave me his card, but I misplaced it so could never really thank him.

The MPs obviously thought I'd been his entertainment for the night; they laughed a lot together as soon as he left. We arrived in Trenton at 6 A.M., very foggy and dismal looking. They put my bag on the platform and told me to take a taxi.

I shared one with two businessmen, one of whom said, "I wonder if it's this foggy in England?" (not knowing I'd just come from there). I didn't say a word; by this time I was afraid to breathe. I'd been awake since we docked at Boston at dawn the day before, after my first sea voyage of five days. The men got out in town and the driver took me to the house. When he got my bag out, he then asked me where I'd come from, etc. He said, "Do these people expect you?" I said yes, but they'd no idea when. He said very emphatically, "God Bless You Girl." I had wanted to turn back before, and that almost did it.

Many Americans were very helpful to the newly arrived war brides. Pat Hobbs, who travelled to the U.S. by air from London, recalls the difficulty she had while waiting in Omaha, Nebraska, for a connection to California:

Looking around all I saw was tall cowboys wearing Stetsons, boots, and jeans; I felt sure I would be shot before I got a flight, so I sat huddled up on the edge of the bench, trying to look as small as possible. I had to call Western Union to let my fiancé know when I would arrive in Sacramento. The ticket man told me to put the dime in and ask for Western Union. When I got through she told me to deposit so much for the telegram. Having trouble with the money, I stood there like a dope not knowing what to put in, close to tears. I heard footsteps coming up behind me. A soft voice said "Can I help you, Ma'am?" I looked around at this cowboy and told him my problem, he made the call for me, then sat and talked to me till the plane left.

Because the army issued her the wrong ticket, Helen Hyde, from Australia, had to cross the U.S. alone instead of with other war brides who arrived in San Francisco with her on the April 25, 1946, voyage of the *Mariposa*. She travelled on a passenger train to

Chicago and then on a troop train to Boston. "I was nicknamed the marsupial soup girl!!" Arriving in Boston in the middle of the night as the only passenger on a "ghost train," she was greeted by the station master, who telephoned her husband, "and it was not long before he arrived to hold me in his arms!!"

Helen Eyles from Esher, England, travelled across the U.S. by train with a large group of war brides. "When a bride would reach her destination and detrain, everyone left on the train would stare out the windows to see what her husband looked like!!" When an unlikely pair embraced, some would say: "What did she ever see in *him?*" or "He married *her?*"

Chapter 6

Don't Give Up Too Soon

Your home in America can't be "a little bit of England"—it's got to be American. The girl will definitely have to "give" a little more than take in the beginning.
—Alistair Cooke's advice to war brides aboard the Queen Mary *in March 1946* [1]

The first few months in the U.S. were traumatic for most brides, even for those who had the advantage of a common language, which turned out to be not so "common" after all. Like Joan Cater, many struggled with pronunciations such as "bananas vs. bahnanahs" and were misunderstood by tradesmen. Isobel Heely describes the experience:

It was almost as hard to go from Australian-English to American-English as from a foreign language. Sewing some cool cotton dresses for the terrible humid heat here in Tidewater I needed "a reel of pink cotton, some press studs" instead of "a spool of thread, snap fasteners." I asked for a "pillar-box" to "post" my letter—needed a "mailbox" to "mail." Couldn't find a "frock" shop (dress), the "tram" was a "streetcar" and so on. It was a whole new language.

On their first American shopping spree in a small town in California, three war brides dashed across the street in the middle of the block. When they reached the other side, one remembered being confronted by a policeman who angrily asked, "Do you know it's against the law to jaywalk?" Dot, with her hands on her hips, looked at him squarely and answered, "How dare you insult us. We come from good families!" His retort was, "Lady, I just saw you jaywalk."

Her answer, "You must be mistaken; we are good girls. We do not jaywalk." He threw his hands up in the air and gasped, "Foreigners!" and proceeded to explain the rules of crossing.

Irene Fehn, from England, started out working as a waitress in her husband's luncheonette in Long Beach, California. The most popular sandwich was a BLT because the customers enjoyed hearing her repeat their order with "tomartoe" instead of "tomayta" as they said it.

Most war brides can remember an embarrassing experience like Joan Cater's:

I happily described a long bicycle ride with Al in Hertfordshire at a tea given for me by one of Oneida's most esteemed ladies. Describing the ride I concluded saying that "afterwards I was simply knocked up." A red-faced Al explained that in England that expression meant "tired." Later at home he explained its real meaning, as defined in America. I felt simply terrible and wrote a note of apology to my hostess.

Some English-speaking brides discovered that their "American" in-laws did not speak English. Australian bride Margo Dlugosinski's most difficult adjustment was "learning to be patient with the Polish relatives and to understand why they didn't speak English in front of me—they couldn't!! The first holidays were awful."

Although Marjorie Bargout knew her husband for three years in England before they were married, he never thought to tell her that his immediate family, his relatives, and their friends were all immigrants from Damascus, Syria. When they met her at South Station in Boston on May 30, 1946, "They all looked very dark and very foreign to me and on the way home in the car were speaking in a foreign language which I did not know was Arabic."

Gert Yescavage's mother-in-law spoke only Lithuanian, but having immigrated to the United States herself, she understood how many adjustments Gert had to make as a newcomer from Australia—understanding helped bridge language differences. On the other hand, an English war bride felt left out at social gatherings in her husband's German-speaking community. Although warmly welcomed, she was unable to participate in the German conversations.

Another woman's mother-in-law was Irish and her father-in-law was German-English. After a few months, she realized that:

> Americans did not think of themselves as "Americans"—they were Italians, Polish, Jewish, etc. Until that time I had thought of everyone in this country as just being American just as everyone in England was English. It took me by surprise and there seemed to be so much hatred between the different nationalities.

Those ethnic prejudices caused problems for many brides. A London woman arriving at a farm in Kansas learned that her in-laws were German-Americans who did not like "Verdamt Englanders." Another woman, who arrived in 1944, found her husband's parents were Slovak and would have preferred him to marry someone of the same ethnic heritage and also the same religion. "I was here only two months," she said, "and my husband was sent to England flying missions—I certainly was lonely, wishing I'd never arrived in America." Her unhappiness was eased somewhat when she was befriended by a woman of Italian descent whose family made her feel most welcome.

Earlier immigrants and other war brides were usually the most helpful contacts and friends made by newly arrived war brides, perhaps because these people had also recently experienced the same homesickness and bewildering adjustment period. Joan Ogozalek, who was greeted at the dock with a "GO HOME FOREIGNERS" sign, appreciated a party given for her by World War I brides in Springfield, Massachusetts.

Many American families had advised their sons not to marry overseas, and a number of GIs had broken engagements back home in order to marry foreign women, so there was bound to be resentment from the jilted American women and their friends. Isobel Heely's mother-in-law, however, was very sympathetic to her son's bride and used a daring tactic to dispel any hostility that might be felt toward her:

She had a fancy tea for me the first week I arrived and invited *all* of my husband's old girlfriends. I got along well with them, and joined their bridge clubs and we laughed at my mother-in-law's courage to invite them all to the "Tea."

Some women would have found it difficult to laugh at being put in such an awkward situation, but Isobel explains that she and her mother-in-law "got on famously." They shared many common interests; both were musical and played piano and organ.

One Australian woman laughed when she remembered describing her journey across the Pacific to San Francisco to her mother-in-law, who told her she must be mistaken—she was sure the way to come to America was across the Atlantic. The young bride said "No," that was not the way she came, but her mother-in-law insisted, "Yes, Etta. That is the way you came." The young bride found a map to prove her point and presented it to her mother-in-law, upon which the latter slowly conceded, "Well, Etta, you *might* be right about that."

American misconceptions about other countries were not uncommon. One Australian bride found people were surprised she was white and could speak English.

Lalli Coppinger, from London, who spent her first six months in the U.S. in a remote Colorado town, found her reception by her in-laws somewhat strange:

I land in the supposed land of friendship and find myself looked over like a rather weird novelty. My brother-in-law's father-in-law, who was in the cleaning business, on meeting me for the first time, actually looked at the suit I was wearing (I'd used coupons to have it made in London) and said, while twisting my lapel through his fingers, "Nice material!" I could have died. No word of welcome, just "nice material!"

In spite of differences, war brides had to learn to get along with their in-laws, because most of them spent their first few months or longer under the same roof, due to the postwar housing shortage and unemployment. Many war brides faced disillusionment in the beginning. In love with their husbands, they simply had not thought about what life in the United States would be like. The Hollywood version of American affluence combined with the image of the free-spending GI impressed women overseas. While a few GIs may have spun tall tales about mansions and servants, most spoke about their homes and families honestly. However, distance and homesickness may have caused the GIs to idealize what they left behind in the States.

Phyllis Totman was impressed by the seeming prosperity of the Americans when she first arrived in the U.S.:

> From the start we had a car. In London, very few people I knew had a car. We had a washing machine. At the time I forgot that although our means were modest in England, my mother sent all the heavy wash to the laundry and it came back washed, ironed, and ready to put away.

A Short Guide to the United States, printed by the American Red Cross for war brides, boasted: "All in all, the lot of the housewife in America is, at present, a great deal easier than that of a British housewife." The reverse proved to be true in some cases. Many war brides were amazed that their homes in America had no indoor plumbing or electricity, and that they were expected to cook on coal or wood stoves. One city girl, who found herself living on a farm lacking all the amenities to which she was accustomed, lost forty pounds her first year in the U.S. She would have gone home, had she been able to do so without having her parents say, "I told you so."

When introduced to her GI husband's sharecropper family in Alabama, Kathleen Thomas from Yorkshire, England, thought they were in the process of moving, because

> there was hardly any furniture and the walls were bare wood. Really dirty and primitive. I didn't have water in the house until my eighth child was two-and-a-half years old. My husband was a sharecropper and I worked in the cottonfields with him. Living conditions were horrible.

One British city dweller was very disappointed to find she had to live on a farm. She hadn't given much thought to what it would be like in the U.S.,

> but did *think* it would be a city. *It wasn't*. People on the farm where my husband had a job as a tenant farmer were *very* unfriendly and very bossy. My husband's employer walked into our bedroom and yelled for my husband to get up. It was very *hard* pumping water and making fire with coals and

kerosene and scrubbing clothes on a wash board. We had an outdoor toilet.

Another British bride, who found her husband's Italian-immigrant parents were poor and uneducated, recalled her new brother-in-law's

witless remark that he'd heard all British women cleaned their husband's shoes, together with all other household chores. I wondered what my mother would have said to that, for we employed two cleaning women and the men in our family cleaned our shoes as well as their own.

Any remark I made about England [my sister-in-law] countered with 'Do they have washing machines?' She seemed ignorant of the fact that England had been at war for the past six years and most of the things manufactured during that time pertained to munitions.

This war bride's first meal with her in-laws proved to be a big disappointment for her:

A meal was thrown on the table—sans tablecloth. I was prepared for the spaghetti, having always associated it with Italians. However, I didn't realize how unattractive it appeared, heaped on a cracked serving dish and then scooped onto mismatched plates, with tiny dribbles of sauce making trails on the table. . . . Wine, normally thought of as a gracious complement to a meal, was put on the table in a gallon jug and everyone liberally helped themselves. How glad I was my parents weren't there to witness my distress.

Another woman, whose father was a British officer, describes her reception by her in-laws as "horrific":

A decrepit taxi took us to an equally decrepit old two-story wooden house, rusty screens bulging in front of the doors. We hauled the luggage into what I can only think of as a malodorous brown cave. A woman sat bare-footed in an ancient armchair. She was wearing a feed sack dress and was tatting. My husband said, "Well, here she is, Mother!" Mother never got up, never stopped tatting, just asked in a whiney voice, "Didja hev a nice trip?" And that was it for welcome.

The father came home from work in his work clothes—and kept them on during the meal—not supper nor dinner—

just a mass of unknown food on odd plates, around which we sat on unmatched chairs while everybody grabbed. I was treated to ridicule about my accent or using an unfamiliar word. There was absolutely no consideration for a different culture.

The bathroom was utterly dreadful. A grubby ring around the old clawfooted tub had me making a big decision. Should I fill the tub *over* the ring and cover it, or *under* the ring so that I would not get somebody else's dirt in my bathwater. The toilet smelled strongly of urine and there were pink plastic drapes at the small window, absolutely covered with thick layers of dust.

My first night had me terrified when a giant spider crawled up from behind the head of the bed. Next morning I remarked that I thought they had a tarantula or something in the bedroom. I was greeted with roars of unkind laughter—"Them's no trantlers—them's house pets. They eats bugs!" All I can say is that the spiders were not earning their keep. Going into the kitchen one night I turned on the light and away scuttled tribes of huge black roaches.

Perhaps even worse than physical discomforts was the isolation. The mutual support the war brides had aboard ship was suddenly gone, as the reality of the vast distances between towns and cities in the U.S. hit home. A shipboard friend could be hundreds or thousands of miles away when needed. Few Americans could understand their homesickness; Americans often took offense when the war bride compared her homeland to the U.S. It was difficult to make friends with American women their age with whom they felt they had little in common. Marjorie Bargout was annoyed by what she felt was superficiality in American women:

I had been through a war with all its rationing, bombings, days and nights in the air raid shelters. Our house, our street was bombed, our windows blown out several times, the women here and I had nothing in common. I was only eighteen, but an American eighteen was a high school bobby-soxer—we were light years apart. Older women were into domesticity and fashion, subjects which bore me to death.

An English war bride from Chelmsford, Essex, found Americans to be childish about the world:

One became extremely tired of hearing about the hard times they had during the war. My God, they should have lived through Dunkirk and the Blitz, Buzz Bombs, Rockets, etc. Dunkirk—I was fourteen years old. You grow up in a hurry, believe me. I saw a boy in my class in a fishing smack and ran down the cliff to help him; what I picked up was shoulders and his head. He'd been strafed while coming back with a shipload of wounded. To my dying day I'll never forget that. Don't tell me about hardships over here. At least not in 1946. It was too soon.

Emotional baggage carried over from the war and the trauma of leaving behind surviving family members intensified initial homesickness. Audrey Smith, from Worcestershire, England, experienced a typical depression during her early adjustment: "For the first six months I was terribly homesick and cried myself to sleep every night."

Regret surfaced abruptly for June Romano:

Six weeks after I got here, my cousin married and I can remember going downtown to the Western Union office to send her a congratulatory telegram. I walked out of that office onto the street and it was as though a blank wall had come down in front of my face. *What the hell am I doing here?* I asked myself.

Whatever the answer to June's question, most war brides were here to stay. Most had children, or a baby on the way, and whatever their disillusionments with the U.S., most were still in love with their husbands. Even if funds were to be had to return home, pride held them back when they remembered those admonishing words, "You made your bed; now lie in it."

Harvesting sugar beets. (8th Air Force men volunteered to help with the harvest.) Lily Vicky and Santo DiNaro. 1944.

A GI and his British bride. Bournemouth, April 10, 1945. (Norma Wylie Edler)

Rainbow Corner, near Piccadilly Circus, was one of the best known American Red Cross Clubs. (Postcard contributed by Vera A. Cracknell Long)

Even at a wedding, doughnuts—the standard American Red Cross refreshment—make their appearance. (Catherine Roberts-Swauger)

Beryl Lynch and Charles Colvin married after nearly seven months of paperwork. West Leedsville, Australia, 1944. (Beryl Lynch Miller)

Wives and fiancees of American Servicemen's Club. Sydney, Australia. (Australian INS Photo; contributed by Stella Coates Frey)

Joyce and Robert Moore. Melchbourne, England, July 23, 1944. (Joyce Rowlands Moore)

Dorothy and Leo Lind honeymooning in Blackpool, England. June 1945. (Dorothy Butterworth Lind)

Tidworth Staging Area, January 1946.
To Southampton and then the States.
(American Red Cross)

At Carleton Hotel, Bournemouth, England prior to leaving for Southampton. (left) (Lily Vicky Blackmore DiNaro);

leaving Southampton (right) Jean Grantham Dahler).

Arriving in New York, February 10, 1946. (Doris Blackwell Hutchinson)

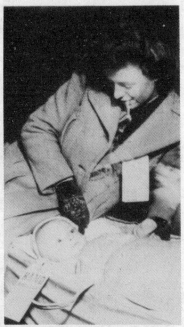

"Here Comes the Bride," (*left*) (*Queen Mary* Archives); *Hand Baggage!* (*right*) (American Red Cross); *Australian bride and twins* (*bottom*) (American Red Cross)

Europe—Liberators and Conquerors

Part Two

Karin Trenina, in her "Moscow Mule" rabbit fur coat, waiting for her fiancé, Lt. Burton Yount, in front of M.P. Headquarters. Bamberg, Germany, 1947.

KARIN TRENINA YOUNT

Chapter 7

Where's Your Husband?

*The day we got married my husband left for the invasion of Anzio.
I didn't see him for two years.*
—*Anna Gonzales, Naples, Italy*

The Italian women who married GIs between 1943 and 1945 faced years of uncertainty and hardship when their husbands were sent to the battlefront or transferred to other bases. Communication was uncertain and many war brides feared they had been abandoned; some of them were. Numbers of distressed Italian women roamed southern Italy searching for their GI bridegrooms. Those who could not return to their families had to turn to the Red Cross for assistance, for Italy's critical food shortage and lack of housing made it nearly impossible to exist without GI rations.

"Beautiful; terrible," were the words Maria Spinoso used to describe her first impression of American GIs. After forty years of helping Maria express herself in English, her husband, Peter, crossed out her words and wrote "We were all very happy and glad to see them come and liberate us from fear." No doubt both versions are valid for a great many Italian women. Due to Italy's unique position of fighting first against and then with the Americans, the country was bombed and shelled by both the Germans and the Allies, and the casualty rate of civilians caught in the crossfire was high. After the September 8, 1943, armistice between the Italians and the Allies, fighting between the Germans and Allies continued in Italy, with opposing Italian factions assisting both sides.

The Allied troops who entered the city of Naples on October 1, 1943, found that the situation of the population was desperate. There was no water, no food. Water and electric power had been cut off since the massive Allied air raids of August 4 and September 6. Many homes, hotels, and public buildings had been destroyed by German demolition squads before the Germans abandoned the city. During the first week of Allied occupation, hundreds of starving women and children were seen searching for edible plants and small birds along the roadside seven or eight miles outside of Naples, for fields nearer to the city had been stripped of everything edible.[1]

Anna Della Casa, one of the eighteen children of a Neapolitan civil servant, remembers being constantly hungry and having to line up before dawn for food rations, which sometimes ran out before her turn came. She and her sisters had to carry water home from the bay in buckets. On her way to the waterfront with her empty bucket one day, Anna heard a woman yell, "They're giving away food!" She entered a crowded store and, hungry and unaware that she was among looters who had broken in during the owner's absence, Anna began to fill her pail with a piece of cheese, some flour, oil, a salami. Then she heard shots outside. "German soldiers were shooting the people right there, with the food in their hands!" remembers Anna, who somehow managed to sneak out and run home.

When the Americans came, Anna's large family was crowded into her married sister's upstairs flat, because their own home had been burned by the retreating Germans. A woman who lived downstairs began washing clothes for American soldiers, and in September 1943 Anna saw GIs for the first time. Holding her sister's baby, Anna had no patience for the GIs who teased that John Gonzales liked her. "Oh, keep quiet," she told them. "Why don't you bring some milk for the baby?" John did, and returned often to visit the family. Soon Anna broke up with her Italian boyfriend, because he disapproved of the American soldier's visits. By December, Anna recalled, John wanted to marry her:

> My parents kind of encouraged me to marry John because I was almost going to have a nervous breakdown.

The air raids came when we were asleep, and you wake up—where's my stocking? where's my shoe? where's my coat? And then never mind, you run out—it was cold. I said I want my shoes. It's cold—never mind! Run, run, run! And while you run the bombs drop! and you see people die. Oh my God, I don't want—That's why my Mom told me, "You marry Johnny. Go, go, go, go, and we'll come one day." I didn't want to come to America, because we were too close in our family, very close. But they said, "Oh, you're gonna send for your mother, your father, everybody." [2]

"My hometown was the last place to be liberated, so when I first saw the American GIs I was overwhelmed," recalls Iolanda McMullin of Gorizia. "I never saw so much cigarettes and chocolate candy." The GIs were generous to the Italians, sharing their rations and not hesitating to "liberate" supplies from the mess hall to feed destitute civilians.

A post exchange in Naples was well stocked with candy, chewing gum, cigarettes, and toothpaste, and a separate women's counter offered face creams, lipsticks, and nail polish for female members of the armed forces. "Men were not allowed to patronize this department, but frequently a soldier waylaid a WAC or a nurse, asking her to buy a lipstick or a box of face powder which he could give to some Italian girl." [3] A Triestina was surprised when the American officer she was dating presented her with some perfume and a card with the message (in Italian), "You stink good." Although there is no common expression in Italian equivalent to the English "You smell good," she still thinks her husband's secretary may have deliberately mistranslated the phrase because she wanted to date him herself.

The GIs brought an element of fun with them, too. The American Red Cross set up rest centers and clubs in metropolitan areas where American troops were concentrated, and Italian women enjoyed being able to forget about food shortages and the recent German occupation. "We found we could have some kind of recreation at the rest center and enjoy dancing and the company of the American GIs," recalls Renata Chiaro, who later married one of the GI musicians who played in the band at the rest center in Rome. "He tried to talk to me but his Italian was kind of wrong—well, bad—somehow we communicated with one another by motions with our hands. He was a good companion and we sure had a lot of fun."

By the late 1940s the Americans had their own radio station in Trieste, and Ken Spitler was one of the GI disk jockeys. Luisa Ermani had a photographer's concession in a Red Cross Club and Ken "dedicated so many songs to me that I finally learned that the Americans had a radio station and that's why so many GIs knew my name." Although she didn't normally date GIs, Luisa consented to go out with Ken on his twenty-first birthday. He proposed on the first date.

Courtship was often carried out under the watchful eyes of a signorina's family, with a "date" permitted occasionally if the couple was properly chaperoned. Many Italian women worked for the Americans and met their future husbands on the job. One woman married the GI who often came to her sister's tailor shop to chat with her as she ironed. Another married a GI she met at the opera. And sometimes the meetings that led to romance were quite coincidental: "I was walking. He was standing on a corner. I bump into him. Then he follow me home."

Because there were few experts on contemporary Italy in the U.S., the War Department had turned to second generation Italian-Americans for the work of military government and intelligence in Italy. These men became deeply involved in Italian life. "In their half-scornful, half-affectionate fashion, they began to make friends," observed H. Stuart Hughes. "Many American soldiers found a woman, or even an entire family, who offered them a second home. Others became engaged or married to 'nice' girls whom their parents had sedulously sheltered from the perils of the streets." [4]

"Marry a nice Italian girl!" many Italian-American parents told their GI sons who were going overseas. Upon receiving orders for Germany, a Chicago GI was told by his parents, "Don't marry a German girl. You go to our hometown and marry an Italian girl from there." A dutiful son, he took a week's vacation in Italy and did indeed select a wife among the girls in his parents' hometown. On some shipping lists, the number of war brides from Italy whose husbands had an Italian surname is over 50 percent. Ines d'Angelo, who met her husband at a party at a friend's house in Rome, attributed their immediate attraction to each other to his being of Italian extraction. It certainly helped facilitate communication when the GI could speak at least some Italian.

Italians did not always react favorably to their women dating GIs. "My mother always told me GIs look for cheap thrills," says a Triestina who never wanted to date a soldier, regardless of his nationality, for soldiers had a bad reputation, and often the girls who dated them did too. Although her sisters dated GIs, she always refused their attempts to arrange dates for her. Eventually, though, she fell for a GI who was in civilian clothes when they met. Her mother's fears were realized when one of the sisters was left behind pregnant and unmarried when her GI returned to the States. Attempts to locate him through the Red Cross failed. She became one of many women left behind with illegitimate children fathered by GIs.

One war bride felt that some soldiers married overseas so they could have sex without worrying about contracting venereal disease, which was rapidly spreading among the soldiers. With much of the Italian population destitute and undernourished, "morality sank to an extremely low level, and prostitution and the black market flourished, feeding on the presence of Allied forces who were well provided for." [5] Estimates of the number of prostitutes in Naples in 1944 range from nearly 4,000 to over 40,000. Soldiers stationed in Italy during the war were quick to defend these so-called prostitutes and often spoke with great respect for these women who sacrificed much to support their families under the most difficult circumstances. British soldier Norman Lewis, who felt that 75 percent of these women would cease to be prostitutes "as soon as they can hope to keep alive by any other means," described their situation:

Nine out of ten Italian girls have lost their menfolk, who have either disappeared in battles, into prisoner-of-war camps, or been cut off in the North. The whole population is out of work. Nobody produces anything. How are they to live? [6]

The red light district of Naples was declared off-limits to GIs, posters warning against VD covered every wall in areas occupied by the Allies, and there were "pro stations," where prophylactics were distributed to the GIs free of charge, on every corner. In some cities, the American Red Cross issued a "Trust Pass" to women who were investigated and found to be of good character and free of disease. "They wanted nice girls to go to the club so that GIs wouldn't go out on their own and get into trouble. The Red Cross attempted to set up a controlled social atmosphere," remembers a war bride from Trieste.

The reputation of any woman who consorted with Allied soldiers suffered because of the rise in prostitution. Italian men resented their women dating Americans and some young Italians shaved the heads of women who dated GIs. Bruna Guarino recalls what happened to her coworker at the Institute of the Innocent in Florence, who was dating an American MP in the winter of 1943–44:

> Two men came out from the shadows and started insulting the girl. She believed they were fascists. The American came to her aid, and the Black shirts pulled her hair up and cut off part of the front. With the same scissors they turned on the American and stabbed him. He was lucky he was wearing a wide white military belt and the scissors never penetrated.

This incident and similar stories in the newspapers made many girls fearful of dating Americans.

Maria Spinoso remembers that pregnant women were harassed and had their heads shaved. They were taunted about being left behind and called "Madama Butterfly" by youths who carried scissors in their pockets to cut the hair of women who fraternized with American GIs. Seven members of a so-called "Barber Gang" were arrested in Rome in February 1945.[7] Many Italian women were careful not to be seen in public with a GI. In *Naples '44,* Norman Lewis described the complex web of relationships and social structure of betrothal and marriage in Italy, and the effect of the Allied soldiers on these traditions:

> The foreign soldiers came on the scene and were in immediate collision with the local boys, who had no work, no prestige, no money, absolutely nothing to offer the girls . . . an American private—who can shower cigarettes, sweets, and even silk stockings in all directions—has a higher income than any Italian employee in Naples. The temptation is very great, and few seem able to resist. Thus the long, delicate, intricate business of the old Neapolitan courtship—as complex as the mating ritual of exotic birds—is replaced by a brutal, wordless approach, and a crude act of purchase. One wonders how long it will

take the young of Naples, after we have gone, to recover from the bitterness of this experience.[8]

But "a crude act of purchase" was not what most GIs were interested in. GI John Horne Burns said many soldiers were not long content with "affection" that had to be bought. Burns describes the situation:

> Consequently after a few tries, with the fear of VD always suspended over our heads, we began to look at the good women of Naples. And here entered the problem of the GI Italian bride. I remember that the Italian girls began to look sweet to us early. Perhaps because their virginity was put on such a pedestal. There were few of us who didn't have access to some Neapolitan home, where we were welcomed, once our entree was definite and our purposes aboveboard. We usually got in through a Neapolitan brother. Then we discovered that there were girls in the family, carefully kept and cherished as novices in a nunnery. It was obvious that these girls were interested in us . . . if we proposed marriage to them.[9]

The ease with which a GI could marry his Italian sweetheart depended on his individual commanding officer. John Gonzales had no trouble getting permission from his commanding officer and the chaplain of his unit, perhaps because his marriage to Anna Della Casa took place prior to Italian Decree 430 of December 28, 1944, which required a marriage form, filled out in triplicate, in both Italian and English. Later, a U.S. Army Review Board required that one of the couple speak the other's language, and instituted a personal interview and question period by an army officer of Italian origin.

One Italian war bride feels that poverty and hunger were responsible for many of the marriages to GIs. She says, "Half of Trieste married GIs, and the other half wanted to!" Maria Spinoso says, "The lack of everything led many naive young girls into the arms of allied soldiers." But her own reason for marrying a GI was "love at first sight," a statement seconded by her husband, Peter.

Peter Spinoso was a gunner on a B-24 Liberator, a "flying box car," when he chanced to meet Maria Donati at a party in Cerignola in 1944. It was love at first sight for both of them, but when Peter was to return to the U.S. after completing fifty missions, everyone told Maria, "once an American leaves you they never come back because they find somebody else." But Peter extended his stay in Italy for another fifty missions, and he and Maria decided that "on the day of St. Maria, September 12th, we would get engaged. So we had a party and everything was confirmed but I said I couldn't set a date to get married because I'm flying missions and I don't know what might happen, but just as soon as the war here in Europe ends I will set that date." On V-E Day, May 8, 1945, Peter took his parachute to Maria's village for her aunt to make the wedding dress. The seventy-two yards of parachute silk produced not only the wedding dress, but also two bridesmaids' dresses and two night-gowns, with still much fabric left over. The wedding took place on May 16.

Two months later, Peter was shipped back to the U.S. Maria recalls what followed:

My difficult and sad existence started then. Pietro had left me with a supply of food and 56,000 Lire which I would need for the birth of the child. The food soon came to an end with the "help" of my landlady and her son! My "Via Crucis" [sta- tions of the cross] at Livorno's PX started then. I must admit that this was helpful as I was able to buy things at a reduced price, which I later sold on the black market.

It was at the PX that I made the acquaintance of my guardian angel—an American Major—who was very kind and showed an interest in me (a purely platonic relationship!). He offered me his ration of cigarettes and his moral support of which I was in great need during that critical period. After he discovered my predicament (family situation) he got the American police to inspect my room and then had me and the other expecting war brides transferred, with the help of the Red Cross, to the "Stork Club" in Livorno. A new existence started for me then. I was fed at the American mess hall and received medical check- ups on a weekly basis.

On March 1, 1946, I gave birth at the Ardenza Military Hospital to my beautiful baby girl Margherite. She bears the name of an American Red Cross nurse who was the only person present at the delivery and who continued to take an interest in me. She translated Pietro's letters for me and wrote my letters as I knew no English.

Meanwhile, Peter was trying to secure transportation to the U.S. for Maria. He wrote to Senator Mead of New York but was told that there was little to be done to speed up the process. Although a petition according Maria nonquota status in the issuance of an immigration visa had been sent to the American consulate general in Naples on January 5, 1946, arranging transportation at government expense was at the discretion of the military authorities overseas.

An August 11, 1945, War Department circular informed theater commanders that the Military Appropriations Act of 1945 authorized theater commanders to provide shipping space for dependents of military personnel when such space was available and considered justified by the commander.[10] Although shipping priority was given to troops being demobilized, military regulations allowed for war brides to be transported to the U.S. in cases of extreme hardship, at the discretion of area commanders.

When *The Stars and Stripes* reported that fifty-six Italian war brides had travelled to the U.S. in October 1945 on the *Monticello* and *Wakefield,* a number of inquiries were sent to public officials on behalf of people who objected to the shipping of dependents before soldiers were returned to the U.S. A November 8, 1945, directive from Army Chief of Staff Lt. Col. Franklin directed that a reply be sent to inform Congressman Frank W. Boykin that dependents of military personnel were not eligible for transportation except in extreme hardship cases, and that all the dependents on the *Monticello* and the *Wakefield* were hardship cases carefully screened by both the army and the American Red Cross. Most of the women were pregnant, ill, or had infants under one year of age. Their living conditions were poor and their husbands had been discharged from the service and had no means of continuing to support a wife overseas. In most cases the young wife either had no family to help her, or the family was also having financial difficulties. "To care for these cases longer in the Theater would have involved an allocation of Army and Red Cross personnel and facilities which would have been incompatible with the Army's repatriation and demobilization program."[11]

In addition to helping with special hardship cases, the American

Red Cross provided weekly orientation classes for Italian war brides prior to their shipment to the U.S. A war bride who lived next door introduced Anna Gonzales to the Naples Red Cross:

She said, "Come with me." She took me to a building where there were American people working and I managed to get an identification card from the Red Cross to go to the PX. They used to have doughnuts, coffee, chocolates. We used to have meetings every day with the Red Cross—you had to be there—meetings about American law, American rules, American everything.

A lot of women were crying, "I don't know where my husband is." There were a lot of GIs who didn't send for their wives.

The Red Cross helped war brides write letters to their husbands and set up mailboxes for the brides to receive mail from the U.S. While John Gonzales, who had been sent home after being injured in Italy, was unable to find out how to bring his wife to California, Anna found the solution in Naples.

"I used to go to the Army camp and ask, 'How can I get my wife here?'" John said. "And nobody knew. The Captain, all the officers didn't know, until she sent me the little piece of paper—what to do—from the Red Cross." Anna remembers:

The Red Cross said, "We have good news from America. We're going to have some forms that your husband can fill out no matter where he is." After they sent this letter I sent one to my husband and he filled out the letter and sent it back to the Red Cross.

One time I saw the Red Cross lady come out with letters and I said, "Hi, Mrs. Templeman. Any news for me?" And she said, "Here. Your husband sent for you now." I was going to San Francisco! I ran and ran to tell my Mom. They had been telling me, "You're married, but where's your husband? Where's your husband?"

It would take several more months before Anna received notification to report to the Hotel Cincinnati in Pozzuoli, where war brides were housed prior to embarkation for the U.S. Here war brides and their children were examined to make sure they had no communicable diseases. Sometimes the residence of brides and babies at the hotel would extend to thirty or forty days when disease necessitated quarantine. Armida Knutson's son had to recover from measles at the Hotel Cincinnati before they could travel to the U.S.

The first contingent of Italian war brides arrived in New York aboard the U.S. Army Hospital Ship *Algonquin* on February 22, 1946, after a difficult two-week voyage. "We incurred very bad weather," Filomena Ruggiero recalls. "The ship almost sank. Two girls who were seven months pregnant lost their babies." Rosalia Lucatorto said that several infants died on that voyage. Her three-month-old daughter suffered from dysentery and had to be hospitalized upon arrival in the U.S.:

> My little girl struggled between life and death for three months and even the specialists at the hospital were amazed that she survived. Those two weeks we spent on the ship were nightmares and we all signed a complaint for the terrible treatment we received on board.

The *Algonquin* continued to make monthly trips between the U.S. and Italy and continued to encounter rough seas. Marcella Gallo was convinced her April 1946 voyage was the last the *Algonquin* ever made, but on May 17, 1946, the ship brought both Maria Spinoso and Anna Gonzales to New York. Maria and her daughter were taken to the hospital when they arrived, for baby Margherite had spent most of the voyage in the ship's infirmary. Anna was among the war brides treated to a bus tour of New York before they boarded trains for destinations in other parts of the U.S.:

> When I reached New York it was my birthday. Some Italian old men came to the bus to give us flowers, doughnuts, cookies. They knew Italian war brides came and they gave us a nice welcome. The strike was still on with the trains, but then they sent a special train for war brides.

Anna asked one of the Italian men to send a telegram for her, and she arrived in Los Angeles expecting John to meet her there. But she found she had to continue on to Oakland alone, and from there she took a ferry to San Francisco. Still there was no husband to meet her. Another war bride wanted Anna to come home with her and her husband, saying they would then look for John. But Anna said, "No. I don't want to look for nobody. If he was not here, I want to go back to my Mom. I'm going to go right back to my family in Italy." With the help of the police, contact was made with John by telephoning a downstairs neighbor (for John had no phone in his flat). John had been completely unaware that Anna was on her way to America.

We started fighting the first day I was here because I thought he didn't want me. "Why didn't you tell me you don't want me? I was gonna stay in Italy. I won't come here. I'll get a divorce and then I'll go back in Italy." But he said he didn't know anything about that I was going to come. His sister didn't give him no letter, no telegram, no nothing.

John lived with his sister who disapproved of his overseas marriage and did not give him the letters announcing Anna's arrival.

Rosalia Lucatorto, who said she had not slept during the two-week voyage to the U.S., had a much better reception from her in-laws. "Relatives and friends came to welcome me, but unfortunately in the middle of it I fell asleep like a log, and I can't remember a thing. My beloved husband told me that I slept for twelve hours and a bomb could not wake me up!"

Ines d'Angelo's husband and his Italian-American family welcomed her warmly at the dock in New York. "I loved them right away," says Ines. Renata Chiaro's Italian in-laws were at the station to greet her, too, but she found the meeting awkward:

It was somewhat embarrassing, because I could not understand them. But they smiled a lot and I smiled back at them. I could not understand my in-laws, either their English or their Italian, because they spoke a dialect that to me was a completely strange language. I was frustrated because I couldn't talk to anybody. And, boy, I made up my mind that I was going to do something about that.

Now, the second disappointment came the same day, when I was told that we would all be living together. Eight people in a two-bedroom house. I was thinking of my big beautiful bedroom and my apartment in Rome—we had four bedrooms.

Maria Brixner was considered lucky by her war bride friends because her in-laws adopted her from the beginning. Her mother-in-law admitted, however, that she had sent a discouraging letter to her son when he first announced his intention to marry an Italian.

Despite apprehensions, the Brixners met their daughter-in-law at the station with flowers, an Italian symbol of welcome, and their misgivings disappeared as soon as they met Maria.

Luisa Spitler's father-in-law announced he approved of his son's bride at a restaurant where they stopped for lunch on the way home from the airport. Luisa found meeting family friends a little disconcerting:

> Every night my in-laws had friends over for dinner or a drink. All their friends were nice people, but invariably all would ask me how I liked the U.S. Not only had I not seen much of this country to form an opinion but in Italy we asked foreigners to tell us about their own country. Much more interesting and diplomatic!

While Italian brides and fiancées were travelling to the U.S. to join their American husbands, there were also a few American women travelling to Italy to marry former Italian POWs. During the war, 51,071 Italian soldiers were interned in the U.S. When Italy changed from enemy to cobelligerent, these POWs were permitted to volunteer for work in Italian Service Units (ISUs) and were paid $8.00 monthly, plus $16.00 in coupons redeemable at the camp canteen.[12] These men

> sought the company of American women, both at dances held for them in camp and during evenings when they were allowed to go into town, usually in groups of four or five escorted by a GI. These good-natured, often good looking young men pursued and at times were pursued by young girls, wives whose spouses were overseas, middle-aged widows, and, in the second instance, by angry husbands and irate fathers.[13]

Scores of letters were sent to Washington on the subject of love and marriage with Italian POWs. Most of them were from young women seeking permission to marry ISU men, but the army did not permit any POW to marry while in this country. A dozen or so Italians, however, took advantage of liberal state laws and married before the Pentagon issued a ban on December 14, 1944. In spite of specific regulations against POW marriages, letters continued to flow to officials in Washington.

On July 11, 1945, General Brehon Somervell issued a stern four-page memorandum to all service commands, stating that sexual relations between ISU personnel and American women were much too prevalent:

> Prisoners of war, even those occupying a special status of Italian Service Unit signee, should not have an opportunity to develop their acquaintanceship with American women to the point where matrimony is contemplated. The women were encouraging the prisoners to go AWOL, and were harboring them, even deserting and divorcing husbands in uniform to be with the Italians. One would think from the volume received at the Pentagon, he noted scornfully, that "one of the functions of the Provost Marshall General is to conduct an 'advice to the lovelorn' bureau!" [14]

Ruggerio Purin, an Italian POW captured in Tunis, Africa, in June, 1943, was transported to several camps in different states before he was sent to Camp Hill Field, Utah, in 1945. He was assigned to work at Fairmont Park in Salt Lake City, where he met his future wife seventeen days before returning to Italy:

> I was treated better by the American Army than by my own Italian Army. I suffered while in the Italian Army. There were various times when I had to beg for food from civilians in order to stay alive.
>
> I remember returning home to Italy after the war was over. It was later that the girl I met in Salt Lake City came over to Italy and our marriage followed. I loved Italy and wanted to stay there, but my wife wanted to return to the United States. I remember how humane my treatment was here as a prisoner of war. Otherwise I would never have returned to live in this country. [15]

Chapter 8

The Liberation of Europe

*Dances were everywhere. Everyone was so happy to be "free"
again.*
—Lisette Brock, Paris, France

All the church bells in Paris were ringing. After five years of war
and degradation under German occupation, the entire population
of Paris thronged the streets as American soldiers liberated their
city on August 25, 1944. *"Merci! Merci!"* they shouted as they waved,
fingers spread in the "V" for victory sign. Some reached into marching columns of GIs to touch them and present a hero with a hoarded
bottle of champagne or wine, a bouquet of flowers, or a hearty
kiss on the cheek.

"The gratitude toward Americans is immense and sometimes
embarrassing in its manifestations," wrote American correspondent
A. J. Liebling:

> People are always stopping one in the street, pumping one's
> hand, and saying "Thank you." It is useless to protest. To

the Parisians, and especially to the children, all Americans are now *Héros du cinema*. This is particularly disconcerting to sensitive war correspondents, if any, aware, as they are, that these innocent thanks belong to those American combat troops who won the beachhead and then made the breakthrough. There are few such men in Paris. Young women, the first day or two after the Allies arrived, were as enthusiastic as children; they covered the cheeks of French and American soldiers alike with lipstick.[1]

Previously solemn French women, many who'd risked their lives serving with the Résistance, many still mourning the death of a relative or friend, unleashed their emotions in jubilant and grateful embraces. Andrée Blais Davis of Nantes, France, described the arrival of the GIs as "love at first sight." Andrée, who had served with the underground faction known as the Lucy Group, said, "With war, then German occupation, there was no time or opportunity to meet many French men." For most women, there had been little time for romance during the war. The liberation was an exhilarating turning point, a rebirth.

French demoiselles were a welcome sight, as well, for GIs who lifted them into their jeeps and trucks and adorned them with their helmets and pistol belts. Wine, women, and song was the order of the day as Americans drank in the hero worship before moving on to face the die-hard enemy troops still awaiting them on the route to Berlin. Names and addresses were exchanged on cigarette and candy wrappers as chance threw a man and woman together for a moment or a lifetime.

"*Vive l'Amérique! Vive Roosevelt!* Honor to the Liberators!" the crowds shouted. A. J. Liebling remembered his colleague shouting back, "I have done nothing. I am only a journalist," to which a young woman answered, "He is so modest! He is adorable!" Another woman exclaimed, "How tall they are!" and showered him with kisses on the left temple, knocking his helmet liner over his right eye.[2]

The crowds were under a spell. To French women, the GIs were heros larger than life, while Americans saw French women as alluring sirens. A. J. Liebling gave his impression of the Parisiennes:

To make a woman really beautiful, liberate her. She visibly exudes a generalized good will that makes you want to kiss her.

These women wore long, simple summer dresses that left their bodies very free. (Elastic for girdles had disappeared from Occupied France years earlier.) Their bare legs were more smoothly muscled than French women's before the war, because they had been riding those bicycles or walking ever since taxis vanished from the streets of Paris, and their figures were better, because the *pâtissiers* were out of business. It was a tribute to the French frame that none of them looked scrawny or knobby. Their hair was done up high on their heads, without silly little ponytails, and they wore wooden platform shoes, because there was no leather. As they bore down on the oncoming jeeps, I understood how those old Sag Harbor whalers must have felt when the women of the islands came swimming out to them like a school of beautiful tinker mackerel.[3]

At nightfall, Paris was once more a city of light, its restaurants packed, people dancing in bistros and in the streets. The parents of sixteen-year-old Lisette Vergnoux gave her permission to attend a neighborhood celebration where she danced with her future husband, Clyde Brock. "Dances were everywhere," recalls Lisette. "Everyone was so happy to be 'free' again."

Many French women enjoyed GI lightheartedness. "Carefree, happy to be alive," Andrée d'Angelo from Marseilles described the American soldiers she met. "French men were more concerned with national and world problems. An American would tell you laughingly, 'I am a plain man with simple tastes.' A French man took pleasure in life's complications."[4]

GIs stationed in Paris after the liberation made the most of their tour of duty as John Neill, a journalist for *Life,* reported in the spring of 1945:

One of the pleasantest sights on Paris streets and park walks these afternoons of warm spring sun is that of eager GIs and dark-eyed demoiselles attacking the problems of language and budding love with much earnest thumbing of phrase books.

The Stars and Stripes and the French newspaper *Résistance* have been a great help. Each publishes daily one or more useful phrases, with translation and phonetic equivalent. An assiduous student of *The Stars and Stripes,* for example, is qualified to engage in such improving conversations as the following:

> GI: Bawn-JOOR, lay fronSAYS sawn marvay-yuhs. [Good-day, French girls are wonderful.]
>
> Parisienne: Voo zet treh jahnTEE. [You are very nice.]
>
> GI: Kuh fett voo sub swahr? [What are you doing tonight?]

These conversational gambits are considerably more useful to the GI in Paris than the ones suggested in Army handbooks, which include phonetical French for "I am lost," "I want insecticide," and "Give my horse water." [5]

Introductions, in some instances, were made by parents who unwittingly chose a son-in-law by inviting a soldier home to dinner. Monsieur and Madame Raymond Buignet of Paris, pleased to meet a GI who spoke French, invited him to share a French gourmet dinner with them instead of his usual canned rations. Before long, T.Sgt. Emery Delongchamp, then with the 709th MP Battalion, proposed to their only daughter, Germaine. She was employed by the House of Lanvin, where colleagues gave them an engagement party and then set to work on a wedding dress with a pattern from the exclusive "Collection Maison Jeanne Lanvin."

In the fall of 1944, GIs were cluttering the desks of their commanding officers with requests for permission to marry French women. On December 9, 1944, the Paris newspaper *Libération Soir* hailed the first union between an American officer and a French woman since the liberation, featuring a photo on the front page of Denise Khaitman and Stanley Schorr as they signed the marriage register. [6]

"We met on my birthday, September 20," recalled Denise. Stan, a lieutenant with an antiaircraft unit, was stationed in Paris at the time. September 20 was also Rosh Hashana, and Stan and some of his buddies wanted to attend a service. They were told that there was a synagogue at a home for troubled teenagers where Denise was a social worker. Stan readily accepted an invitation to attend Denise's birthday party afterwards. A friend noticed how taken he was with Denise and told her he would ask her to marry him. Denise shrugged it off saying, "I'd never marry anyone as short as him." Stan stood just over five feet tall, slightly taller than Denise.

"Stan and I only had two dates and he asked me to marry him." Denise was willing. "I liked his dark eyes and his refreshing innocent look. But I told him he had to ask my father—in those days a father's answer was important." Denise's mother was crazy about Stan from the start and did not protest. Her father was concerned about possibly not seeing her for long periods of time, but gave his consent after Stan reassured him he would bring her back on visits.

The Church expressed doubt about the advisability of such unions. Cardinal Suhard, Archbishop of Paris, spoke against marriages between French women and soldiers of the Allied forces, referring to failed marriages from World War I. On February 10, 1945, he issued instructions to parish priests to notify his office of any proposed marriages with American or British nationals. The warning was no more of a deterrent than were language differences.[7]

America was known to many Europeans as "the land of divorces," remembers Christiane Buchanan of Soissons, France, a teacher who helped organize a welcoming committee to improve relations between the GIs and the civilian population. But when she fell in love with a soldier from Appalachia, she decided to take her chances.

V-E Day, May 8, 1945, brought thousands of cheering women like Yolande Dauphin into the streets and into the arms of American soldiers again. A GI swept her off her feet as they danced in the streets of LeVesinet, and then he led her to the altar on February 16, 1946. It was a bittersweet marriage for a fifteen-year-old girl. Yolande explained that her GI

> had received a "Dear John" letter from his wife in the U.S.
> His divorce was processed quickly and we were able to marry.
> My only parent was my mother who was 48 years older than
> me. She gave her consent hoping this was for the best. I decided
> to escape being a "batarde" by getting the first man to marry
> me. We had a free honeymoon in Chamonix, paid for by the
> French government as a goodwill gesture.

After some GIs suddenly broke off their engagements, or their marriages to French women turned out to be illegal, the hero worship faded. When Jacqueline Campbell of LeHavre announced her engagement, her three older sisters were afraid she would be disappointed. "We had heard about a few girls from LeHavre who had returned from the U.S. after finding out that the GIs they were engaged to were either already married or had no intention of going through with the marriage to them," Jacqueline explained. Disreputable soldiers were also "exploiting our lack of food and clothing and were selling blankets, C-rations, etc., at outrageous prices or for very 'personal' favors," recalled Huguette Study of Nice.

Paul Trunzo, who met his wife Olga at a dance on June 16, 1945, wrote about her apprehensions regarding GIs in his diary:

We had a marvelous evening. We again enjoyed each other's company the following Tuesday at a Red Cross sponsored dance. Our next date was for the following Saturday night, but she didn't show and wouldn't date me anymore. Much later I learned that she was falling in love and remembering all the stories about the GIs "loving and leaving." She put on the brakes as far as our relationship was concerned.

For four months we would dance, talk, enjoy a drink together, and I would take care of her desire for candy and cigarettes. I was totally committed and always had the feeling that she was playing a reluctant part. My perseverance was finally rewarded on October 2, 1945, when she consented to go with me to see a USO show, *The Rockettes*. I kissed her for the first time that night.

We were wed on Friday, December 28, 1945 . . . the first happy event to occur in her small town of Montois la Montaigne in over six years. We held a large reception for most of the town with No. 10 cans of turkey, potatoes, fruit cocktail and many, many large cakes.

Even if a French woman preferred to avoid the Americans, it was very difficult, since they became a primary source of employment for many French citizens. Even if one was not directly employed by the Americans, communication with them was still often necessary, as it was between Rachel Berquez and Arthur Plamondon. Rachel met a GI over the wire while she was "a telephone operator at the Post Office telegraph-telephone in Compiègne, France. Arthur was a switchboard operator. In our city, after being liberated, we had several branches of the armed forces. Around January 1945, we had 10,000 GIs under tents on the golf course."

Some American servicemen and women communicated so well with the French that they decided to settle in France with their brides and grooms. Pat Livingston Bounin, an ex-WAC, and her husband Claude took an apartment one block away from the gardens of the Champs de Marseilles. They met at a nightclub on V-E Day. Pat wanted to stay in France and said she considered "Frenchmen more chivalrous than Americans." Bill Loomis and his French wife Ginette, who met during a liberation celebration when she ran up on the Champs-Elysées and kissed him, also decided to stay. Many Americans in France found jobs as civilians with the American army. Others worked as artists or journalists.[8]

Historian and reporter Theodore H. White, working in postwar France, recalled that overall:

Americans were welcome, American reporters particularly so. The embossed press card, the tricolored *coup fils* of the accredited correspondent, was a *laissez-passer* anywhere. . . . Gasoline was tightly rationed for Frenchmen; but an American reporter was entitled to 120 liters a month. Down the empty boulevards, down the Champs-Elysées, one could sweep at forty miles an hour, parking anywhere, free of traffic regulations, while the police smiled.

Not only was the government indulgent of the Americans; so were the people. I recall going to visit the D-Day beaches in Normandy. . . . Coming off Omaha Beach, I pulled out into the main road, speeded up, swerved out from behind a truck, and forced a motorcyclist into a ditch, where he tumbled to the ground. I was horrified, and ran to pick him up. He rose, glaring, brushing himself off, and turned on me, then recognized my accent. Was I an American? he asked. I said yes and began to bumble apologies and offer help. But he smiled, said it was unimportant: all Americans were friends.[9]

The French in North Africa also cheered the arrival of the GIs. In Casablanca, Morocco, Eliane Lasry was "Ecstatic!" when she saw Americans in battle dress marching into the city in 1943. "As our saviours," she said, "they seemed 'taller' than other men in every way."

Wedding bells started ringing for GIs and French women in North Africa as early as the summer of 1943. Victor Sotnik applied to his commanding officer for permission to marry in June 1943. "He told him he was crazy. We had a war to fight," recalled Victor's wife, Alichka, of Algiers. "But Victor insisted. Col. Elliott Roosevelt, who was Commanding Officer of the 3rd Photo Group, gave permission to marry. Victor was the second GI in the Mediterranean Theatre of Operations to get such permission. We were married in August."

Love flourished right through the bombing of Algiers. Trying to keep her mind on her job as a civilian with the twelfth Air Force Service Command, Nadia Goëau de la Brissonièrre found the attentions of one GI to be as distracting as the explosives going off in the street:

I was so scared to even look at him that I might lose my job. He kept coming past my desk and one day he asked a civilian friend to introduce us. I thought he was the most handsome soldier standing there in his uniform. There was a lot of bombing every day. One time we were so exhausted from all this we laid down in an ambulance to sleep. Both of us were startled as the ambulance began moving. They stopped and we took off. The next morning I was sitting at my desk typing, as I looked up, there stood a PFC. He was holding a tiny match box from Bill. He handed it to me and said he was waiting for an answer. I opened the little box. There was a small gold ring and a note, "Will you marry me." I turned to the soldier and said, "Oui."

As American soldiers advanced on the European continent, they were generally given "red carpet" treatment wherever they went, regardless of the dubious reputations of soldiers worldwide. In Belgium, Carmen Kergis of Bièrges remembered, "It was not really 'proper' to go out with a soldier even if he was American. Of course, a German soldier would have been unacceptable. I would have been ostracized! But the Americans, how we loved them all; we thought if we survived until we saw them, we would never die anymore."

Sylvia Gardner of Liège learned that an engagement could take place without the usual formalities: "In Belgium a man must ask a girl's parents for her hand, everything is much more slow and formal (so are the boys) but the Americans just came and proceeded to conquer the Belgian girls as far as they advanced over the land." Sylvia wed an American officer in the Forest of Ardennes.

A paratrooper recalled landing in Holland in September 1944 at the city of Nijmegen, where his outfit was to take the bridge from the Germans: "Those gallant Dutch were all around. It was like a holiday and the girls all hugged and kissed us. They even threw flowers—it was all unreal. Then they brought us good, cold beer." [10]

A Dutch war bride, Gertrude Reichenbach, recalled the arrival of the GIs in Arnhem:

> We were liberated on the 17th of September and that was the same day of the airdrop of Arnhem and that of course was a failure . . . the liberated area was south of the rivers, the northern part was still occupied and had no food; it was just terrible. During that time we had the 1st and 9th Army in that part of Holland and then it became a rest center. My brother worked for the Americans as interpreter. He brought one of these soldiers home and he was to become my husband.

Dutch war brides often made a trip to the American cemetery in Margraten on their wedding day. Bridal bouquets were placed on the graves of GIs who died liberating their country. [11]

Although friendship was encouraged with Americans, European and American government officials had mixed opinions about marriage. The American chargé d'affaires in Luxembourg, George Platt Waller, was decidedly against such marriages. At the request of American Headquarters European Theatre of Operations, the government of Luxembourg waived its lengthy legal prerequisites for marriage between soldiers and Luxembourg women for a period of one year. Waller expressed his disagreement in a letter to the secretary of state in Washington:

> I had hoped that during this war some effective means would be worked out by our military authorities to prevent marriages

between members of our armed services and women of French, Luxembourg, Dutch, Belgian, and German nationality. In the case of Luxembourg I feel very strongly on the subject because among the recurring annoyances with which I have had to cope during the past fourteen years have been the cases of Luxembourg women married during the last war to American soldiers and officers who have been pursuaded to return to their homeland by their husbands and then neglected, abandoned, and frequently divorced without their knowledge in order that their husbands might marry Americans.

When a soldier comes to me to inquire how he can get married, I discuss the matter in a very frank and kind way, and point out to him the practical certainty that his marriage will prove a source of unhappiness to himself and of misery to his partner.[12]

Maya Cellina, a school teacher from Luxembourg, and Sgt. Anthony Usewicz were not discouraged by these warnings and went ahead with their marriage on September 29, 1945, in the Sacred Heart Church in Luxembourg. Maya had met Anthony while she fled the Germans, who had tried to kidnap her as they retreated. She ran toward Mandorf, about thirteen miles away, in the direction of the advancing American lines. Anthony, riding in a jeep, was among the first GIs she ran into.

By January 1946, at least 6,000 French and other European women had married American soldiers.[13] As the transportation program got underway at the end of February 1946, hundreds of brides prepared to leave their homes and families. "It is much better for you to be happy 3,000 miles away, rather than miserable living right around the corner," Simone Verhaghen Howland's mother in Brussels assured her. Another bride from Antwerp wasn't so sure; she turned back en route after crying all the way saying, "I can't go through with it. He will have to come with me here."

The first official contingent of 206 war brides and 9 babies entrained at the Gare Saint Lazare on February 28, 1946, while an army band played *The Marseillaise*. Several hours later they arrived at LeHavre and detrained at Camp Phillip Morris as the German

POW band there played *Here Comes the Bride*. Other brides from Belgium, Holland, and Luxembourg were assembled at the Hotel de Paris, a reconverted hotel for GI dependents in Paris. At the camp, seven French women were on hand to help. The Red Cross was there with coffee and doughnuts.[14]

Germaine Delongchamp remembered five cold nights in the Nissen huts: "German POWs were working there and brought us wood for two pot-bellied stoves. The 'rest room' was a tent where there was a bench with five holes in it!"

"The documentaries and lectures at Camp Phillip Morris tried to persuade us that it was no longer Cowboys and Indians, and that not every American had been born with a silver spoon in his mouth!" remembered Simonne Migden of Besançon, France:

> But some of the brides clung to their illusions. I recall the elegant Parisian who had knowingly wed a sharecropper. Yet, having read *Gone with the Wind* too many times, she could not shake her vision of her white columned Tara-like mansion staffed with a retinue of black servants (fortunately she did not call them slaves)!

Simonne also related an incident in the theatre barracks where a Red Cross worker asked those who were expecting to raise their hands:

> An embarrassed silence followed. Finally, the head nurse said, "It's not a disgrace but an honor to be pregnant." Immediately a hundred hands went up, mine included. We were given special food rations, vitamins and the lower berths in the ship cabins.

On March 6, 1946, the United States Army transport *General W. Goethals* left LeHavre after a twenty-minute delay caused by a stowaway, Madame Lulu Politzer of Paris, who couldn't bear to part with her war bride daughter, Rosette Adelson. Altogether, 426 wives and 15 babies laughed and cried as they left their native shores.[15]

Simonne Migden left with the next group shortly after on the *Vulcania*:

> Some of the women who had married officers complained bitterly about being mixed with the wives of mere privates and demanded preferential treatment. Instead, they got their

first lesson on the meaning of American democracy: On the
ship everybody was equal and nobody was more equal than
the others.

In contrast to their jubilant and hopeful beginnings after the
liberation, many European women experienced tragedy and disappointment as they prepared to start a new life in America. Collette
Bollens of Paris was a passenger aboard the converted Liberty Ship
Zebulon Vance, later referred to as "The Death Ship" by the crew
because of this infamous May voyage:

> We were like cattle so tight on narrow bunk beds, some
> 200 women and children in the same room. Many were seasick
> and since I was OK the officer in charge put a Red Cross arm
> banner on my arm and declared me Red Cross help. The babies
> sick and dying were a nightmare. I believe it was in the food
> they ate that was the cause of their illness. When we got to
> New York after 12 days at sea, the ship stopped before port
> and the dead babies were loaded out in small plain wood cof-
> fins—that was my first impression of America.

Thirteen babies out of the 57 children and 369 adults who crossed
over on the *Vance* died as a result of an infectious diarrhea epidemic.[16]

Another type of nightmare awaited Georgette Baker of Liège,
Belgium, who arrived in May 1946 aboard the *Santa Paula.* When
she was reunited with her husband in Mississippi she found "a totally
different person than I had married, a beer drinker, no job, no home,
no nothing but one room in a hotel."

An eighteen-year-old bride from Marseilles, who expected a
Tara-like existence in Georgia, was rudely awakened when she
reached her destination:

> My husband had told me and my Mom and Dad—when
> Jackie come to America she will never have to do anything
> like house cleaning, dishwashing, ironing, cooking, making
> bed, etc. She will have two colored maids. They will take
> care of her like a baby.
>
> It was a great big shock for me when I saw Mom-in-law
> had to build a fire in her stove so she could cook the food—
> how terrible. And there was not anyone waiting on her and
> certainly no plantation—no help of any kind. We lived in pieces
> of board and carton box for a house, two little rooms, no

water, no kitchen or bathroom. As things turned out to be, I became his "Bonne à tout faire" (maid of all trade).

Gertrude Reichenbach of Holland was more bewildered than anything else by her welcome in Philadelphia at the end of October 1946:

> There were people, neighbors, who came wearing masks and were drunk and they wanted to see the Dutch girl with the wooden shoes. Of course, I didn't know those people were neighbors down the street. I thought, oh boy, all Americans are crazy.

The masqueraders hadn't intended to frighten the newcomer; they were simply celebrating Halloween.

Chapter 9

Remember, They Are Still the Enemy!

Don't gum up the victory!
—*headline from an editorial in* The Stars and Stripes *protesting the GIs' practice of distributing gum and candy to German children*

"Be on your Guard. DON'T FRATERNIZE WITH GERMANS" warned hastily lettered signs posted by the roadside as reminders to GIs marching through Germany during the spring of 1945.[1] As Germany prepared to surrender, the Allied Joint Chiefs of Staff, anticipating problems controlling the social activities of GIs about to begin a lengthy occupation, issued Order Number 1067 in April 1945:

> Germany will not be occupied for the purpose of liberation but as a defeated enemy nation. In the conduct of your occupation and administration you should be firm and aloof. You will strongly discourage fraternization with the German officials and population.[2]

And yet, when the Americans occupied a German town, the establishment of a military government necessitated constant contact with civilians who were registered, rounded up for labor details, questioned about possible Nazi affiliations, and restricted from travelling more than three miles.

Armed GIs were sent to eighteen-year-old Annemarie Ploderl's home in Starnbergsee, Bavaria, to search for her father, who had been a chauffeur for some German officers during the war. The soldiers marched Annemarie at bayonet point to an army office and interrogated her regarding her father's wartime activities. She answered calmly in English that she didn't know anything except where he was, and she gladly volunteered that information. Annemarie and her mother were grateful when they picked up her father and brought him home, where he would have been in the first place had he been able to obtain transportation himself. Having settled that case, the Americans decided that English-speaking Annemarie, first approached at gun point, could be of assistance to them as a clerical worker.

Annemarie accepted the needed work readily. Like her, many German women were relieved that the war was finally over and had prayed that the Americans would get there before the Russians. Annemarie's grandmother had prepared a hiding place for her in the attic just in case the Russians arrived first.

But the American soldiers were also feared by some women. "The first American troopers were no gentlemen," reports Dorothea Dodson, who was in Fussen-Algau on April 9, 1945. "My parents and I were robbed of our watches and camera." Else Dickel and a friend hid in an attic for three days when U.S. troops first arrived. Just up the street from her parents' home in Kassel, a neighbor was raped in front of her husband.

Most American soldiers, however, treated civilians kindly and many Germans looked upon the invasion of American troops as a liberation from war. In Frankfurt am Main, liberated Russian work battalions were looting houses and attacking German civilians. Frau Paul Klost tried to fend off one of these men when he tried to force his way into her house. Sgt. Victor Gribas heard her screams as he was walking down the street near his medical depot and rushed over to see what had happened. He found Frau Klost lying on the sidewalk stabbed through the shoulder. Gribas carried her into the house, dressed her wound, and was then introduced to her daughter, Theresa. The mother's injury provided Gribas with an excuse to make daily visits in spite of the ban on fraternization. Only two months away from demobilization, he found he was falling in love with Theresa.

"After having been 'liberated' by the Russians and lived under Soviet occupation for about three months, the U.S. Military were greeted like *saviours and gods* by us," recalls Ina Lathrop of Berlin. "Their ever cheerful outlook on life was like balsam on our weary souls!"

In East Germany, Barbara Scott felt that a special situation existed between some Germans and Americans:

There were only a few Americans left in a number of "stations" across the Russian Zone to guard the telephone lines between Frankfurt and Berlin, and I suppose the common experience we shared with our soldiers gave us an edge over the American girls back home. Our life was often spiced with intrigue and incongruous situations. The Russians were our common adversary then, long before the "Cold War" had begun.

The nonfraternization policy was almost universally ignored by GIs, recalls Margaret Bouchard of Berlin. "No one really enforced it; there was too much of it going on."

GIs thought nothing of crying out, "Hey Fräulein! Would you like some American chocolate?" as twenty-four-year-old Daniel E. Militello did to sixteen-year-old Katharina Trost on April 3, 1945, in Bad Nauheim, Germany. The town had surrendered without resistance to American troops just a few days earlier. Peace seemed imminent to Katharina and four girlfriends as they enjoyed the exceptionally warm spring weather in the town park. Katharina accepted the chocolate, but refused to give Militello the kiss he wanted in exchange. She liked the friendly brown-eyed GI, though, and made a date with him for later that afternoon. Her mother decided she'd better go along to have a look at the soldier, and she liked him, too. By the time the war ended thirty-five days later, Katharina and Daniel were in love.

German nationalists could be harsh with women who showed any sympathy toward Americans. In Austria, which had been annexed to Germany in 1938, Pauline Julius of Tamsweg took pity on the American POWs being marched through town by retreating German troops:

One of the soldiers collapsed and fell in the road near a puddle of water that collected from rain that had fallen the night before. I rushed over to him and revived him with a hand full of water from the puddle. Then I helped him to his feet. Three hours later I was arrested and placed in the city jail. After two days, the Americans captured the village, released me, and my life began to take shape. I was fed and taken into their protection. We set up a First Aid station and I worked there as a nurse.

Many Germans, especially former soldiers, felt the Americans were still the enemy and resented any association between German women and GIs. Gia Hawthorne remembers:

Boys cut German girls' hair off to show they were Ami-whores, which is what they called us. The boys I knew wouldn't even look at me and a couple of my girlfriends would only talk to me when they were sure nobody was around to see them. People dumped garbage in front of your door. At the store they made you wait longer.

The label "Ami-whore" was applied indiscriminately to prostitutes and to women who merely worked in an American facility, even when the latter had no contact with GIs outside of their jobs. Ostracized by family and friends, women who might not have dated GIs under other circumstances were eventually forced to seek friends among Americans and other women who dated them.

Else Dickel of Kassel gave her mother a shock late one night when she called to her in the dark, "Mamma, wake up. I brought a soldier home." The GI who had been accompanying her on the way home from her job at the PX had missed the last bus back to the base. When Else's mother went into the living room to make up the guest bed for the young man, she screamed and made a hasty retreat when she saw the curly-haired young man in the U.S. Army uniform. She had thought her daughter had brought home a German soldier, for many of them were returning from prisoner of war camps at that time. Else's father had a long talk with her.

I had to make sure he left at 5 o'clock the next morning before the neighbors saw him, and I had to stay home for three days and not go to work at the PX. But like most young people, the more my parents opposed my seeing him the more I wanted to see him, so finally I started spending the night at a friend's house so I could see him, then I rented a room for the weekends so we could be together. I had to get a special pass from the military so I could go to the club on base to be with him. It was hard for me to do all those things behind my parents' backs, but I was so in love with him that really nothing else mattered to me.

A German woman who worked as a translator for a graves registration unit, whose job was to locate the graves of American soldiers, was treated as an outcast by her family even though her earnings were necessary for survival.

Many of my friends wouldn't speak to me because I was working for the Americans, so it stood to reason that sooner or later I would find American friends to substitute for the German friends I had lost. They felt I was working for the enemy. My mother could not understand at all, since my father had died in an American prison camp.

Most young women in Germany and Austria had known only war, hunger, and fear throughout their teenage years. They had been drafted out of school into nursing, the military, war-related industry, and compulsory labor on farms. Families were separated and millions of civilians had died, cities were reduced to rubble, and disease spread rapidly among the undernourished population. In Berlin, for example, 95 percent of the city center was destroyed, and only one in four houses was habitable in the rest of the city. Houses were overcrowded and unheated; fuel, electricity, food—everything was rationed. The official food ration in July 1945 was 1240 calories, but in reality only 850 calories per person were available, less than half that considered necessary to sustain a person on an average work day. In Berlin alone, 4,000 people died each day in August 1945, and half the babies born that month failed to survive.[3]

"I was 18 years old then and had seen so much suffering. There was not enough food, apartments were without heat, the threat of death hung on every day," recalls Hilde Robichaud of Vienna, Austria. Like Berlin, Vienna was jointly occupied by the four Allied powers, and Hilde soon got used to the curious sight of four military policemen patrolling the city in a jeep. "The American was the driver, next to him sat the Englishman, the two of them conversing amiably. In the back seat there sat the Frenchman and the Russian, stoically, unable to communicate with each other." Hotels, pensions, and army barracks that had not been damaged by the bombing were occupied by the occupation troops. Hilde found the Americans intriguing:

> I remember two American soldiers standing on the opposite side of the street, baseball glove on their hand, throwing a ball back and forth—"as if they were children!" I thought. Long before I met my husband-to-be I was fascinated by these young men; they seemed so carefree, happy, and well fed, friendly, gentle with children and animals. At an outdoor cafe, they would sit and drink their Coca-Cola from a straw, while reading "Funny-Books." I wished that I could erase all the sad memories of the past years and act as young and spirited as they did.

Maria Reed had just turned fourteen when the village of Hainstadt, to which she had been evacuated, was taken by the American troops without resistance early in 1945:

> The war was not over, but these first GIs I met were very kind to us. They did not treat any of the people as enemies. I remember well how much they liked us children. They gave us chocolate bars, chewing gum and other goodies which we had never tasted. After their mess hall was set up, the cooks gave the left over food to the children. We took this food home to our hungry families and feasted.

Giving leftover food to civilians was actually not allowed officially. *The Stars and Stripes* even printed an editorial titled "Don't gum up the victory," protesting the GIs' practice of distributing gum and candy to children.[4]

As the soldiers who had witnessed the liberation of concentration camps were rotated back to the U.S., they were replaced by new troops who had not seen these horrors or experienced combat in which their buddies were killed by Germans. These replacement soldiers were more likely to be friendly to Germans, especially to young women.

Although fraternization was not allowed, contact between GIs and civilians in occupied Germany and Austria was an everyday occurrence. The administration of the occupation required large numbers of civilian laborers, and many women were hired as interpreters, secretaries, typists, clerks, and workers in the kitchens and laundries of the U.S. Army. Some women had no choice in the matter: German municipal offices were required to provide services needed by the occupation army. But within a short time, many were eager to accept jobs with the Americans, because one meal a day was provided and food was scarce.

When Maria Higgs received a postcard from the German labor office instructing her to report to work at the base occupied only a week before by American troops, she had to comply. Food was rationed, and without work one would receive no ration card.

> Twelve girls were needed in the kitchen and messhall and I was very unhappy at first that I was among them. We thought we would come back the next day to work. *No way!* We were sent to the kitchen at once. Six of us had to clean up the mess hall from breakfast and the others had to do the dishes. The dishwater had so much soap in it that my hands were raw in minutes. The water was almost boiling. Tears were running down my face, but I was afraid to say anything. Here I was, standing in my best dress crying and washing a whole army's dishes.

Her tears soon changed to laughter when the women were served the food left over from the GIs' breakfast. Pancakes, bacon, bread and butter, jam, coffee—"None of us could remember when we had last seen so much food—and it was all for us! It didn't matter that we all threw up afterwards. Our stomachs just couldn't take it." [5]

Back in Frankfurt in 1946, Maria Reed's family was similarly dependent on the Americans:

> We had very little of anything. My mother's friend was doing laundry for GIs and was paid with coffee, cigarettes, soap and other items we could not get. She had more customers than she could take care of, so my mother, who used to have her own laundry and ironing done, started doing laundry for the Americans also, for the same kind of pay. This way she could trade cigarettes for potatoes, etc., and our life was better. This way I met a few American men and could observe the difference between American and German men. It was obvious how much American men appreciated women. They were generous, complimentary and thoughtful in such a casual way, which was a totally different behavior pattern than that of Ger-

man men. They always looked good in their uniforms and smelled good. I think all Americans used "Old Spice" After Shave.

Aside from the obvious need for food, young German women were attracted to the GIs because they were starved for male companionship. Over three million German soldiers were killed during the war and more than twice that number were prisoners of war. Ina Lathrop of Berlin, who was fourteen years old when the war started, recalls:

> After the beginning of the war in 1939 mostly old sick men stayed behind. All my friends' brothers were drafted before men really interested me. My very first date was with an American soldier who was 20 years older than I (and I only accepted his invitation to a *concert* because of the music, and I welcomed a uniformed escort to the Russian sector. It was more like going out with an uncle and we expected nothing more)."

Some women were eager to have fun now that the war was over, and the GIs were young and available. Regina Shelton describes the desperate gaiety she felt during the war, feelings that surfaced for many young people during the grim occupation years:

> Sometimes I don't feel like dancing, but sometimes in the depth of grief I am overcome by a sudden surge of hunger for lights and laughter and music that I want to dance until I am unconscious, to snatch at happiness, and to forget what has happened and what may still be ahead.[6]

"When those GIs came we thought they were gorgeous!" recalls actress Anneliese Uhlig. "They had beautiful teeth, they were so *healthy*, clean, well fed. Do you know how long it had been since we had seen a man who wasn't crippled in some way?" Only one of the boys from Anneliese's high school friends survived the war.

Lya Cutcher described the GIs as "different in every way" from German men: "Short haircuts, well fed, relaxed manner (to the point of being sloppy and impolite) and childlike in many ways, friendly, generous, braggarts, and often running the gamut from kindness to abusiveness toward women. The latter usually triggered by alcohol."

Margarete Bohling of Berlin recalled:

German men were very scarce and unwilling to court a girl as was customary then. Americans in turn were able to fulfill all these expectations and were fun to be with. Also it was great fun to finally use the English I had learned in school for so many years. Their treatment of women varied, some very kind and compassionate, trying to help in every way, while some were driven by a hatred toward the enemy and were letting it out on their women.

But abusive GIs were in the minority, reports Margarete.

Stories about GIs and German women appeared frequently in the American press, and wives in the States sent a flood of concerned letters to their husbands overseas. "Bring Back Daddy" clubs were formed and American wives appealed to General Eisenhower and other officials to return their husbands to the U.S.[7] On July 2, 1945, *Life* featured a photograph of a pretty woman with a small child; the caption read, "Unwed German mother succumbed to the Nazis' 'patriotic baby' program. The worried authorities hope that she and others like her do not switch over to lonely U.S. soldiers."

In spite of concern and opposition to lifting the ban, all restrictions on fraternization were lifted in Austria on August 24, 1945.[8] In Germany, the Allied Control Council lifted the official ban on October 1, 1945, after the feared Nazi resistance movement had failed to materialize, but the U.S. military government continued to discourage fraternization.[9] Certain civilian establishments and some areas of town were declared off-limits to GIs, and Germans were restricted from U.S. facilities.

The respectability of German women and the integrity of German nationals were consistently under attack. A British woman wrote a scathing letter to *The Stars and Stripes* in March 1946, complaining that German women were permitted to stay overnight in the compound shared by army officers and War Department civilian employees in Frankfurt. Chaplains in the European theater believed that to be an example of the looseness of American army discipline, and expressed relief that "the scandal has come out at last in the open."[10]

Gen. Joseph T. McNarney, commanding general of U.S. forces in the European theater, ordered tighter discipline in the European theater, and all military units in the Frankfurt area had to stand reveille at 7 A.M. daily. "It must be remembered that they're still our enemies," warned Gen. J. M. Bevans on the Armed Forces Radio Network in March, 1946.[11]

By April 28, 1946, *The New York Times* reported the morale of occupation troops in Germany had seriously deteriorated and there was a steady increase in rowdyism and the use of foul and insulting language to women, "even in the presence of those women who wear the American uniform." When American dependents began arriving in Germany, brassards with small American flags were worn by wives and daughters of occupation officers to protect them from getting the greetings Fräuleins got. Some GIs "were quite rude and not very nice in what they said to a girl," recalled Marie Ditzler. The word "Fräulein," which merely means "miss," took on a derogatory connotation when used by some GIs during the occupation.

Correspondent Dana Adams Schmidt summed up the situation for *The New York Times* in May, 1946:

It is Saturday afternoon and the soldiers are still there with their frauleins. In every park they are thick in couples and in groups on the grass. The first sugar ration for adults since V-E Day has only just been distributed, and the soldiers have plenty of PX supplies. More important, there are few young Germans left. No sugar, no men. Thirty-two percent of the babies born in Bavaria last month were illegitimate. In the next war they say all the Americans will have to do is send over the uniforms.

Perhaps the most serious consequence of the nonfraternization policy was the large number of illegitimate children. In the first year of occupation, 94,000 illegitimate children were born in the territory of the three Western powers.[12]

War Department policy allowed for a soldier to be returned to the U.S. if he wished to marry the American mother of his child, but no such privilege was granted if the mother was an alien. In cases of disputed paternity, no foreign court had the right to try a U.S. serviceman. The army "encouraged a soldier to make reasonable provisions for the woman during the pregnancy and for the care of the child," and failure to make such provisions in cases of admitted paternity were subject to disciplinary action. However, a soldier could not make an allotment to a German woman; it was considered "aiding a belligerent nation" to give support to a subject of an enemy country. Even if the army could find its way out of that contradiction, there was little chance of disciplinary action against a soldier resulting in any assistance to the mother of his child.[13]

In many cases, there was no dispute about the paternity of children born to German women and American soldiers—the couples were unmarried only because marriage was not allowed. Abortions, though illegal, were readily available during the first postwar years, as were many illegal goods and services on the black market. A carton or two of cigarettes or C-rations could purchase an abortion, and many women who did not want a child took the risk of terminating their pregnancies. In May 1948, two doctors in Vienna were caught trying to dispose of the body of a woman who died during an attempted abortion, and a prominent gynecologist in Darmstadt was sentenced to three years of hard labor for having performed seventy-seven abortions between the German surrender and July 1946.[14] Far more women opted to have their babies and hoped that eventually they would be permitted to marry the GI fathers. The army refused to make an exception to permit marriage in the case of pregnancy on the theory that this would be rewarding lawbreakers while punishing those who abided by the law.

To discourage GIs from taking their fraternization seriously, The Stars and Stripes published eight cartoons a month showing drunk, disorderly GIs with fat blowsy German Fräuleins. When Germans protested these cartoons by Don Sheppard, a young GI from Mill Valley, California, the army decided "repeated publication could be offensive enough to the Germans to jeopardize our occupation program." In June, 1946, Sheppard was ordered to tone down the cartoons, and only three could be printed per month.[15]

While General McNarney continued to refuse permission for GIs to marry their German sweethearts, American wives in Frankfurt complained about U.S. officers being seen in public with German women. The first two rules on Lt. Joseph Curatolo's Officers Club membership card were "do not bring Germans as guests" and "do not become familiar with any of the help." The first rule was easy to ignore, however. If challenged, a GI could simply claim his date was not German, since there were millions of displaced persons in Germany after the war. Lia Parker and her friends often went to American clubs in Mannheim:

> As Germans we weren't allowed, so we said we were Polish. They knew better, but let us come in anyway. Sandwiches were served. I always looked for the heel of the bread because it was thicker, and 'Spam' luncheonmeat was the first good food I had in years.

Often no questions were asked when a GI or officer brought a date to the club. Joe Curatolo's fiancée, Isolde Müller, was such a frequent guest at the officers club that she helped plan a party to welcome American wives who had just joined their husbands in Germany. Joe thinks the meeting may have been less than cordial, for Isolde and the other German fiancées wore long gowns for the party, and the American wives, not expecting a formal event in occupied Germany, appeared in short dresses.

The army tried to indoctrinate soldiers about the pitfalls of fraternization before sending them overseas. Replacement troops for a constabulary squadron going to Germany in March 1947 were given the following reprint from a *Reader's Digest* article in their ship's newsletter:

> By the spring of 1946 the American Army in Germany had become a sorry remnant of the proud force that overwhelmed Hitler's Wehrmacht. The unpleasant story of its disintegration under the pressure of a short-sighted American public and an election-minded Congress has never been fully told. American units were decimated by frenzied redeployment of their best men. Many of these remaining were utterly demoralized by Fräuleins and drink, and were commanded by tired, indifferent officers. Crime of every kind, from almost universal looting and pilfering to murder and rape, was rampant. In the Munich area alone the Military Police average 200 arrests a night.
>
> The constabulary trooper must continually cope with skulduggery. Black marketeers, proving that the average GI is a sucker for a grinning kid, will place children on their trucks to divert attention from the contraband aboard. Or an expensive camera is left where the trooper can slip it into his pocket.

Smugglers of refugees may send a good-looking girl to engage a lonely constabulary patrolman in conversation while the fugitive slips by.

Black marketeering and smuggling were not the only problems the constabulary had to deal with; murder and suicide were common in the turbulent postwar period. From early May to June 1946, five young German women were found dead in the billets of American soldiers in Litzingen, Nürnberg, Kassel, and Bad Kissingen. In two separate cases, the women were alleged to have shot themselves while the soldiers were away because the soldiers were to be redeployed to the U.S. In another case, a soldier admitted accidentally shooting a nineteen-year-old German woman in her apartment. On June 21, 1946, a twenty-year-old German woman was sentenced to life imprisonment for shooting an American military police sergeant. She claimed to have taken his pistol with the intention of killing herself because he had rejected her love.[16]

Crimes like these made the army even more anxious to deter soldiers from getting involved with German women. A GI who later married a German woman recalls the nonfraternization lectures he heard as a young corporal at the overseas replacement depot in Goldsboro, North Carolina, before he was shipped to Germany in August 1946. These speeches, given by a colonel standing on a stage in front of an enormous American flag, made a big impact on this GI:

I arrived in Germany, having been briefed that Germans were all NAZIs with unholy, bestial natures who would lure pure American soldiers into dens of vice with women who reeked with venereal disease. It was emphatically emphasized that no German female could be found without venereal and other disease because Hitler had established brothels, encouraged all females for sexual and reproduction purposes.

Venereal disease was a major problem in Europe during and after the war and reached epidemic proportions in Germany. In July 1946, the VD rate exceeded one in four among American troops, probably the highest in U.S. military history.[17] Soldiers were fined for public petting and recommendations were sent to Washington to institute severe punishment for soldiers infected with venereal disease. In some units, men were docked a day's pay for every day they were hospitalized with VD, and it was recorded as a disciplinary matter on a soldier's service record. A less punitive deterrent was attempted by the periodic publication in *The Stars and Stripes* of the names of companies which had reported a ninety-day period without any new cases of venereal disease.[18]

The nonfraternization policy did little to curb the growing VD epidemic in Germany. Women were arrested on the street and in frequent nightclub raids and were examined for VD and forced to go to treatment centers. On May 9, 1948, *The Stars and Stripes* reported that loitering women (i.e. suspected prostitutes) were being arrested in Frankfurt at the rate of 250 a week, and 40 percent of them were said to suffer from venereal disease. GIs were punished when they sought treatment for VD, with punishments ranging from fines of $5 (for public petting) to $325 to serving time at hard labor. Although these fines might have been a real hardship for GIs who earned as little as $21 a month, so many GIs were engaged in black market activity that the fines had little effect. The punitive measures made GIs reluctant to seek treatment but did little to curb their relations with prostitutes.

In many cities, photographs of women who were known to have VD were posted in the barracks or in public places frequented by soldiers. The corporal from Goldsboro, North Carolina, recalled that the faces on these posters were colored green to indicate that the women were diseased, and the letters VD were stamped boldly across their faces.

With the German economy destroyed by the war, many women turned to prostitution to survive. Unofficial estimates set the number of prostitutes in postwar Germany at 10 to 20 percent of the female population. Sex was available to the GIs for a chocolate bar, some cigarettes, or a few cans of C-rations. Soldiers who wanted a woman often turned to prostitutes because they were readily available, the business deal could be quickly agreed upon to avoid detection by "purity patrols," and—most important—there were few "nice girls" available. Many soldiers didn't want to risk taking the time for the social amenities necessary to strike up a friendship with a "nice girl." Hans Habe, in *Our Love Affair with Germany,* reports that 3,000 prostitutes invaded the town of Kassel within a few months and "the 'nice girls,' afraid to be punished for even talking to an

Allied soldier, carefully kept indoors."[19] No "decent German woman" wanted to risk being picked up by the police and labeled as a prostitute just for talking to a GI on the street, so they avoided them as much as possible. Some soldiers made the mistake of thinking any woman could be bought. "No manners, rough and rowdy, *crude,*" is how one woman described them. "At first they had no respect for anyone, treated people (girls) like they owned them and some done like they pleased." ·

Because the GIs had such a bad reputation, many women agreed to a first date with a great deal of ambivalence. Shy Hanneliese Tannenbaum, who had spent three years in a concentration camp because she was Jewish, failed three times to show up for a date her coworkers at the railroad station arranged for her with a Jewish GI who spoke German. Finally a coworker brought Joe to the office to meet her, and that Saturday they went to the movies. She agreed to meet him again the next day at the railway station, but remembers:

I was ashamed to wait in front of the Station so I stood across the street. We never met; I was so mad. As I came to the office the next day my co-worker gave me hell. Joe had been there and had to walk back to Frankfurt 12 miles on a warm summer day. He was dead [tired] when he got there. Well, from that time we got very friendly and after about 3 months Joe asked me to marry him.

Ursula Hunter was another German woman who resisted going out with a GI. She worked at the cigarette counter in the Munich PX, a job she had been entrusted with because she had no boyfriend. (It was believed that many of the women who had GI boyfriends would smuggle cigarettes out for them to sell on the black market. Cigarettes were the most common currency during the early postwar years.)

"The first time Ceth came into the PX I was standing there behind the counter. I was an awkward, skinny girl," recalled Ursula, who had taken the job because one meal a day was provided.

"She's new isn't she?" Ceth asked one of the other women. "We've got to fatten her up. I'm going to bring back a nice club sandwich for her."

"She won't take it," warned Ursula's coworker. "She doesn't accept anything from GIs."

"Then you give it to her, and tell her it's from you," said Ceth, undaunted. The two practiced this deception for some time and Ursula was amazed at the kindness of her coworker. Meanwhile Ceth chatted with Ursula every time he came to buy cigarettes, but five months passed before she accepted a ride home from work from him. "But I told him my girlfriend had to come along, too," Ursula recalled:

> I always made him drop me off a block away from my house, and then I'd watch to make sure he was gone before I started walking home because I didn't want him to know where I lived. And I didn't want the neighbors to talk.

Ursula feared that the neighbors would gossip and would disapprove of her friendship with Ceth because he was black. Later he would often tell her, "Keep your head up high and act like you own the joint."

Ursula remembers that Ceth often had little gifts for her:

> . . . but I never accepted his gifts. He'd always have to bring it back. My grandmother had always said, "Don't accept gifts from men because they'll present you with a bill later on."

> One day I invited him in for coffee because my aunt wanted to meet him. He told me later you could have knocked him over with a feather when I told him my aunt wanted to meet him. So, he came, I made ersatz coffee—we didn't have real coffee then, you know. And Aunt Lina just loved him. He was always a perfect gentleman. He could just wrap my aunt around his little finger.

When Ceth first saw Ursula in the PX he had told her coworker, "I'm going to marry her." "Fat chance," was her reply. Although some efforts were being made to get the army to relax the ban on marriage with Germans, an interracial marriage seemed out of the question.

Chapter 10

Winning the Paper War

I'll stay over here fifty years if necessary, but I'm going to have my Trudie.
—GI's plea to President Truman for permission to marry a German

---

A year and a half after V-E Day, GIs in Germany were still not permitted to marry. Sgt. Daniel Militello, who met sixteen-year-old Katharina Trost in Bad Nauheim on April 3, 1945, thought he could circumvent the military prohibition against marriage with German citizens by returning to Germany as a civilian. Katharina was pregnant when Daniel left for the States in January 1946, and he promised to return to her soon.

In spite of appeals to both his senator and his congressman, Militello was unable to secure a passport to return to Germany. A personal letter from General Eisenhower in April 1946 notified him there was nothing the War Department could do to help him. Undaunted, Militello got a job with the Merchant Marine as a mess steward on the *Thomas H. Barry,* which arrived in Germany on April 17 with the first contingent of American wives aboard. Militello left the ship in Bremerhaven and returned to Katharina in Bad Nauheim, where he registered with German authorities as an American Displaced Person.

He and Katharina were married by German civil authority on June 13, and their son Robert was born six weeks later. When Militello went to the American consulate in Frankfurt to register his son as an American citizen born abroad and to arrange transportation to the U.S. for his wife, he was arrested, sentenced to thirty days in jail, and ordered to return to the U.S.—alone.

From his cell, Militello managed to smuggle his story out to the press, and soon newspapers in the U.S. and Germany reported the plight of the young veteran under headlines such as, "Is it a crime to marry?" Militello also wrote to Cardinal Spellman, who replied that Catholic chaplains had protested the marriage ban.

Joseph T. McNarney, Commanding General of U.S. Forces, European Theater, notified the War Department that the prohibition against marriage with Germans applied to all persons subject to military law under Article of War 2. Civilians who violated the law were to be expelled from the U.S. zone of Germany, and the German spouse would be denied a military exit permit (the document required for a German national to leave occupied Germany).[1]

Thanks to the intercession of Congressman Elsaesser of New York, however, General McNarney approved an exit permit for Mrs. Militello in October. She and baby Robert flew to the U.S. on American Overseas Airlines on November 11, 1946.

The Militello case illustrates the awkward position in which the military government in Germany found itself: permission to marry could be refused, but the legality of marriages which took place without permission had to be recognized.

"I'll stay over here fifty years if necessary, but I'm going to have my Trudie," said one of three GIs who remained in Germany after discharge from the army to remain near the women they loved. On January 23, 1946, the three sent a letter to President Truman appealing for relaxation of the ban on marriage with Germans. They told Mr. Truman that they represented hundreds of American soldiers and civilians who were pining to marry Fräuleins.[2]

A number of couples had managed to have German wedding ceremonies without military authorities finding out about them. Sometimes a chaplain helped arrange a secret wedding for a GI. More often, a GI who wanted to marry took his discharge in Germany and then worked for the military government as a civilian employee. These men enjoyed considerably more freedom than soldiers and were permitted to live off base. One former officer married a German woman in Austria where he was employed by the United Nations Relief and Rehabilitation Administration (UNRRA). "But the bureaucrats found out that we were living happily in the country and ordered us to leave," his wife recalls.

For another couple married in Berlin in November 1945, a secret wedding was just one in a series of risks they took to be together. They met before the end of the war, but when Germany was divided after the Potsdam Conference on July 17, 1945, her town became part of the Russian zone and all American troops were withdrawn to Berlin. Soon after, her GI returned to bring her to the American zone of Berlin:

> At this time Berlin was very unsettled, so it was easy to get permission from the Russians to go in and out of their zone. It was ten days later when someone tapped on our window. My soldier friend had come back this night with another soldier to pick up his girlfriend and me to go to Berlin. They were armed to their teeth, since the Russians were very unpredictable, and they wanted to be prepared for any trouble that might occur.

> My parents and I had a conference about my leaving. They thought it would not be proper to go without being married, but they finally consented to let me go. It was a terrible ride, roads were at times impassable from the bombings. We had no problem at any of the checkpoints and made it to Berlin.

> The other girl and I had two rented rooms, and our two American soldiers lived just one block from us. We had a hard time getting food, so the boys brought us their dinner every day.

> My fiancé knew that he would get his discharge papers in October. In order to stay in Germany, to be with me, he secured a job in Berlin as a civilian working for the Engineers, a government job.

Her fiancé was to return to the States on leave before beginning his civilian job, but somehow his leave papers were lost and he had to return to Berlin without going home first. On the flight back to Berlin, he met an American major who advised him to get married before he signed the contract for his civilian job. A bottle of wine from the major graced their wedding feast of dry white bread with strawberry jelly thinned with water.

When the Berlin airlift started in 1948, a friend advised the couple to leave for the States. Travel to the U.S. seemed impossible because, having been married without the permission of the military government, the wife could not get a military exit permit. But, for a bottle of whiskey, a sergeant they knew provided the necessary form and promised he would destroy the evidence once the two were safely airborne on their way to the U.S. A seat on the plane was provided by a high-level military government friend in appreciation for some repair work the husband had done for him. This war bride may have been one of the most frightened women going through customs in New York at that time—she was so afraid of being discovered that she still doesn't want her name revealed.

On January 2, 1946, the army announced that soldiers would be permitted to marry Austrian citizens who passed a political, moral, and physical examination. Within fifteen days, 300 applications for marriage were filed.[3] The German marriage ban remained in effect, but GIs began to find some loopholes in the system. One of them was Public Law 471, passed by Congress on June 29, 1946, to facilitate the admission to the U.S. of alien fiancées or fiancés of members of the armed forces of the U.S.

"I think the only reason I was able to come under this law was because they forgot to exclude Germans," says Isolde Curatolo of Heidelberg, who came to the U.S. as a fiancée on May 27, 1947. A November 4, 1946, statement from the Judge Advocate General supports Isolde's assumption, and points out that the War Brides Act, Public Law 271, also failed to exclude ex-enemy alien spouses:

It may be argued that it was not the intent of Congress to allow German wives to enter this country, but the law as it stands today definitely does not exclude them. Furthermore, it must be borne in mind that, once a marriage has lawfully been performed either contrary to the theater commander's orders or previous to the issuance of the theater commander's orders, that marriage is a legal marriage and has been so considered by the competent legal authorities of OMGUS.

. . . the commanding officer of the occupied territory . . .

may justifiably make regulations for the guidance and discipline of the armed forces under his command but he may not overrule or ignore an act of Congress which is the law of the land and under the applicable provisions of which he must function. He may prohibit marriages and provide for the punishment by court-martial of those members of the military service who choose to disregard these orders; but, once such a marriage has been performed, he may not, by way of punishment, refuse to grant an exit permit to the spouse. . . .

It should be noted that the policy . . . which allows German fiancées of American military personnel to leave Germany while forbidding wives the same privilege, discriminates against marriage and in fact appears to clothe immorality among the American forces in Germany with a pseudo-legality. Such policy further makes both partners to a perfectly legal act, marriage, liable to punishment, because the military regulations of CT, USFET, prohibits marriage of U.S. members of U.S. forces with Germans.[4]

A secret cable from Chief of Staff Dwight Eisenhower, marked "Personal," directed General McNarney to accept applications for exit permits from German spouses and to issue exit permits to all German spouses who qualified under Public Law 271 and met existing security requirements.[5] On December 5, 1946, McNarney, in a message marked "secret top priority," asked Eisenhower to reconsider:

I cannot too strongly emphasize my personal opinion that the time has not yet come when we should permit unrestricted marriage between Americans, particularly soldiers, and German women. There are many reasons for this, but one of the principal ones is the extreme youth and susceptibility of a high percentage of our enlisted personnel, combined with the surplus of German women who are in straitened circumstances, to put it mildly, and who will take calculated advantage of these young soldiers. This may be a paternalistic attitude, but I consider it a serious problem, and that it is our responsibility to protect our own people.[6]

McNarney was also concerned about the problem of having to provide food, post exchanges, clubs, schools, living quarters, and medical care for German dependents of military personnel.

Eisenhower's brief reply was sent the same day:

I appreciate and am sympathetic with your problems. However, requirement to issue exit permits is clearly statutory and affords no recourse. Still believe marriage can be discouraged and partially controlled by theater regulations which you may prescribe, i.e., forbid marriage until the individual is under orders to leave ETO.[7]

On December 11, 1946, the ban on marriage between GIs and German nationals was officially lifted.[8] Many German war brides will be surprised at this date, for the many restrictions the army used to continue to discourage marriage led many to believe that marriages were not allowed until much later. Couples who took on the army paper war when they sought permission to marry often felt that they had broken new ground when they succeeded. (Many women responding to our survey indicated that they were the "first" to marry in Germany.) A three-month waiting period was required before servicemen could marry carefully screened Germans, and then the marriage could not take place prior to one month before the American was scheduled to depart from the European theater. The paperwork process often took much longer than the required three months.

By the end of December, 2,500 GIs had submitted applications for permission to marry. On March 27, 1947, *The New York Times* announced the first officially sanctioned German-American wedding in occupied Germany. The happy couple, who had met in September 1945, were former Sgt. Peter Rupeka of Hempstead, New York, and Erika Schaefer of Frankfurt, Germany. Peter had remained in Germany as a War Department civilian employee after his discharge from the army in the hope that he and Erika would be permitted to marry. By April 21, 1947, forty-four Americans had received permission to marry German women. Military government officials expected 6,000 more weddings within the year.

In the U.S., many people wrote letters to the War Department and to members of Congress to protest these marriages. "Are we going to forget so soon?" asked a woman from Texas whose brother was killed fighting the Germans. Her letter to her senator said:

What ever [were] the finest men of our land sacrificed for? As one of the family with a broken heart and home as a result of the horrible war I resent it, and feel that any American man who would stoop to marry a German should have to pay a price, either revoke his citizenship or take severe punishment.[9]

A New Yorker who fought with the 508th Parachute Infantry Regiment in France and Belgium protested marriage and immigration of German women, saying that the sacrifice of the men who died fighting the Germans was not being respected or valued. "A canvas of American people will prove beyond doubt that we are almost 100 percent opposed to German women as our wives," said another New Yorker in a letter to General Eisenhower.

The War Department adjutant general answered these letters, saying that a relaxation of the nonfraternization ban had always been planned and was now being instituted because of the successful progress of the de-nazification process.[10] In other letters he said the new marriage policy was dictated by public laws that forced the commanding general of the European theater to provide exit visas and transportation

for those German Nationals who managed to circumvent the theater directive and became dependents of personnel of the United States occupation forces. It was considered impracticable to continue the prohibition of these marriages in the face of laws, outside the Army jurisdiction, which extended obvious benefits to violators and thereby penalized the majority who obeyed the ban.[11]

On the other side of the debate were the many GIs who wanted to marry their German fiancées, many of whom had waited years for the regulations to be loosened. The fact that so many of these courtships lasted several years without diminishing the affection of the parties involved suggests that these were not casual infatuations based on short acquaintance.

Sometimes a woman's parents also imposed a waiting period and advised a soldier to return to his home in the U.S. for a visit before marrying their daughter. Maria Garner's mother and father in Ried im Innkreis, Austria, were understandably concerned about her "engagement" to Lloyd Hixon: she was only ten years old when they met! Maria had seen Lloyd and some other GIs walking a little dog in the street near her house. She offered to be their guide and showed them the sights in town and struck up a friendship with Lloyd. When Lloyd returned for a visit five years later, he wanted to marry Maria. Her parents didn't reject Lloyd outright; they said he could come back when she was seventeen and marry her then. Of course, no one expected him to return, and Maria's faithfulness became a family joke, until the day Lloyd returned in 1952 to claim his bride.

Many GIs became frustrated with the long permission process and wrote to their legislators demanding their right to the constitutionally guaranteed "pursuit of happiness." The May 9, 1948, issue of *The Stars and Stripes* reported that a veteran who had been refused permission to marry his German fiancée had attempted to renounce his U.S. citizenship so he could return to Germany to marry her. The Department of Justice replied that a U.S. citizen could not renounce citizenship while living in the U.S.

Overseas, a GI not only had to file a written request for permission to marry, but he could be required by his commanding officer to file a preliminary notice of intent at a prescribed time prior to the actual application for permission to marry. A commander who was firmly opposed to marriages between his men and German women could create even more difficulties than the usual army red tape. Some soldiers were transferred to another base after they applied for permission to marry. At a new base, the application process had to be started all over again.

Maria Higgs and her future husband had known each other for two years when he applied for permission to marry her:

It was not an easy undertaking. Such a paper war! Hermann was 37 years old at the time; almost ten years older than me. He had been married before, and it seemed to take forever to get the papers proving that he was really divorced.

Before the application was approved, Hermann was transferred to another base, where he had to start the paperwork all over again. After two years, he was transferred again, this time back to the States. Maria recalls:

He was to ship out during the first part of January. He went to the Chaplain's office every day to see if the papers had come in. I could not believe all the run around we were getting. But there was nothing to do—just wait.

Back in the States, Hermann started the application process a third time. That June, Maria was finally granted permission to travel to the U.S. as a fiancée.[12]

Overseas, both the GI and his fiancée were subject to interviews and counseling by the chaplain and commanding officer. The personal opinion of these officers carried a great deal of weight; a Jewish chaplain refused to sanction or perform any marriages between German gentiles and Jewish soldiers in February 1947.[13] Protestant and Catholic chaplains also were more likely to sanction marriages when both parties were of the same faith.

A German fiancée's past was investigated to make sure she had not been a member of the Nazi party. She also had to be of good moral standing; a police record of arrest for prostitution would make her ineligible for both marriage and immigration to the U.S. Both partners had to be free from venereal and other communicable disease, and the German prospective spouse had to be free of tuberculosis and twenty other diseases listed by the U.S. Immigration Department.

It is interesting to note that in one case, an American soldier who had tuberculosis was given permission to marry while in the hospital. Erika Herman recalls:

> We had so much of the paperwar behind us that we were to the point of getting the required physical examinations; to our horror a spot was discovered on my husband's lung, a fact that threatened to draw a big X through our marriage plans.
>
> My husband was admitted to the Army hospital in Salzburg awaiting transfer to a hospital in the States. A month passed, a terrible time, and one day my husband stood at my door with a 5-day leave in his pocket from his doctor. Matt had convinced his friendly, compassionate doctor to give him this leave on his own responsibility, to give us the chance, if we could manage it, to marry within the 5 days. We were on the road from morning til night to get the last stamps of approval, and were successful. Matt returned to the hospital as a happily married man.

The discovery of tuberculosis did cancel many marriage plans and caused long delays in others. When Francis Maginn applied for permission to marry Elsbeth Weber, a Swiss national, her medical examination revealed that she was in the final stage of a pneumothorax cure for tuberculosis which was no longer contagious:

> The application was returned with a big fat stamp across the forms: DISAPPROVED. It turned out that I belonged to the same category of undesirable women as German prostitutes, girls with VD, ex-Nazis, ex-Youth Group members, camp followers, you name it. I felt like a piece of garbage and Francis wasn't any happier. The Army refused to recognize the fact that I was cured.

Francis turned in applications at regular intervals and considered various ways to get around the army's prohibition, such as getting Elsbeth pregnant, but they realized the army wouldn't make an exception for that. He even thought about deserting, but she told him she wouldn't marry a deserter. Early in August of 1948, after being engaged for a year and a half, Francis drafted a letter to his commanding officer in which he demanded "an immediate discharge from the U.S. Army on the grounds that the Army was interfering with his civil and constitutional rights as an American citizen and the pursuit of happiness." He showed his CO a draft of the letter and said he would submit an official letter in triplicate the next day. Elsbeth relates the results:

> We were married within one week!!! *No way* was the U.S. Army going to lose one of their precious regular Army GIs who was willing to put in 20 or even 30 years! Inconceivable. So he got a two-week leave so fast it made his head spin! By that time of course I had discontinued both pneumothorax treatments and I guess even in the eyes of the Army I was *whole* again and no longer undesirable.

Like other diseases, tuberculosis spread rapidly among the over-crowded, undernourished population of postwar Europe. In October 1946, 17,000 cases of tuberculosis were reported in Hamburg alone, five times the prewar level.[14]

Else Dickel and Wally Smith already had two children when they were refused permission to marry in 1951, because Else's medical examination revealed a tubercular spot on one lung. Wally paid for her stay in a sanatorium in the Black Forest, but when he had to return to the States after being in Germany for seven years, her family situation made it impossible for her to get the rest needed to cure the disease. "He's forgotten you and now we're stuck with you and your kids," her mother accused time and again. In desperation, Else elected to have a lumpectomy, radical surgery, new in 1954, to remove part of the diseased lung. Because her mother was only willing to care for one child while Else was hospitalized, she had to place her youngest daughter in a childrens' home until she recovered. Wally returned to Germany and they were married in December 1956, after she had a clean bill of health.

Other marriages were delayed because a GI who had been married previously had to prove he was legally divorced. In Annemarie Gossler's case, she was given a hard time and made to feel somehow responsible for the fact that her husband-to-be had divorced his American wife. Annemarie quickly set the interviewer straight, for Tom's wife had left him for another man while Tom was overseas, long before Annemarie even met him.

George and Margarete Bohling's marriage plans caused a bit of concern in official circles and had rumors of bigamy circulating in her neighborhood. George filed a "Declaration of Intent to Marry a German National" in May 1949, with the marriage to take place prior to his scheduled departure from Europe in 1951. During their two-year engagement, they went to church together on base every Sunday. Margarete had a "church pass" to permit her to enter the base:

> So the army priest knew us and knew of our intent to marry when the time came. One Sunday after church he called us into his office and asked if we wanted to get married and we of course said yes. An American civilian priest from Fordham University was in Berlin as a guest and married several young couples. We had about four days to get ready for the wedding and it had to be kept very quiet. August 30, 1950, we got married in a German Catholic Chapel and as far as the army was concerned we were still waiting to get married and our papers were all filed and mounting.

In Germany, as in many European countries, a civil ceremony is legally required, and the church ceremony is optional. When the time came for the required civil ceremony, the church register in George's home town showed he was already married, and he was called in front of his company commander to explain. "All turned out well in the end," says Margarete, "but we were worried for a while. Our civil ceremony took place July 6, 1951. Needless to say we celebrate August 30 as our wedding anniversary."

Soldiers under the age of twenty-one were required to submit letters of consent from their parents along with their request for permission to marry. A commander could also require an enlisted man to set aside a portion of his pay as savings, and failure to do so could result in permission to marry being denied. Or a soldier could be asked to show intention to reenlist or give proof of his prospects for employment in the civilian sector.

The marriage applications of couples who were "color blind" were routinely denied or "lost." Ceth and Ursula Hunter, after a most unusual proposal, decided to marry in church without applying for permission from the army.

"He proposed to me in the cemetery," remembers Ursula. When Ceth wanted a date on a Sunday, Ursula told him she always visited her grandmother's grave on Sunday, but he could come along if he wanted to. While she arranged flowers and tidied up the grave, Ursula found herself telling Ceth that her grandmother had raised her after her parents died and how her grandmother had died during the last days of the war when they were unable to get medication for her. Ursula remembered Ceth's reaction clearly:

> He just stood there and, without looking at me, he looked at the grave and said, "Well, Grandma, I want to marry your little girl. Is it OK with you?" Then he turned to me and said, "Well, it's OK with her. Is it OK with you?"

In March 1947 Ceth and Ursula were married in church, delaying the official civil wedding until it was time for Ceth to leave Germany. Once a soldier married a German national, he was required to leave Germany and could not be stationed there again. Before Ceth's tour of duty in Germany was to end in 1950, the Korean War began. The Hunters didn't want to risk Ceth being sent to Korea, as had happened to several friends who had applied for permission to marry. Ceth managed to extend his tour in Germany until 1954, when he was transferred to Texas. Ursula remained behind with their two sons until Ceth was able to return in 1955. "He didn't want to bring us to Texas because they didn't like mixed marriages in Texas—remember, this was 1955!"

Although Ursula reports that most people accepted their mixed marriage, a few incidences of racial prejudice stand out in her memory:

When Ceth was promoted to Warrant Officer 3, the major made a toast, "To Mr. Hunter and his lovely wife Ursula." I turned to the woman next to me, an officer's wife, and said, "Come on, you're supposed to drink," and she said, "I'm not thirsty." And she was black!

When we first came here in 1955 Ceth told me that in New York no one notices you. But, right after our arrival we went to a pizza place in New Jersey; I'd never had pizza before. As we walked in, everyone in the place turned around and looked at us, and I said, "Daddy, I thought you said nobody in this country ever stared at you!" When they heard me say that, they all turned back around quickly.

Some interracial couples who faced overt racist hostility in the U.S. returned to live permanently in the wife's home country. A German urologist married to a black American doctor was often taunted by people in her husband's hometown when she and her child went to the neighborhood market or used public transportation. Her husband reenlisted in order to be stationed back in Germany and they decided to make their permanent home there.

Like many war brides from overseas, Ursula Hunter never wanted to leave her country to come to the U.S., "But, whither thou goest, I will go . . ." she quotes from the biblical story of Ruth. The army, however, feared that scores of women in war-torn Germany and Austria would marry GIs to get the privileges accorded to army wives: housing, medical and dental care, PX and commissary shopping privileges. To avoid the expense and administrative costs of such an undertaking, the army made it clear that alien wives would not be entitled to any military privileges overseas and required a soldier to leave the European theater within thirty days after marriage to a German. Conditions in postwar Germany and Austria were still desperate for many people, and many thought that they would not see economic recovery—or even the rubble of the bombed cities cleaned up—in their lifetime. It was a depressing prospect for young Germans, and no doubt some did want to marry Americans in the hope of having a better life in the U.S.

Many war brides report their friends envied them. "It was considered a blessing to get out of war-torn Germany at that time," recalls Margarete Bohling. Anne Drexler says her friends envied her "and were happy for me because I was going to the U.S. where the streets were paved with Gold."

It didn't always work out that way, though, for a GI who seemed wealthy in Europe (where many supplemented their soldiers' pay with black market trading) often found it difficult to support a wife and children back in the States. With the uniform as a leveler, class distinctions and background were hard to determine, and a woman often could not tell if her husband-to-be was from a social class similar to hers. Language differences added to the problem. A GI who said he had been to high school made a good impression, but what was called high school in Germany was equivalent to college in the U.S. A woman who did not speak English well could not detect grammatical errors and speech patterns which might indicate a GI was uneducated. Conversely, there were so many refugees in Germany after the war, and so many whose homes had been bombed, that a GI couldn't tell what social class his fiancée belonged to. Working class women masqueraded as countesses, and educated women worked as clerks in the PX.

The requirement that the GI leave Germany within a month after marrying a German national often caused a rather unhappy honeymoon. Either the husband returned to the States alone, leaving his wife uncertain of when she could follow, or, if the couple were fortunate, she could travel with him, which meant that the weeks after the wedding were spent in frenzied activity. An exit visa had to be applied for in haste, medical examinations and immunizations were needed, and the sad farewells to family and friends often overshadowed the happiness of the wedding. Even if the couple travelled on the same ship, they were separated for the duration of the voyage, for the ships were so crowded it was necessary to house the GIs together, with war brides and children crowded into cabins no better than those the troops shared.

For women whose husbands were sent back to the U.S. alone, life in Germany and Austria was very difficult. Lia Parker was married just before her husband had to leave Germany in 1948, and discovered to her dismay that, due to laws still on the books from the Hitler regime, a German woman who married a foreigner lost her German citizenship: [15]

> I didn't have any rights as a German and got nothing from the Americans, so I became a stateless person. Our son was born September 22, 1948. I had to go to a German hospital. My insurance was cancelled; my Dad had to pay for the bill. My husband helped as much as he could. I didn't have a ration card, they told me since you are marrying an American let him support you. I don't have any happy memories, lost everything—my hope chest, linen, china, silver, all my clothes—came to America with one cheap suitcase.

Without ration cards, food could only be purchased at exorbitant prices on the black market.

Burgunde Duchatel also mentions what a problem loss of citizenship was, but her life was somewhat easier because her husband remained overseas as a civilian government employee, and in-laws on both sides were understanding:

> To the German government of the time, I was a stateless person (no ration stamps); to the Americans I was an Enemy National.
>
> Our daughter was born November 15, 1946. We registered her with the American Consul as the daughter of an American Citizen and she became a citizen at birth. Still, all baby food, etc., was mailed to us by my husband's parents, as the PX only carried baby powder and things like that. I was not allowed in, so my husband bought baby clothing, and my mother always claimed little Viola was the most dressed up baby she had ever seen. She would holler, "embroidered silk dresses in bed?"

Some couples avoided the problem of having to leave Germany so soon by having their honeymoon before the wedding. Many lived together while waiting for approval of their marriage applications. One war bride says with a chuckle, "Many of us have to add a year or two to our wedding anniversary date." Having told their American in-laws they were married overseas, some couples had a quick Reno wedding secretly after their arrival in the U.S.

Anneliese Uhlig and Lt. Douglas Tucker were married July 1,

1948, at Schloss Mirabel in Salzburg, Austria, but she found the wedding ceremony an ironic conclusion to the long paperwar they had fought with the army:

> Now we are supposed to say "yes" to something that we've taken for granted for some time already. We certainly would have been married long ago had it been permitted to marry a German sooner than four weeks prior to a soldier's return to the States. Our wedding trip lasts one evening as we celebrate legally as "husband and w." (w for wife) in Berchtesgaden. We reassure ourselves with the golden band on our left ring-finger and ignore the signs: "Für Deutsche verboten." (off-limits for Germans).[16]

It often took some ingenuity to come up with the things needed for a traditional wedding in Germany and Austria. Bertha Brandstatter of Passau, Germany, was one of the many women whose wedding gowns were made out of a parachute: "It cost a carton of cigarettes and it took many hours to separate the seams, and then a very good seamstress to make a gown out of it!" Karin Trenina and her mother shared a blouse her mother made with parachute silk, and Karin's only suit was painstakingly tailored and pieced together from two pair of her fiancé's "officer's pinks" trousers. Other women borrowed wedding gowns or had them sent from the U.S. by their future in-laws. One bride's borrowed white shoes were several sizes too large and had to be held on with elastic.

Karola and Wayne Parkin will never forget their Cinderella wedding, complete with horse-drawn carriage and an eight-piece orchestra borrowed from a nearby hospital unit:

> The wedding cake is one of a kind and will never be duplicated. Wayne got some of the ingredients on the black market and the German bakers at the hospital made the cake, which was delicious. To decorate the cake was magic. No decorations were available, so around the bottom layer they used Kellogg's Corn Flakes. On top of the bottom layer and on the layer above they used half circles of pineapple slices. Other decorations were improvised in this fashion and to me at that time it took the blue ribbon.

Many couples had to wait and have their weddings in the U.S. German fiancées generally flew to the U.S. from Hamburg or Frankfurt, and they or their fiancés paid for the trip. The twenty-two-hour flight, with three stops for refueling, was little better than being tossed around on the stormy Atlantic in a converted Liberty Ship. A GI who sponsored an alien fiancée had to deposit $500 with the State Department, to cover the cost of returning the fiancée to her country in the event that the wedding did not take place within three months. "He only married me for that $500," one war bride says with a laugh.

Some German and Austrian fiancées became engaged after a lengthy correspondence. Some of these couples had never even seen each other when they agreed to marry. Mary Grill of Bad Mitterndorf, Austria, wrote a letter to John Berthiaume of Massachusetts in May 1947. "Your dear brother, Paul, wrote to me telling me all about you and he encouraged me to correspond with you. I hope you will not be angry with me," began her first letter. The military censor passed the letter, without removing the edelweiss she had included as a talisman, resealed the envelope, and stamped it No. 2930.

John, a shy romantic, decided to reply. In dictionary German, he wrote to Mary, "I am happy to know you will be my friend. I will try to be your best friend."

Mary had met John's brother Paul when he was stationed in Austria with the eleventh Armored Division. Her friend, Margarete Kaisereiner of Steyr, met Paul on a blind date, and they became engaged before he was shipped back to the States. Mary and Margarete were both nurses at the same hospital in Gmunden at the time.

After a six-month correspondence, John travelled to Austria to marry his pen pal. During that same week in November 1947, Paul and Margarete were married in Spencer, Massachusetts.

"Nobody in my family could understand how I could leave my country and marry a stranger," remembers Mary, who also had her doubts about the outcome of her adventure. On her way to Vienna to meet John upon his arrival in Austria, her aunt's parting words kept echoing in her mind: "How can you marry a man you've never even seen?"

A woman from East Berlin came to the U.S. on December 14, 1948, to marry a man she had never met. The GI had written to her in April 1947 after he got her address from her cousin who lived in New York.

Thinking back, it is hard to explain the reason. It would be untrue saying "because of love" since we had never met. Neither was I an opportunist nor adventurer. On the contrary, I was always cautious with people, making friends rather slowly. I felt comfortable with him and believed we would get along. It also meant to escape the dreary existence under the communist regime. It was not easy, there was no slow getting to know each other. Five days after meeting him, we were married.

Another German fiancée had difficulty convincing immigration authorities that she was indeed a fiancée when she arrived in New York in December 1948 with three teenage children from her deceased German husband. Her eldest son had befriended Maj. C. P. Schroeder when he was stationed in Germany and had prompted the correspondence between them. She had not met the major, however, before she came to the U.S. to marry him, just days before the expiration of the Fiancées Act.

For a number of couples, a lengthy correspondence deepened romance begun while the soldier was overseas. But exchanging letters was not simple in those days. "We had to have a middleman as we could not write to America direct," recalls Brigitta Henning. "We had to have someone in Military Government send and receive our letters." She met her GI in June 1946 when the handsome MP stopped fifteen-year-old Brigitta to ask directions. He was surprised to hear her answer in English. "My husband met me that one day, but adopted my whole family," remembered Brigitta. When her husband-to-be learned that the family were refugees, he helped her father and brother get jobs in the nearby town of Göppingen and procured medications for Brigitta's brother, an ex-POW still recovering from war wounds. Before marriage in Germany was permitted, the GI had to return to the U.S. After corresponding a year and a half, Brigitta flew to Forest Hills, New York, to marry her former MP.

Those who had to make the trip to the U.S. by ship faced the dismal gray barracks at Bremerhaven, which served as a temporary shelter for the war brides travelling under army auspices. At this processing center, many war brides were suddenly faced for the first time with the magnitude of their decision to leave home and family for a new life in the U.S. To Maria Higgs, "It seemed like everyone in Germany was leaving!" [17] Anneliese Uhlig Tucker was overwhelmed by the "mountains of baggage and still larger mountains of documents and forms" that accompanied the travellers.

Mrs. Tucker noted the contrast between the departing war brides and the American wives arriving in Bremerhaven to join husbands stationed with the occupation forces:

> Women and children from two worlds pass through this small, crowded place . . . tomorrow they leave for separate continents. Some to leave a devastated world whose wounds they too bear. Others see the shocking reality of a devastated country, whose ruins they had only known from magazines. [18]

For German wives travelling with children from a previous marriage, it was necessary to get a quota immigration visa for the children. Sometimes busy consulate staff members missed this important little detail, causing much stress and heartache when travel plans were suddenly canceled or delayed due to lack of a visa. The Tuckers, along with Mrs. Tucker's son Peter, were among ten passengers scratched from the list of the *Daniel P. Sultan* in August 1948. Telegrams to Washington eventually resulted in a visa for Peter, and the Tuckers were able to board the small gray Liberty Ship *Blanche F. Sigman* a few days later.

Children born to a couple, even before marriage, were automatically granted American citizenship if the GI father had their birth recorded at the American consulate and attested to their paternity. A visa was not required for these children.

Once "in the pipeline" for the U.S., German wives were granted all the privileges of military dependents for the first time. Their meals and other needs were provided, and they were entitled to medical care while awaiting shipment from Bremerhaven. By this time they had been thoroughly examined and usually were in good health, but the discovery of certain diseases could still cause them to be inadmissible to the U.S.

War brides from many other European countries also travelled from the port of Bremerhaven. Cabins were assigned alphabetically, so women of different nationalities were often thrown together. The psychic wounds of the war had not yet healed sufficiently for this to be easily accepted by the women and shipboard animosities sometimes developed. For some German war brides, this was their first confrontation with the prejudice they would meet in the States, where some people considered every German a Nazi.

By the time the German war brides began arriving in the U.S., the media fanfare that had greeted the earlier voyages of British brides was already old news. An occasional German bride or fiancée would get a write-up in her husband's home town paper, but for the most part little notice was taken of their arrival. The few who were greeted by reporters often found the experience bewildering.

"I don't kiss in public," said Isolde Müller of Heidelberg to reporters who wanted to photograph her kissing her fiancé, Joe Curatolo, when she arrived at New York's La Guardia Airport on May 27, 1947. Joe, who had eagerly waited for Isolde with an armful of red roses and an engagement ring, received a "proper" German handshake instead of a warm embrace.

During the last weeks of December 1947, record numbers of war brides arrived just under the wire of the expiration of the Fiancées Act. Eighteen European fiancées were sent to Ellis Island because, although they left their homelands prior to the December 31 expiration of the act, flight delays caused them to land in New York after the deadline. Immigration authorities permitted these women to stay in the U.S., but three war brides enroute from Germany were put off by a Royal Dutch airliner in Scotland when airline officials realized they would arrive in the U.S. after the deadline. Another woman was left behind in Paris by Air France.[19] One wonders whether these women and their fiancés were able to accomplish the paper process to try again after Congress passed Public Law 450 on March 24, 1948, to extend the Fiancées Act until December 31, 1948.

For many women in Germany and Austria, the complications involved in trying to marry the GI they loved were too much. For some, the War Brides and Fiancées Acts came too late. One woman in West Germany fondly remembers the GI she met at a club on Christmas 1945, and wonders if he is still alive and well:

> He was shy but spoke to me. In time, we developed an idyllic closeness that lasted 9 months, 7 days and two hours. Through my inability to decide what I should do, it unfortunately all came to an end after 1½ years. This man was com-

pletely good. He took care of my mother and me, for we were all alone after my father was killed in action in Italy January 2, 1945. We were never hungry when he was there; with his love and kindness he made our lives easy.

A woman in East Germany will never forget the GI with whom she fell in love when the American headquarters was directly across the street from her home in 1945:

I had no direct contact with the soldiers until one of them brought me to the Red Cross after I fell on the street and badly injured my knee.

I was 18, not bad looking, but was reserved around men. I had just lost my boyfriend, who, at the age of 19, was killed in action in Russia in March 1945.

And now it was June, I was young, and a beautiful summer was beginning. I noticed one of the soldiers because he used a black umbrella to shield himself from the sun when he was on guard duty in front of the headquarters. I saw that he often watched me and he even spoke to me occasionally, but I pretended not to notice.

One day I received a large box of candy with a bouquet of roses carefully tied on top. The roses grew all along the fence of the American headquarters. Even today, when I visit my hometown, I can still sometimes find roses along that same fence, but there aren't many left.

One day a neighbor said to my sister, "Doesn't your sister see that that American practically eats her up with his eyes?"

I wasn't convinced yet that I could fall for another man so quickly. But one day I gave in to his pleading and agreed to meet him. His kindness and love soon thawed my heart and I fell in love with him. I didn't want my parents to know, but it wasn't possible to keep it a secret in the long run. My older sister was the first to find out that I was going to have a baby.

"Why didn't you tell me sooner?" she said. "Then we could have done something about it."

The father of my child reacted the same way. "It isn't good for you to be alone with the child. I still have to go to war in Japan."

But I wanted to keep the child, and nothing in the world could have convinced me to give it up. He was being transferred to Kassel and wanted to take me with him. He asked his superiors, but it wasn't allowed. I had packed my suitcase in preparation, but the journey was never to take place.

On March 15, 1946, I gave birth to a daughter. I named her Rosemarie. My parents had meanwhile forgiven me. My maternity coat was made from a wool blanket _____ had given me, but I never heard from him again.

I tried several times to contact him at the U.S. address he had given me and even sent photos of Rosemarie. I received an answer to my letter, too, saying it must be another Mr. _____ I knew, for these people had no son. But the photos of Rosemarie were not returned.

My daughter looks just like her father, and when she makes a bouquet of flowers I always think of the roses on that first box of candy.

I am now nearly 60 years old. I have never regretted keeping my daughter. Because I am disabled from an operation in 1974, I am permitted to visit my sisters in West Germany. Coming home is always especially painful for me, for I always see handsome, young American soldiers at the train. They are friendly and wave to the people on the train; sometimes they even wave to me.

Other women who were left behind are bitter about the experience. "I accuse!" says a German woman who married an American army deserter in Austria in February 1946. Although he registered her child as his in an effort to help her, she never heard from him again after he was arrested and returned to the U.S. in May 1946.

"In 1950 I met another American. He followed me everywhere and I finally gave in to him. It was a grand passion. (To my misfortune, I am very romantically inclined.)" She had two children with this man and had to place them in a home because she couldn't care for them. They couldn't marry because she was still married to her first husband; a divorce was too expensive because she would have had to hire a lawyer to stand in for her absent husband.

Terrible things happened. My "great love" beat me and had other women. When I was pregnant with our third child it was time for him to return to the U.S. I went to the train station to see him one more time, but he ignored me. Earlier he had said I should wait for him; he would send money and return quickly.

Unbelievable suffering followed. I was condemned by the world for loving a GI. Letters to Agencies and Councils in the U.S. went unanswered. No one cared if my children and I perished. You see me as guilty, but why me alone? There was a man who also wanted these children but evaded the responsibility in the end.

Ingeborg Siebert, who lives in Salzburg, Austria, is much more forgiving toward the GI who left her behind:

I was a war bride, too, as we were called 40 years ago, but my story has no happy ending. I still have a little wood-carved casket in which I keep his loveletters, carefully tied together with a blue ribbon, along with his photographs and engagement ring. Once a year on May 11th I re-read the letters.

It was the first great love of my life, which I will never forget. One day he had to leave because his company was moving to Germany. I couldn't follow because the borders between Austria and Germany were closed. He was able to write to me through a soldier still stationed here.

Well, you know, a man is a man and so it happened to me as to many other women. Another woman entered his life and I was left behind.

I spoke to him once on the telephone. Then he came by one day to ask for his engagement ring back, while his wife waited in the car, which I found most unfair. One shouldn't open old wounds.

Memory is the only paradise from which one cannot be expelled. I do not wish to find William. I only wish my William—once my William—well; I hope he is happy and that life has been good to him. That is my heartfelt wish.

Chapter 11

I Want That Flag!

---

*I had been cooped up for five years under the German Occupation,
with no opportunity to move around, and I like to travel. When I
met this lady, I said to myself, rather than staying in Denmark,
we'll go see some of the United States.*
—*Jørgen Nielsen, Danish war groom*

When the American army liberated the forced labor camp at the
IG Farben Factory in Frankfurt in April 1945, the GIs distributed
food, candy, and cigarettes to the inmates of the camp. "Do you
want a candy bar?" a soldier asked Tamara Hupka. "No," she replied.
"I want that flag." The soldier gave her the American flag that
was flying from the radio mast of a tank. Tamara still has that flag
hanging framed on the wall of her home in Omaha, Nebraska.

Tamara's arduous journey to Omaha began in the town of Khar-
kov, in the Russian Ukraine. As the German army advanced in
the spring of 1942, SS troops killed forty-five people in Karkhov,
including Tamara's parents. When the Russian army returned five
months later, she was drafted into the army and, not long afterward,
seventeen-year-old Tamara was among eighteen noncombatant female Russian soldiers taken prisoner by the Germans. Grazed on
the neck by a German bullet, Tamara awoke in a hospital in Warsaw.
She was among the first female soldiers captured by the Germans.

"They didn't know what to do with us," Tamara recalled, "so

they put us in the Jewish concentration camp where they had women." There she escaped being killed in a gas chamber when the guards, noticing she did not have a number tattooed on her arm, realized she was not Jewish. She and other Russian prisoners were then sent to a labor camp in Frankfurt, where they worked in a factory rolling sheet metal for Messerschmidt fighters.

In 1944 she was selected to be a servant for several months in the home of a German widow, Frau Elsa Genz, whose son had been killed on the Russian front. The two women became friends, a friendship that would prove helpful after the liberation, when Tamara and two friends narrowly escaped being repatriated to Russia.

"We were thought to be deserters and they were going to 'rehabilitate' us," said Tamara, who learned that Siberia was the destination for Russian soldiers being repatriated from Germany. There seemed to be nowhere to turn for help, for the U.S. military had to cooperate in the repatriation of former prisoners. The three young women went to Tamara's friend, Frau Genz, who gladly hid them in her house. Food was a problem, until some GIs happened by looking for someone to do their laundry in exchange for food and cigarettes.

Elmer Hupka, of Crete, Nebraska, brought his laundry and returned later to ask Tamara for a date. Eventually Tamara went to work in the mess hall where Elmer was a cook, and when Elmer's tour of duty in Germany was over, he asked Tamara to marry him. The service was performed by his commanding officer and attended by the GIs from his company. The bride wore white, a gown made from a liberated parachute.

Before her husband's overseas duty ended, Mrs. Hupka travelled to the U.S. on one of the official war bride voyages. She recalls her delight at unexpectedly finding a friend on board:

Who did I see on my very first day on the ship? Anna, my friend from prison camp. She had married another GI and was on her way to Chicago. She was a front-line sergeant in the Russian army—in combat all the time until she was captured. She was rough, tough. She pulled me through. That was the best reunion of my life! I see her twice a year, in Omaha or Chicago. We never miss Christmas together—never in 36 years." [1]

Another woman from the Russian Ukraine, Rosa Eranorna Dad-nora, was also seventeen years old when one person from every family in her hometown of Izym was ordered to go to Germany to work in September 1942. Because her father was ill and her brothers too young, Rosa had to go. For three years she worked in a textile mill in Alsace-Lorraine making mattresses for the German army. When a plan to slow up production was discovered by the Gestapo, Rosa and others were taken to Strassburg and imprisoned. They were destined to go to a concentration camp, but during an American bombing, the prison walls were broken and, while the female SS guards were hiding in the bomb shelter, the prisoners escaped. It was December 1944, and the prisoners suffered cold, hunger, and fear as they fled toward the American lines. Those who fell back were killed.

Rosa reached the American lines and went to work at the American ninety-third Evacuation Hospital. A few weeks later she met Carl White. They were married August 20, 1945, in Rotenburg, Germany.

Citizens of Soviet Russia were expected to bring their spouses home and raise a family in Russia, recalled Rosa. Her report is confirmed by a recently declassified secret memo, dated July 21, 1945, on the subject of Soviet-born wives of liberated British POWs, who were not permitted to leave Odessa with their husbands. The U.S. European theater commander stated that instructions in the U.S. and British zones provide that women of Russian origin who claim the nationality of other United Nations by reason of marriage were to be brought to the notice of the proper repatriation officials of the countries whose nationalities they claim in view of their marriage, without undergoing interview by officials of another country. Women who were interviewed earlier and had been claimed as Soviet citizens were not to be turned over to Soviet officials without specific concurrence of appropriate officials of the country whose nationality they claim because of their marriage.[2]

Rosa White, however, recalled:

All citizens of USSR were being repatriated at that point after the war, in many instances against their will. I ran away shortly after the wedding to another country. [Belgium] I did receive permission to wait in that area for further developments. I heard of one Russian girl having been sent to Russia, having taken her husband and child, too. I came to this country with full permission of USSR Consulate in Belgium (and passport).

On March 21, 1947, the Supreme Soviet of the USSR officially decreed that citizens of the Soviet Union· were forbidden to marry foreigners. This prohibition had no parallel in any other country.[3]

Rosa White and Tamara Hupka were among the displaced persons caught up in the chaos of postwar Europe. In Germany, 9.5 million slave-laborers, political prisoners, concentration camp inmates, and prisoners of war had been released by the Allies.[4] Many of these people were detained in displaced persons camps set up by UNRRA, the United Nations Refugee Relief Association. Others had had enough of camp life and struck out on their own.

Under terms of the July 1945 Potsdam Agreement, the Allies agreed to accept twelve million ethnic Germans expelled from Poland, Czechoslovakia, Russia, Estonia, Hungary, Romania, and Yugoslavia.[5] Three million of these expellees were already in West Germany by November 1945, and their ranks were swelled by the refugees who fled from Soviet-occupied Eastern Europe.[6] Many died during these massive migrations of people, and families were often separated. Many young women ended up desperately alone in West Germany. Sometimes a lonely GI could take the place of the family a woman had lost.

One of these women was Gisela Blake, who was drafted in 1944 into the German National Labor Service in her native Silesia and was sent to Czechoslovakia to work on a farm for one year. Back in Silesia during the last days of the war, she and her mother tried to flee to Germany. The train, crowded with panic-stricken civilians, was strafed by Russian airplanes and attacked by bandits who stole most of their belongings. Gisela and her mother tried to continue by bicycle, but these were stolen by Russian soldiers. When one of the soldiers grabbed Gisela's accordion, however, she refused to let go of this prized possession and held fast until the accordion ripped in half. After acquiring a horse and buggy from a farmer, she tried to convince the Russians she and her mother were French and were trying to return to France, but they didn't believe her and the two women had to continue on foot. "Thousands of Russian troops swarmed over the countryside and would take horses and ride them to death," Gisela recalled. "There were hundreds of dead horses on the street." Her mother was unable to continue the journey and returned home to await her husband's release from a POW camp.

Gisela made her way to Munich, where she lived in a bomb-damaged building in a room with only three walls. Living conditions were worse than anything she had experienced before. Although there had been rationing and shortages during the war, "afterward there wasn't anything—if you had nothing to trade there was no food." When the U.S. Signal Corps offered one meal a day to teletype operators, Gisela was glad to go to work for the Americans. Many of the women had American boyfriends who would give them things scarce on the market, and Gisela sometimes worked two shifts, her own and another woman's, for a bar of soap or butter that the other woman would give her. Eventually Gisela also had an American boyfriend.

"I would have married a German man, but there weren't any around then. German men were in prison camps," said Gisela, whose brother returned from an English POW camp shortly before her marriage to a GI in 1948. "I was at an age when I wanted to get married and have a family of my own."

In Czechoslovakia, Baroness Elisabeth Baratta was also conscripted into the German labor force and sent to Germany to work in a factory from 1942 to 1943. On her return to Czechoslovakia she was employed by a Czech firm, under German control, located on the outskirts of Prague. She hated the crowded air raid shelters near the factory:

> When the air raids came during the day I always went into the hills. I could see the planes passing over on their way to their targets. The planes were silver things high up in the sky, and I could see the bombs falling out of them into the city, which was bombed several times.

On May 8, 1945, two out-of-gas German tanks were abandoned in the courtyard of Elisabeth's home. All of the next day Russian troops and tanks rumbled through the town. "The people were all so happy because the war was over," recalled Elisabeth. "They gave flowers to the Russians and Slibovice, a Czech national drink. There was much joy at the war's end. I was happy, too."

But her happiness was short-lived. Russian officers were quartered in their home and Elisabeth spent a terror-filled night hiding under a bed while drunken officers demolished the furniture and fired shots into all the paintings on the second floor of the eighty-room castle that had belonged to her family for over 200 years. In town, forty women were raped while their men were locked into cellars. A friend of Elisabeth's was raped several times and was infected with syphilis.

Late in May, Elisabeth, her mother, and two younger brothers were imprisoned by the new leftist government and Elisabeth was forced to do heavy work for three months. Her mother's health suffered from the conditions and poor food in prison. After their release on August 31, 1945, recalled Elisabeth, "I was at this time so scared of the Russians. I nearly fainted every time I saw a Russian on a street car." In November, Elisabeth left Czechoslovakia for Germany with a letter of safe passage from the American chargé d'affaires, a man who had often enjoyed the family's hospitality before the war. (One year later, when her father returned from a Siberian prison camp, her parents and brothers managed to buy passports to Italy on the black market. The family, who had lived in an eighty-room castle, had been reduced to living in one room in Prague. Their escape to the West was accomplished just in time— a warrant for their arrest had been issued for the next day.)

Elisabeth had no trouble getting past the Russian guards at the border. They could not read English, but when they saw the American embassy seal on her letter, they let her through:

This paper did wonders by the Americans. At this time Germany was in chaos. You had to get a permit to work before you get food rations and a residence permit. I had no papers other than my letter from the Ambassador's office, no passport. My cousin at this time had a job with the Americans. Count Waldendorf invited the Colonel of the American forces to dinner. At this dinner, I asked the Colonel's translator if the colonel could help me. The Colonel couldn't give me a job because I couldn't speak English, but he said, "Come to my office every month and I'll stamp your card so you can get some food and a place to live."

For four or five months Elisabeth relied on the colonel to stamp her card, until she got a good job in Regensburg. Later on she moved to Munich:

> I met my husband going between Munich and Regensburg by train. The train was already starting to move when I saw this American running by the window where I was sitting asking "Regensburg?" I said, "Ja" and he got on the train. He got off the train at Regensburg too. I had to walk home, there were no taxis. He had a jeep waiting for him and wanted to drive me home. I was very sceptical, but I had a suitcase and had to walk 15 minutes in the dark, so I took a chance and accepted the ride.
>
> The next day was Sunday. I came back from church and there was this American again with his jeep. He said he was leaving, but he had the afternoon off. Do you want to go to the Red Cross dance? I said OK because it was afternoon. The dance was like a tea garden. The music was excellent and I enjoyed it. I had a milkshake and just loved it.

Allen Honey was in Regensburg looking for his plane and crew, for they had been shot down there during the war, but he was stationed at Erding, near Munich. When he found out Elisabeth was moving to Munich, he asked where she would be staying and surprised her with a visit. Although Allen always acted as a gentleman, Elisabeth was still reluctant to become friendly with him. Because Americans were known to be rather forward, she thought she'd better establish some ground rules immediately if she and Allen were to continue seeing each other.

"I don't want to go to bed with you," she told him. Allen assured her that he had no intention of trying to take advantage of her. Their friendship and mutual respect gradually grew into a deeper fondness.

For three years Elisabeth had a well-paid job selling prefabricated houses, but money was not worth much. "At that time a carton of cigarettes was worth a whole month's pay for me." Elisabeth said that Allen helped her and the German family she lived with a great deal:

But everything he did for us was legal. He did not have anything to do with the black market. He could have had much, but he didn't take anything.

In November 1948 Allen was sent back to the U.S. because of illness (he had ulcers). He told me that he will send for me or he will come back for me. I was a little sceptical. After all, such a long way, different continent and getting home to his old friends, I thought he would change his mind. But in February 1949 he returned to Germany.

They were married in August, 1949.

Marie Stejskalova of Pisek, Czechoslovakia, was also sent to work in Germany in 1941, and she stayed there when the war ended. She met her GI husband-to-be, Earl W. Avery, February 2, 1949, at the train station in Augsburg. "I was very happy in 1949 when the Czech officer came to ask if I go home. I said no," Marie recalls. "I also told him I will marry an American GI." Earl was later hurt on maneuvers and sent back to the U.S., but he came back before Christmas 1952, bringing many presents for Marie from his parents and brother and sister. They were married March 4, 1954.

During the war, American troops had advanced into Czechoslovakia as far as Plzen. Ed Lucas was stationed there with a tank battalion when he met Ann Kadlecova. They were married in Plzen on August 22, 1945. She arrived in the U.S. on July 4, 1946, aboard the *Henry Gibbins,* along with nearly one hundred Czech war brides and many from France. Only a small percentage of Czech war brides married their GIs in Czechoslovakia as Ann Kadlecova did. Most Czechs who married U.S. soldiers were refugees in West Germany, as were Elisabeth Baratta, Marie Stejskalova, and Ilse Ingrid Hardy.

Ingrid Hardy left Decin, Czechoslovakia, on the advice of a family friend, to try to get to the American-occupied zone of Germany in the spring of 1947. The family feared that the outspoken young woman would be sent to work in Russia if she remained in Decin. Ingrid describes her flight:

I took no luggage of any kind, not even a change of clothes. It seemed the safest and would not cause any suspicion. No papers or identification either. Had I been caught by police my answer would have been that I was looking for my Russian boyfriend, as this was believable. I rode the train next morning to the border city of Cheb, not inside but on top of the train, hanging on for dear life, getting the soot right in my face. Train service at that time was still few and far between so the trains were crowded to the limit and even the rooftops had no empty space.[7]

At the border town of Cheb, a farmer advised Ingrid to hide in a haystack near the border until the changing of the guard at 2 A.M.

Past midnight it started to rain, slowly, steadily. This was a blessing—it kept noises down. The haystack kept me warm and dry for a while but soon coldness took over my body, and when the farmer alerted me that it was time to go I was almost relieved. He said: 'Go down on your knees, creep across that empty field—the grass is high enough to shield you from any moving lights. When you reach the forest it will be German territory. Good luck, young girl!' I gave him a hug and handshake and started to crawl. My clothes became wet, my dress ripped, my knees became sore and began to bleed. Occasionally I could hear the sound of guards talking and I knew there were others out there in the rainy night taking their own chances on getting across no man's land. What must have been a fifty-minute crawl seemed like hours. Suddenly dogs barked; I heard shots being fired and felt a burn . . . and I woke up in a hospital in Bavaria. I was *free*.[8]

Ingrid was lucky. She had only a surface wound on her ankle; no bone damage. The Red Cross gave her clothes, many of which had been donated by churches in the U.S. She was given a displaced persons identification card and sent to a DP camp in Weissenburg, near Nürnberg:

On arrival at the camp we had to be deloused. That was a shock! Some women went from person to person and sprayed powder in front and back beneath our clothing; such an icky feeling. This procedure was repeated before every meal, every day. We lived from day to day. Some days food wasn't enough; plenty was cooked but perhaps 50 new people would arrive, so we shared.

Actually we were free to go as we pleased, but where would we go? In camp was much despair and sadness. Many of the elderly missed their homeland and loved ones. They couldn't adjust to commune living. Lost children looked for their parents and parents searched for their children. Everyone was wondering, will life become normal again? [9]

Ingrid was eager to find a job so she could leave the camp, and she was eventually offered a job working for the Americans in Garmisch-Patenkirchen:

'Hurrah!' I was ready to go, anything to get out of the camp— to make a future for myself. Next day the commander gave me a train ticket. In a dress and coat trimmed with artificial fur from some lady in Michigan, USA, I walked down the hill and caught the train to Munich. [10]

After working in Garmisch for one year, she got a job in Munich working for two Czech emigrees who had opened an import-export business. While in Munich, she recalls:

It happened several times to me that American soldiers talked to me on the street, but I would walk on, as I couldn't understand what they said. Girls who were seen with GIs were looked on as undesirable citizens. When GIs said something in German, usually it wasn't proper words. It is my belief the soldiers didn't know what they were saying. I'm sure that back in the USA they wouldn't address a girl on the street with the words 'Come here with your panties in your hands.' Soldiers usually were always first taught the dirty words and jokes in another country. To me it was no joke.

On June 4, 1949, however, Ingrid met Ralph Hardy, whose warm blue eyes and concern for her well-being appealed to her. When they went out, Ralph brought his secretary along to translate, but eventually Ingrid grew leery of this arrangement, for whatever they said to the secretary would be much shorter when she translated it. One day Ingrid learned that the endearments Ralph was fond of addressing her with—"Hello, Beetlebrain. How are you, Knucklehead. Goodbye, Bubblebelly!"—did not mean "Honey, Sweetheart, and Darling." There were no more dates with the secretary along after this; Ingrid bought a German-English dictionary and began writing down questions before meeting Ralph.

It is my belief that at first there was no romantic feeling between Ralph and me. Ralph was 33 years old and I didn't believe he was not married. He didn't look like the dream man I imagined. Ralph's hair was receding, his teeth were not straight, and I only was fascinated with his eyes—so blue and warm. Ralph told me later that his first impression was that of a lost orphan. Who would ever wear high heel shoes with socks! I needed someone to look after me. Ralph wanted to help me get to America, where I would find a better life than Germany had to offer at that time. He even went so far as to sell his car and personal clothing, and went with me to the American Consulate to apply for a visa. Since I was a displaced person, I fell under the "Volks German" quota of Czechoslovakia and there was not even a waiting period. Ralph put money down for a passage on a ship to America and wrote to his parents, asking them to sponsor me but they declined. He later told me that his brother and wife would have done it, but by that time we had fallen in love and I was waiting to leave Germany with him.

After dating Ralph for several weeks my landlady expressed her surprise that I went with an American soldier and he never brought me cigarettes or liquor which could be sold on the black market. I would rather have died than to ask Ralph for something; besides I didn't sleep with him. It would be different if we were engaged. Many of the GI's rented rooms for their girls and gave them living expenses but I worked and paid for everything myself. Ralph later told me he respected that and it certainly helped later when we sought permission to get married—no bad flaw on my character.

On my 24th birthday Ralph came with his arms full of packages. It overwhelmed me. I was brought up not to accept gifts from men but on the occasion of a birthday it was different. A lovely gray skirt, a white blouse, nylons and a box of Tootsie Rolls! I had been so starved for chocolate that I ate all 48 Tootsie Rolls in one evening. In the early morning hours I awoke, went to the bathroom and heaved, and heaved, until it came up. I have never touched a Tootsie Roll again.[12]

Having an American boyfriend or fiancé could make a crucial difference in the precarious existence of a DP in postwar Germany, and not only because a GI was able to obtain scarce luxury items such as Tootsie Rolls, soap, cigarettes, and coffee. He sometimes was the only hope for survival for an entire family. Life among the DPs was dangerous in 1945: gang wars, robberies, rape, and murder became everyday occurrences. Some people were desperately seeking provisions to survive; other were wreaking vengeance for wrongs committed by the German government.

Talvikki Manninen, who fled from Finland and then Poland just ahead of the advancing Russian army, described conditions among the refugees:

> The displaced persons in Germany were a large and mixed lot. One could see not only Russians and Poles, but also Czecho-Slovaks, Swedes, Danes, Ukrainians, Estonians, and many more. American occupation authorities tried sending many back to their own countries. Truckloads of them were brought to the borders of their nations, but before long they trickled back into the big cities where aid and rations were more easily available.
>
> People had to have identification. Many wore a small flag to distinguish themselves from the Germans. I made a tiny Finnish flag out of scraps of blue and white cloth and fastened it on my coat. That flag proved to be of great help on many occasions.[13]

In the middle of May 1945, Talvikki received the news that her husband, an Estonian who had been drafted into the German army, was missing in action and presumed dead. On June 19 she gave birth to her second daughter, without any assistance. Three hospitals had been unable to take her, and the midwife arrived after the baby was born. The difficulty of finding food for herself and two babies was alleviated somewhat by the presence of nearby U.S. troops:

> The American soldiers had set up a field kitchen in our yard. Huge kettles of food cooked there all day long and wonderful odors drifted in through the windows. The soldiers had strict orders not to give food to civilians who were often hanging about. Children, thin and pale, were gathering in little flocks around the cooking area, grabbing discarded cans in the hopes of finding a little food left in them. They searched for partly

spoiled fruit which the cooks had thrown away. Every garbage pile was searched, and it was no wonder that all kinds of diseases raged. Sometimes we were recipients of one friendly soldier's gifts of coffee or pancake flour. These gestures of kindness we appreciated very much and we made a party out of the goodies he gave.

Then came that momentous evening in our little kitchen apartment—Suddenly there was a knock on the door and someone stood in the doorway glancing uncertainly at each of us. We were shocked! It was a tall soldier in U.S. uniform and full gear who stepped in and looked at us. "We are going to be ousted," I thought.

But his sober face changed to a broad grin and I heard: "No, hyvaa paivaa!" (well, good day to you). Before I could say anything he continued, nodding his head in my direction: "Are you the Finn? I'm a Finnish-American. Norman, is the name. My father immigrated to America from Finland at the age of 16. I was born in Michigan."

One of the cooks had mentioned that a girl wearing a Finnish flag on her coat was living in this building and he had decided to investigate. As he talked the door opened and another soldier in full gear walked in. His name was Uuno and he was also a Finn in the American army.

A somewhat brighter period followed for us. Whenever and wherever possible, Norman and Uuno were ready to help. They brought us everything they could lay their hands on. A big portion of their weekly rations found its way to our table in spite of the no fraternization rules for the soldiers.[14]

All too soon, the two soldiers had to move on and Talvikki was destitute once more. On Christmas Eve, 1945, however, Norman, on a two-day leave from Regensburg, suddenly arrived in a jeep on which he had painted "Vikki" in big white letters. With armfuls of food and presents, Norman brightened what would otherwise have been a gloomy holiday.

Poverty and hunger still threatened us all. People were committing suicide due to their hopeless situations. Although vaccinations were offered in all parts of the city and serums were given out by the U.S. army for all those who had been exposed to typhoid fever and other diseases, the contagions spread. More and more quarantine notices could be seen in the neighborhoods. To my sorrow, Christel, who had never been very strong, was stricken with a virus.[15]

Norman came for another brief visit in January 1946 and told Vikki he wanted to help her immigrate to the U.S. However, he was sent home before he could attempt to make arrangements. In mid May 1946, an American soldier brought Vikki a letter from Michigan:

There is only one sure way to assure your and the children's future, and that is marriage with me. Think about it and let me know through "army mail" what your decision is. I love you!

Norman [16]

It was a difficult decision for Vikki. She wanted to return to Finland where her eldest son Harri was living with her aunt, but it seemed unlikely that she would be able to make her way back and support the three children on her own. With Norman, her children would have a home and she could ask her aunt to travel to the U.S. with Harri. She decided to accept.

It took thirteen months and many long trips to the U.S. Consulate in Munich to get the papers in order. Vikki and Regina passed the physical, but Christel had a heart murmur, rickets, and malnutrition. The doctor thought she would probably not survive a boat trip, but he permitted her to fly. In June 1947 they arrived in New York:

We didn't leave the plane until we had passed quarantine. Then we were taken to the immigration office to have our passes checked. When it finally came to be our turn the official took the three bundles of papers, one for each of us, and checked them. But he didn't seem to know how to disentangle himself from them. Three different countries of birth and Regine on a Polish quota. He scratched his head and looked at me and then again at the bawling youngsters and finally stated that there must be something wrong with the papers. With red ink he scribbled something over the papers and then disappeared to summon someone to take us away.[17]

They were taken to Ellis Island. In a large room crowded with immigrants, Vikki found space for herself and the children among the canvas cots covered with gray blankets, which she later discovered were crawling with lice. Cockroaches covered the floor at night.

After five days, there was a lengthy hearing, at which she learned that the Munich consulate had given her and Christel permanent visas and Regina only a visitor's visa because the Polish quota was filled at the time of their departure.

I was spiritually and physically exhausted. Before another two days passed we were called in for another hearing. They had another witness. It was Ruth, Norman's sister. We were meeting for the first time, from across the courtroom, under very depressing circumstances. We were not allowed to speak to each other. Ruth took the oath, and the cross-examination began.

"Who is this girl?" Ruth was asked, and the examiner pointed at me.

"She is my brother's fiancée, Vikki," she answered confidently.

"How do you know that," the other examiner asked quickly. "Have you met her before?"

That, of course, was something she couldn't prove.

"I would know her anywhere from pictures and descriptions my brother gave me," she stated.

The cross-examination went on and on, but at last they were finished. The decision was quick and simple. I was an innocent victim of some oversights at the consulate in Munich. I was allowed to enter the United States of America. . . .

At Ruth's home we found Norman, who had just arrived from Michigan, waiting for us. He looked so much taller and slimmer in his new blue suit than I remembered. I guess I hadn't looked at him with the same eyes before. Now for the first time in eighteen months, we saw each other again. How strange it seemed. I felt a mixture of fear and relief; apprehension and joy.[18]

Talvikki and Norman were married June 27, 1947, in Chassell, Michigan. Norman was a loving father to the children, including

Harri, whom they sent for as soon as transportation from Finland could be arranged.

Ruth Applebaum's path to the U.S. was by way of London, England. Born Ruth Schuftan in Poland and raised in Germany, she went to London in 1939 to work as a nanny for a Scottish family. When she left Germany, Nazi soldiers slit her luggage to shreds and she arrived in England, frightened and friendless. A kindly bobby lent her the fare to London. For a tiny wage, Ruth took care of three small boys, cooked, scrubbed, and ironed. "They were a good family," she recalls. "On my day off the mother would pin directions on my coat and send me off to see the sights. And they also sent a permit to my mother.

"But three days after that permit reached Germany the two countries were at war." Ruth's mother and other relatives died at Dachau.

In 1942, the British government assigned Ruth to a first-aid station mobile unit. "After a bombing it was our job to race to the scene to administer aid. We were on 24 hours, off 24. Sometimes I'd be washing my hair and the siren would sound. I'd slap my helmet over my soapy head and off we'd go."

Late in 1944, Ruth met Air Force Sgt. Joe Appelbaum at a dance in London:

I saw Joe heading for a girl sitting near me. But someone else got there first. He looked around, and there I was . . . sitting in a corner, tired and alone. I suppose he figured he'd give me a break. At any rate, the dance floor was crowded, so we talked instead. The next night Joe proposed. I thought to myself, 'What a crazy American,' but when he kept on coming down—a day and a half on the train—to see me for an hour, I saw he was serious, and I gladly said "yes."

Three months later, on January 5, 1945, after a warning by a chaplain and official approval by Washington, Joe and Ruth were married. "What a wedding it was. I begged rations for weeks and finally had enough sugar and oleo to bake my own cake. It was all primitive but wonderful. A week later Joe went to the continent."

After she arrived in the U.S., Ruth was asked how she felt about her adopted country. Her answer:

If you saw me stand before my mirror and practice the words that come hard, you'd know how I want to belong. If I told you that I applied for my citizenship my second day in Chicago you'd have an idea. If I hadn't loved Americans, why do you think I would have married Joe? [19]

Scandinavian countries also contributed to the numbers of war brides and fiancées of American servicemen. An average of thirty-five wives of American citizens travelled from Sweden to the U.S. per year during the early postwar period. Many of these couples met when the husband-to-be was interned in Sweden during the war.

"While on an aircraft salvage mission I met this 'beautiful Swenska Flicka' " reports Steve Condur of Pennsylvania, who was an eighth Air Force turret gunner on a B-17 bomber.

On April 11, 1944, Steve's B-17 was attacked by enemy aircraft enroute from England to Posnen, Poland. Swedish fighters escorted the damaged plane to Malmö, Sweden where the crew was interned. A member of Condur's crew described the internment as a vacation, for neutral Sweden was spared much of the hardship of the war. Americans interned in Sweden were relatively free and enjoyed Swedish hospitality. Steve met Karin Lindvall of Malmö at a dance in the city folkets park (peoples' park) in Ameralen. The meeting made a lasting impression on Steve:

I left Sweden before war's end, returned to England, then to USA, but my life was no longer the same. Two years after the war I completed arrangements under the GI Fiancée Law for Karin to come to the States. In August 1947 we were married in the town of McAdoo, Pa.

Karin will never forget that when she arrived in New York, Steve met her wearing a blue suit and a large blue and yellow tie: "Swedish Flag Colors—pretty loud tie."

Karin's initial adjustment was difficult because of the unaccustomed heat and humidity, and due to a severe case of impetigo she developed the first week, perhaps contracted aboard the ship, which was crowded with refugees. It "kept me low and miserable until cured (six weeks). Facial eruptions prevented my meeting people anxious to meet me."

Another Swedish fiancée of a former B-17 crew member entered the U.S. on May 14, 1946, under the quota allowance for Sweden (not counted under the Fiancées Act). Lt. Brown of Akron, Ohio, met May-Britt Kaal of Taatvik, Sweden in New York, bearing a gardenia corsage.

A member of the U.S. Coast Guard, Virginia McDaniel applied for a civilian job with the War Department when the women's reserve of the Coast Guard was phased out at the end of the war. In September 1946 she arrived in Munich, Germany, where she met Jørgen Nielsen, a Dane. Both worked for the Civil Censorship Division, which censored German telephone, telegraph, and mail communication.

Because so few native born Americans knew German, most of the personnel came from allied countries whose citizens knew both German and English. Americans like myself were called WDEs—War Department Employees. The allied personnel were known as ACEs—Allied Civilian Employees. A big bone of contention between the two groups was that ACEs were paid about one third of what WDEs were paid for the same work. This was at the behest of their own governments because they did not want the U.S. taking away all of their people.

The section of the Army forces of Occupation that we worked for was called Civil Censorship Division, but it was known to us as CCD—'Crooks, Characters, and Danes.' This was because almost half of the personnel came from Denmark. Crooks referred to BTOs: big-time-operators. Actually they were small time, but they did do a lot of black-marketing. The 'characters' applied to a lot of us—one example: an ex-Wave who wore her converted Navy uniform complete with battle ribbons, and came to war-time Germany with 26 pair of shoes and an uncounted number of hats. Almost half the people working on the post were from Denmark, and although English was the official language, what you heard most of the time was Danish.

We really had no problems with military bureaucracy because Denmark was an ally. We did have to get military approval which took about 30 days, and was mostly based on approval by the Lt. Colonel who commanded the post that we were stationed at. Ours was a whirlwind romance. We were introduced on my birthday, February 21st, but did not have our first date until the beginning of June, and we were married July 16th [1947]. That six-week period included the month it took to get military approval. We were almost constantly together during that period. Although we came from different countries, our economic circumstances were relatively the same; we were both interested in the same things, and the things that were important to us were the same.

When my husband and I decided to marry, I found that because I had been in the service during war time, I could bring him to the US under the "War Brides" law. We were married July 16, 1947, and we returned to the U.S. in September 1947.

Since my husband has never had more than a trace of an accent, when we were being processed, he was always being asked where his bride was, and he would have to explain that he was the bride. I was at the same time having to report with all the GIs. When it came to the physical examination, I reported in ahead of time and explained the situation since no way was I going to show up with all those men.

When they got to Bremerhaven, they were delayed for three days because a ship had struck a mine in the harbor. Men and women were segregated in the overcrowded billets, but when the billeting clerk learned that Jørgen was the "war bride," she assigned Jørgen and Virginia a room of their own. She had married a Czech and was taking her own "male war bride" home.

Anna Della Casa in Naples, Italy. December 1943, just before her husband left for Anzio beachhead. (Anna Della Casa Gonzales)

Maria and Robert Brixner in Florence, Italy. December 1945. (Maria Fontana Brixner)

Maria and Peter Spinoso. Montichio Bagni, Italy. May 16, 1945. (Maria Donatini Spinoso)

Carmen Kergis, Bièrges, Belgium, April 1945. (Carmen Aupaix Kergis)

When Gertrude and Joseph Reichenbach were married in Heerlen, Netherlands, on May 7, 1946, there were only two modes of transportation available: a horse and carriage or an army jeep. (Gertrude Consten Reichenbach)

Formalizing the first official marriage between an American officer and a French woman, Denise and Stanley Schorr sign the marriage register on December 9, 1944, City Hall, Paris. (Denise Khaitman Schorr)

French and Belgian war brides leave Paris for the LeHavre staging area. March 1946. (American Red Cross)

John Stefaniak and buddies befriend German children in Nürnberg. 1945. (Esther Stefaniak)

Karin Trenina modelling suit her mother made out of two pair of her boyfriend's "officer's pinks" trousers. Bamberg, Germany, 1945. Bottom: looking like "Lily Marlene"—under a lamppost in Berlin in 1946. (Karin Trenina Yount)

The photo Mary Grill Berthi-aume sent to the brother of her friend's American fiancé in May 1947. In November they were married.

Contact with German women was inevitable, in spite of the non-fraternization policy. Fulda, West Germany. 1946. (Else Dickel Smith)

Co-author Barbara Smith Scibetta with her grandparents in Kassel, Germany, in 1951. (Else Dickel Smith)

Ursula and Ceth Hunter were married in church in Munich, Germany, in 1947. (Ursula Hunter)

Bertha and Walter Brandstatter. Note the wedding gown made out of a parachute. Passau, Germany. January 19, 1949. (Bertha Brandstatter)

Karola and Wayne Parkin posing in front of a bomb-damaged house. Augsburg, Germany April 24, 1947. (Karola Parkin)

The Far East—Victors and Vanquished

Part Three

Tomoko and Joseph Hamelin in front of Emperor Hirohito's summer palace, 1953.

TOMOKO YAMAGUCHI HAMELIN

Chapter 12

Murdering Devils

---

*I was only 13 years old. Scared. Many of my older girlfriends
shaved their heads so they looked like men!*
—Tomoko Hamelin, Zuschi City, Japan

The first American troops to land at Yokohama, Japan, in August
1945 found a ghost town. Homes that survived the bombing were
boarded up and there wasn't a soul in sight. All the girls' high
schools in the city were closed down, and the girls had been evacuated
to the remote countryside. Wartime images of Americans as murder-
ing devils, along with the recent warnings in Japanese newspapers
about anticipated looting and rape, sent women into hiding.[1]

Tomoko (Yamaguchi) Hamelin recalled the frenzy as the Americans entered Zuschi City. "I was only 13 years old. Scared. My
older girlfriends shaved their heads so they looked like men!" Tomoko refrained from this drastic measure, partly assuaged by a less
fearful image of Americans drawn by an uncle who had attended
Harvard University in the 1920s.

Ryuko Ozawa's mother warned her that "when the American
troops arrived, they would rape and murder girls like me and that
I must hide and not let myself be seen."[2] But when the Americans
arrived in Tokyo, their behavior was quite different.

Gen. Douglas MacArthur, commander of the occupation forces
in Japan, was anxious to dispel negative stereotypes of GIs and pro-

mote good relations with the Japanese to ensure a peaceful occupation. The general decreed that any soldier who so much as slapped a Japanese would get five years in prison; rapists faced the death penalty.

The Japanese were convinced that American troops would give themselves over to pillage and rape in the traditional manner of conquering armies. Edwin O. Reischauer, future American ambassador to Japan, wrote:

> . . . the Japanese were visibly relieved and openly appreciative of the discipline and good will our soldiers demonstrated, while the latter, half expecting at first to feel knives in their backs, were puzzled and then charmed by the essentially well-mannered and law-abiding Japanese. The result was a strange fraternization between American battle veterans, who often had a bitter hatred of the Japanese they had just been fighting, and Japanese civilians who had lost loved ones and all their possessions in American air raids.[3]

"I relax," said one woman about her reaction to the news of Japan's defeat and the arrival of the Americans. "Tokyo flat after war from bombs. Here and there a tall building but all around flat. Some cried when the Emperor say Japan lost war, but not me. Older women went to train station every day to pay respect for dead, sometimes only boxes, no bodies."

Half a million American soldiers were stationed in Japan within the first month of occupation. General MacArthur was generally successful in promoting Americans as friendly occupiers, and soon desperate civilians aproached GIs for cigarettes, chocolate, and chewing gum to trade in the black market for scarce food rations to keep their families alive.

"Stores were boarded up because there was no merchandise," recalled Hertha Rogers of Kobe. "All aspects of living were completely changed by the war. Every item of consumption was rationed and distribution centers were set up by the government. We stood in long lines for hours for all rations . . . our sugar ration was ½ pound per person once every six months during the last two years of the war." Ration cards became useless when goods ran out.

Despite General MacArthur's warnings to the occupation troops regarding their behavior toward the Japanese, there were cases of looting, rape, and murder; however, the violence was not widespread.[4] Diversions for GIs were sought and barely three weeks after the Americans landed in Japan, Gen. Robert L. Eichelberger, commander of the U.S. Eighth Army, cut the pink ribbon across the door to the first Red Cross club in Yokohama. Japanese onlookers watched as the general entered the building, formerly a cabaret, and pressed their faces against the windows for a glimpse of the cake and coffee being served to enlisted men at the bar inside.[5]

Hundreds of thousands of destitute Japanese women became heads of households after their fathers and brothers were killed or disabled. They had to find ways to provide for their families. The number of starvation deaths kept rising. In Tokyo there were 1,291 reported deaths from malnutrition between November 1945 and April 1946; 267 bodies were found in the streets during April alone.[6]

A cultural upheaval accompanied economic desperation. On January 1, 1946, Emperor Hirohito, worshiped as the descendant of the Sun Goddess Amaterasu, abjured his divinity.[7] For centuries, the Japanese had been taught from childhood that the grandson of Amaterasu became the first sovereign of Japan, and his descendants had continued to govern in unbroken succession. The Japanese believed that Hirohito was destined to rule the earth, and that his people were braver and more intelligent than other races.[8]

The superiority of the Japanese had been repudiated. Ancient laws and traditions were questioned, especially by the young. After eight months of occupation, many Japanese women had traded wooden sandals for high heels and Western-style clothes.

The breakup of the male-dominated social structure and the enfranchisement of Japanese women were major social changes in the postwar years. Breaking with tradition, many women lived away from home and sent money to support the rest of the family. Some women joined unions or became involved in politics. By April 1946, the first Japanese women were seen policing streets in Tokyo and patrolling railroad stations, once exclusively male occupations.[9] Few women continued to follow the codes demanding obedience to their parents and husbands.

"My Papa almost died with shame when I announced that since I had learned English I would take a job working with the American Army," said Ryuko Ozawa. "He started to shout that I could never do such a thing, but Mama was firm and said it was all right but I mustn't fall in love with any of them, for she still didn't trust them completely." Like so many families in Tokyo, the Ozawas were left in difficult circumstances after losing their home in a fire bomb raid which killed 88,000 people.[10]

Julie Grant went against family tradition when she refused to marry the Japanese husband chosen for her and was subsequently ostracized:

> I found this situation unbearable and, before long, wrapped up my few belongings in a cloth and left. My eldest brother pawned his only suit to get money to help me start out alone. With no home and my money running out, I had to find work. A kindly Nisei man [second generation Japanese-American] and his wife who worked for the American military gave me a job as housemaid. They taught me English. One day a young American soldier came . . . he was twenty-one; I was eighteen. From then on, we continued to see each other regularly.[11]

Postwar Japan rarely offered traditional sources of livelihood, such as farming or work in a family or locally-owned business, largely due to the devastation of repeated bombings and the upheaval in government. The United States military community was often the only source of employment. One woman who went to Yokota to work as a typist at an air force base said, "Everybody, young people, especially young women were so independent. Because of the war everybody had a deep scar. They turned to different ways after the war. Many young people, women, ambitious."

Kyo Wittrock of Tono, Iwate Prefecture, worked as a housekeeper between 1946 and 1948 for an American couple:

> Captain and Mrs. She head nurse, he in hospital office. Americans nice to Japanese women during occupation. Never met bad people. Where I working, give bread, sugar, very nice. At that time we don't have much sugar in Japan and they give it to us.

Kyo's father had an import-export business in China before the war broke out in 1937. He managed somehow to escape back to Japan. "Took one month to get back," she said, "no food, he so sick, malnutrition, died." During the occupation, Kyo lived with her brother, who had found work with the American FBI.

Kobe, where Hertha Rogers lived with her widowed mother,

was about 60 percent destroyed, primarily by incendiary bombs which caused huge fires in residential areas. She explained how the aftereffects of these fires could be as devastating as the fires themselves:

> These incendiary bombs and the fires they caused created such intense heat that inevitably after a heavy bombing raid we would have a tremendous rain. These rains—almost daily occurrences—saturated the land to such an extent that after the rainy season in the summer of 1945 the land could absorb no more moisture and huge landslides descended from the hills. Our home, which was spared the bombings, was destroyed by such a landslide in early October of 1945.

Hertha left Kobe to find her first job with the American Red Cross in one of the servicemen's clubs in Osaka. Her knowledge of English enabled her to later find a job in the rail transportation office in Kobe as an interpreter, teletype operator, and secretary to the officer in charge.

Although contact with Japanese citizens was restricted, fraternization was not officially banned. General MacArthur stated that such a ban would not only be useless but unenforceable and prove "violative of the inherent self-respect of the American soldier." In April 1946, however, when MacArthur asked U.S. Army chaplains to help end "promiscuous relationships" between GIs and Japanese women, he was responding to pressure from "American homes expressing grave concern and deep distress over published reports suggestive of existing widespread promiscuous relationships between members of the occupying forces and Japanese women of immoral character." The general pointed out that there was a tendency to "misconstrue the word fraternization, to clothe it with the sole meaning of immorality, and greatly to overemphasize and misinterpret the relationship between members of the American occupation forces and the Japanese people." [12]

Many women sought employment in geisha houses, which were predominantly frequented by U.S. troops. Geisha women, trained in the art of conversation, usually entertained men by singing, dancing, or playing musical instruments. A famous geisha, often associated with the theatre, could command hundreds of dollars for a single performance, but many were no more than indentured servants. In September 1945, a reporter for the *Chicago Daily News* described the geisha house he visited, an old pagoda-roofed mansion several miles outside Tokyo:

They are dressed in the standard wartime costume of Japanese women: A blouse and mompei, or trousers, which bag unbecomingly in the seat and come to a tight fit around the ankles.

Some wear glasses and look like prim old-fashioned school teachers. You wonder what they are doing here. Many of them are back from recently closed factories, where they have worked during the war. Thousands more are coming they tell you.[13]

Japan's Ministry of Health and Welfare sought to curb the sexual interest of GIs in the general female population through organized prostitution. Women recruited for this purpose were called "pan-pan" girls. Prostitution in Japan's war-torn economy earned more than any other industry.[14] Many women who could not find employment turned to prostitution as their only means of survival for themselves and their dependents. A woman registered as a prostitute forfeited any possibility of ever marrying a GI, for her record eliminated her as a candidate for marriage.

American commanders were distressed over the rise in venereal disease. An average yearly infection rate of 13.4 percent for the entire Eighth Army was compared to a high of 27 percent in February 1946. By July 25, 1946, Gen. Robert Eichelberger reported that the venereal disease rate had been reduced by 50 percent. In his opinion, this downward trend was the result of a vigorous education campaign by the Army Surgeon's office, new recreational facilities and travel opportunities, and placing many hotels, night resorts, and restaurants off-limits.[15]

Money could also be a problem. GIs were paid at the official exchange rate of fifteen yen to the dollar. This ordinarily would make for a comfortable, if not luxurious, situation for most soldiers. But during the early months of the occupation, both the U.S. and Japanese governments took actions which, unintentionally, made things rough on the GIs. The U.S. failed to fix the value of the yen to the dollar; at the same time, the Japanese increased the amount of currency in circulation by more than 60 percent between August and December 1945. As a result, the realizable exchange value of the yen was more like seventy yen to the dollar, about one-fifth the official rate. An evening's entertainment, at the few places accessible to a GI, could end up costing $20, or about a month's pay.[16]

A GI who wanted to date a Japanese woman was severely limited by numerous restrictions. He couldn't take her anywhere in an army vehicle; the only other transportation available was by oxcart, ricksha, or trolley. He couldn't share his army food, even if he bought it with his own pay from the PX. Neither could he buy Japanese beverages or drink Japanese water or have his army food cooked in a Japanese kitchen. He couldn't go swimming or fishing anywhere near Tokyo. Barracks were off-limits to all Japanese females except servants. Japanese bathhouses, banks, and civilian areas were fenced off, and even private residences were off-limits.[17] None of this, however, seemed to deter ingenious GIs from dating Japanese women.

"General Eichelberger made many areas off limits for GIs, but I had a pass that permitted me to go everywhere," explained Walter Gentile, whose job was to build schools all over Japan. "All theatres were off limits, but I was young and loved girls so I went often to theatres: Takarazuka, Noe plays, Buraki, Bugaku . . . off-limits places were great fun. I got written up about 30 times for being in off-limits areas, but when the citations would come into the office, we agreed to tear them up, so no one ever got in trouble." Walter met his future wife, Cheiko, while she was just a school girl trying to survive by typing for the Americans. He used to walk by her desk and knock on it and wave at her. Cheiko was young and shy, still dressed in her sailor-type Japanese school uniform. Walter admits, "She didn't know what to make of this crazy American."

Hertha Rogers was caught breaking the rules on one occasion with an American in the Counter Intelligence Corps:

One Sunday afternoon in early 1947, one of my coworkers, a serviceman who also worked at the rail transportation office, called on me and suggested that we take in a show at Takarazuka, a little village between Kobe and Osaka. The only claim to fame there was the theatre which offered a variety of performances from Japanese plays to musicals, but the biggest attraction was a group of dancers who could highstep like the Rockettes of New York's Radio City Music Hall.

Servicemen at that time were prohibited from riding Japanese trains except in the specially provided GI cars. There was a direct rail connection from Kobe to Takarazuka, but that train had no GI car. On the trip over my date decided that he would take a chance and ride the off-limits Japanese train. However, on the return trip he felt he should not push his luck too far. So we took the train with the GI car from Takarazuka to Osaka, transferring there to the Osaka-Kobe line. My travel was limited to the prefecture of my residence and I could travel beyond this area only with the permission of the U.S. Army Counter Intelligence Corps. A prefecture was roughly the size of a county in the U.S. Takarazuka was in Hyogo Prefecture, but Osaka was not. That Sunday, not having planned to go outside the prefecture I had not obtained permission to go to Osaka. On our return trip when we transferred to the Osaka-Kobe line, I noticed that one of the passengers on the GI car was an agent with the Counter Intelligence Corps. We nodded hello and then my date and I went to find a seat. I was hoping that this Counter Intelligence agent would not check the records and find that I had no permission to be in Osaka.

But much to my chagrin, the very next day Agent Jim Flannagan and a second lieutenant called on me at the rail transportation office where I worked. Jim Flannagan introduced his friend Lt. William Rogers who proceeded to question me as to my whereabouts the day before. He stated that I had been seen in Osaka and that the records did not show that permission had been granted or had been requested and not granted. I did not deny this. He stated regulations are made to be kept and he enumerated the times that I had asked permission to travel and that heretofore I had not been denied. This kind of admonishment went on for quite some time, it seemed to me, and I was beginning to think that here was a newly promoted second lieutenant who just had to pull rank.

He said, "Business aside, will you have dinner with me tonight?" I could hardly believe my ears, for here was this stuffy young man who had been haranguing me about keeping regulations and making me feel like a criminal, and now he was asking me out to dinner. I accepted, for this change in character intrigued me and I decided that I would like to know

more about this strange young man. That was the beginning
of our courtship and it wasn't long and we were in love.

Serious relationships between Japanese women and GIs were
generally disapproved of by Japanese society. Family members rarely
took the young woman's plight into consideration. Her choice of
a Japanese mate had been seriously reduced by the war, and she
would naturally become attracted to the Americans with whom
she worked and lived in close proximity.

When Julie Grant told her family about the American she was
seeing, one relative became so enraged,

. . . he beat me about the hips with a bamboo cane. I still
feel pain from the blows—even now, decades later—when the
seasons change.

But my determination could not be broken. Two months
after our initial meeting, the young man asked me to marry
him. But our storms were not over. His mother in the United
States worried about him because of his youth and took steps
to have him recalled immediately. On the evening of our parting, he visited my room and assured me that he would come
back. But, as he left, a sudden fit of despair seized me. The
razor blade cut my wrist, and the red blood spurted. When I
awoke, I was in a hospital room.

For some inexplicable reason, he had had a foreboding not
long after leaving me. Returning quickly, he found me uncon-
scious in a pool of my own blood and carried me to a hospital
before he left for the United States.[18]

In spite of the difficulties Japanese women had to confront when
they became involved with GIs, they continued to be attracted by
their open friendliness and kindness, compared to the reticence and
aloofness of the average Japanese male. Tomoko Hamelin had dated
a few Japanese men whom she described as "polite and quiet." Her
family, well-to-do textile manufacturers before the occupation, had
hoped for a good match with a Japanese male until she fell in love
with a GI. Tomoko, who'd had a maid herself while she was growing
up, was working at the time as a housekeeper for an American
family. Although she found Joseph Hamelin too demonstrative at
first, she was impressed by his concern for her and the welfare of
her younger sisters as well. "I thought he was a nice human being,

although a bit too forward! I took my brother as a chaperone for the first three dates; he would have come with us many more, if Joseph hadn't complained."

General Eichelberger issued a watch-dog ban on public demonstrations of affection between American soldiers and Japanese women; higher echelons generally disapproved of any type of romantic relationship. This lack of tolerance was not only indicative of racial intolerance, it also suggested that Japanese women were "tainted," although it was apparent that: "Most available girls are neither the haughty geisha nor the *daruma* geisha hostesses nor prostitutes (*imbai*) but ordinary girls who have broken away from family controls." [19]

A double shadow fell over a relationship between a Japanese woman and an American. Not only was there racial intolerance on the part of the Americans, but a man of a different race was unacceptable to a Japanese family wishing to insure a pure racial bloodline. "The Japanese are even more proud than the Germans for being a pure-blooded race," explained Hertha Rogers, whose mother was full-blooded Japanese, but whose father was German, a former POW from World War I who later settled in Japan. He made his fortune in the import and export business and as the first manufacturer of safety razor blades in Japan. Her mother, a music teacher from Osaka, had been disowned by her family for marrying against their wishes.

Until her father's death when she was nine, Hertha attended an English school, but when war was declared, the German Consul ordered her to attend the Kobe Deutsche Schule.

I became a member of the Hitler Jugend at the time when the blonde Aryan race was held in such high esteem and I was of mixed blood. I felt discrimination but somehow I managed to make it through those periods. Even among my Japanese relatives I felt that I did not quite belong. I remember when I was very small and we visited my Japanese grandmother she patted me on the head saying, "If only your hair was black and straight."

Kuniko Jenkins was not only concerned about the difficulties she and Sgt. Richard Jenkins would have to cope with as an interracial couple, but she also told him, "I not a pretty person," referring to the radiation scars on her face. Kuniko had been a nineteen-year-old nurse in a Hiroshima hospital when the atomic bomb was dropped on August 6, 1945. When she met Richard several years later, the devastating long-term effects of radiation exposure were becoming apparent; the incidence of many types of cancer known to be caused by radiation had risen sharply throughout Japan.[20] When Richard asked for Kuniko's hand in marriage according to tradition, he assured her parents "that we were in love, and that we would look out for and take care of each other."[21]

Chapter 13

Persons Ineligible for Citizenship

*Suppose you do marry this yellow girl. I'm on the selection
board and your name comes up. I'd pass you by. We don't
want officers with yellow wives. What about your children? Y'
can't send half-Jap boys to the Point.*
—General Gruver to his son, Major Lloyd Gruver, in
Sayonara, *by James Michener*

In the Far East, all Asians, whether enemies or allies, were subject
to racially restrictive U.S. immigration quotas and laws which made
marriage to American citizens difficult and sometimes impossible.
The Chinese Exclusion Act of 1882, which had been extended to
the Hawaiian Islands in 1898 and the Philippines in 1902, prohibited
naturalization. The Oriental Exclusion Act of 1924 specifically excluded the Japanese.[1] Persons ineligible for citizenship were not permitted to immigrate to the U.S. and were discouraged or prohibited
from marrying American citizens.

The exclusion of the Chinese, our allies during World War II,
was a political embarrassment. Chinese in America, many of them

students who'd been sent abroad by wealthy parents anxious to protect their children from the dangerous situation in China resulting from the warlord civil wars of 1911–1937 and the Japanese invasion in 1931, were active participants in the war effort, with 13,000 Chinese fighting in Europe and China. Of the 15,000 Chinese seamen who served in the U.S. Merchant Marine and on British ships during the war, 3,000 were members of the National Maritime Union (NMU). The Chinese Seamen's Patriotic Association, working closely with the NMU, had to struggle to get these men the right to take shore leave in American ports.[2]

Public opinion, in the U.S. and abroad, rose against the Chinese Exclusion Act, which was based on the notion that the Chinese were an "inferior race." [3] Critics pointed out that this racial attitude strongly resembled the genocidal Nazi ideologies the U.S. denounced, making U.S. policy appear hypocritical.

President Franklin Roosevelt addressed this issue, proclaiming that it was "only through the unity of all people that we can successfully win the war, regardless of race, color and creed." [4] The Magnuson Act, which Roosevelt signed into law on December 17, 1943, repealed the Chinese Exclusion Act. Although this act allowed the Chinese to apply for citizenship, a quota was set of only 105 immigrants per year.[5] This legislation was a symbolic gesture rather than a sincere reform.

The War Brides Act of 1945 waived the quota temporarily and allowed the wives and children of Chinese-Americans who had served in the U.S. armed forces to enter the U.S. Unsatisfied with a temporary waiver for servicemen only, the Chinese Benevolent Association, representing 40,000 Chinese in New York City, appealed to Congress in April 1946 to abolish all discriminatory laws against the Chinese.[6] Thousands of Chinese men in the U.S. had left Chinese wives behind in prewar days and were still subject to the restrictive annual quota of 105. Dong Zem Ping, a Chinese wife whose husband had left for America years before World War II and then enlisted when the war started, posed as a war bride in order to join him, sadly leaving her son born in China behind until later legislation allowed her to reveal the situation and send for him. Yee Wing, who had been separated from her husband in America for fifteen years, also came to the U.S. under the provisions of the War Brides Act: "Because he was in the service, he was allowed to become a citizen and that opened the door for him to bring me and our daughter over." [7] Additional legislation was passed, entitled the Act of August 9, 1946, to put Chinese wives of U.S. citizens on a nonquota basis. [8]

Many proxy brides were included among the Chinese war brides. It was still customary in Chinese-American families to arrange a son's marriage to a young woman in China whom he'd never seen. An animal was often chosen to "stand in" for the groom in a Chinese ceremony. The parents of an American-born Chinese man, who'd been a chicken farmer in Stockton, California, before the war, selected a Chinese bride for him after he was wounded in the South Pacific. His family did not want him to die unmarried. The proxy ceremony was conducted with a rooster standing in for the bridegroom. He recovered from his wounds and in 1946 went to China to collect his new bride. They returned together to make their home in San Francisco's Chinatown.

Some Chinese-American parents, anxious to perpetuate Chinese traditions, sent their sons back to China after the war for a wife. Louis Chu, a Chinese-American World War II veteran and author, described a father's reasons for preferring to import a bride for his son in his novel, *Eat a Bowl of Tea:*

> And we always say that *jook sing* [American Chinese] girls are no good. That's why everybody goes back to China to get married. A village girl will make a good wife, they say. She will not run around. She can tell right from wrong. She will stay home and cook rice for you. [9]

Jane Wilson, a Sunday school teacher in Minneapolis, Minnesota, who taught English classes for Chinese war brides, recalled the arranged marriages among the Chinese in her community after the restrictions had been lifted for veterans:

> This was just what the Chinese had been waiting for so all these boys hot-footed it to China where their mothers had a bride all picked out for them, and this time he could bring her back to the U.S. with him. All this could be accomplished in a month—certainly two months. Back to the laundry, and now there was a fresh set of hands in the tubs!

Although most Chinese war brides married Chinese-Americans, there were marriages between Caucasian servicemen and Chinese women as well. Perhaps the most famous military man to marry a Chinese woman while serving in China was Maj. Gen. Claire Chennault, the "Flying Tiger" Ace. Anna Chan was working as a journalist when she was assigned to interview the general. Coincidentally, he had previously become acquainted with her father when he served as Chinese Consul in San Francisco before the war. General Chennault found himself courting her entire family to win a reluctant approval for their marriage. Even though they admired him, her family was concerned about their different backgrounds, race, religion, and the fact that the general was much older than Anna. Persistence won out in the end and they were married at the general's home in Hungjao on December 21, 1947.[10]

Most of the 6,000 Chinese war brides married Chinese-American soldiers and did not speak English.[11] Just how many applications to marry Chinese women were filed is unknown; however, one lieutenant who supervised evacuations of war brides and children in the Canton-Hong Kong area recalled that out of several thousand applications submitted to his office, only 800 were approved.

Although citizens of the Philippines had originally been excluded with the Chinese under the Exclusion Act, the Philippine Islands became U.S. possessions after the Spanish-American war. The U.S. government agreed to grant the Philippines independence in 1944, and had granted an annual immigration quota of fifty;[12] however, the Japanese took control of the Philippines in 1942.

After the Philippines were liberated from the Japanese on July 5, 1945, the U.S. was anxious to establish good relations with the Philippine government and secure the right to retain armed forces and navy personnel on strategically crucial military bases and other areas of operations in the Philippines. Questions regarding the assignment of immigration quotas and U.S. citizenship for Filipinos were put aside to deal with more pressing security and economic problems.[13]

In his broadcast from Washington on July 4, 1946, President Harry Truman stressed goodwill between the two nations:

Our two countries will be closely bound together for many years to come. We of the United States feel that we are merely entering into a new partnership with the Philippines—a partnership of two free and sovereign nations working in harmony and understanding.

The United States and its partner of the Pacific, the Philippine Republic, have already charted a pattern of relationships for all the world to study. Together in the future our two countries must prove the soundness and the wisdom of this great experiment in Pacific democracy.[14]

Soon GIs were anxious to form partnerships of their own and applied to marry Filipina women. As liberators, they had been welcomed early on by the Filipino population. Carrie Roa of Manila recalled their enthusiastic reception in her battered city:

The general feeling among the Filipinos towards liberating U.S. Armed Forces was one of delirious gratitude. The door of the Filipino home was open and the red carpet brimming with hospitality.

The American soldier she eventually married had been among the many guests in her family's home. Although American soldiers were welcomed, parents had the usual reservations about romantic alliances, as Carrie explained:

My father [one of Manila's best-known couturiers] was very skeptical and quite vocal about it. My mother, rest her soul, gracefully accepted it quietly. I guess they both felt that marriage by itself was already complicated without compounding it with the pervading air of prejudice and East-West differences. At the time, I was not able to comprehend what they were trying to tell me, thank God. My father did his best to convince us to settle down in the Philippines—even to the extent of a job offer.

No matter how welcome the GIs were as liberators, dating GIs was not in keeping with strict Filipino standards. Americans were stationed in every province and in many towns social contact with Filipinas was not allowed. Nevertheless, women coming from devastated areas were often driven by poverty to seek work on military bases, and, as women left home, family rules were forgotten. In Filipino society, however, as in many other societies, women who had relationships with American soldiers were thought of as mainly uneducated and from the lower classes. It was believed that their main goal was to improve their standard of living through marriage to a U.S. serviceman, which was also the commonly held opinion of military authorities.[15] However, marriages between Filipina citizens and Americans were tolerated (albeit reluctantly by authorities opposed on racial or economic grounds) out of diplomatic necessity.

There were often questionable motives for marriage and misconceptions about the motives of others on both sides, in many cases all over the world. Some Americans felt that GIs were attracted to Asian women because they believed them to be subservient to males, and many women did indeed think the streets in America were paved with gold, but no two situations were exactly alike and motives were just as varied.

In reality, marriages were taking place between GIs and women from every level of society, most often for love. Occasionally, a bizarre marriage was reported such as the union between Virgil C. Lehnus, an American soldier, and a girl from the savage Igorot tribe in the Philippine Islands. The union, performed in November 1942, was annulled at Hays, Kansas, after the soldier testified that he wed under threat of death. Lehnus explained that he had escaped the Japanese but was captured by the Igorots. He was nursed through an illness by an Igorot girl chosen by the tribe's chief. Once recovered, he learned that according to tribal law he and the girl were to be married. He escaped after the wedding only to be recaptured by the Japanese and held prisoner for the duration of the war.[16]

On the other hand, American soldiers also married into some of the most socially prominent families. Gloria (Pablo) Montesclaros of Manila, daughter of a Supreme Court justice, married Capt. Mel Montesclaros on February 3, 1946, in the Archbishop's Palace in Tayuman. Mrs. Sergio Osmena, wife of the president of the Philippines, attended the wedding along with the wife of Bienvenido Gonzales, the president of the University of the Philippines. The couple had met at a wedding reception where she mistook him for a chaplain. Mel Montesclaros had been born in the Philippines, which had undoubtedly made him more acceptable to her family. Gloria said:

> My future husband knew how important family background was to Filipinos. He brought his family album in his duffel bag, just in case. When he made his first visit to me he brought his album to show my parents. They were duly impressed. The whole family liked him and trusted him right away.

Gloria, like Carrie Roa, was not allowed to go out on a date unchaperoned. Carrie explained that a single girl had to be chaperoned when she left the house with a male—for any reason: "My mother acted as chaperone or else my father would not give him permission."

An accurate estimate of the number of Filipina war brides is difficult to ascertain, since immigration tables often group totals for Asian women together. No sizable group of Filipinas is accounted for until 1952, when tables show 667 entered as the wives of U.S. servicemen; however, Carrie Schaller and Gloria Montesclaros left the Philippines with nearly one hundred other war brides on September 27, 1946, aboard the *USAT Republic,* the fourth known war bride contingent.

A journalist covering the departure of the *Republic* wrote that Carrie and her husband Donald Schaller were optimistic about their future and "so much in love with each other that they consider racial prejudice inconsequential. . . . All in all, the brides were anything but cowed by warnings of racial barriers." [17]

Gloria was met with open arms by Mel's parents on her arrival in October 1946; his mother had thoughtfully brought her fur coat along and dropped it on Gloria's shoulders, knowing she would be cold. Her shipmate, Carrie (Schaller) Carmona recounted the opposite type of reception which she received:

I arrived in Baltimore two weeks ahead of my husband and was met at the train station by my mother-in-law, sister and brother-in-law, who, I learned later, campaigned among the Schaller family to put me back on a ship bound for the Philippines. My brother-in-law was convinced, at that time, that he was doing my husband a favor by sending me back.

It was hardly the red-carpet welcome her family in the Philippines had given her husband. Carrie was beginning to understand what her parents meant by East-West differences and why they had apprehensions about her marriage. But like so many brides before and after her, she decided that her home was with Don, and now that she was in America, there was no going back.

Although Chinese and Filipina war brides were allowed entry to the U.S. under the War Brides Act, since they became eligible for citizenship under new provisions in immigration law, Japanese

women and GIs were not allowed to apply to marry, since the
Oriental Exclusion Act was still in effect. Although legislation was
amended by Public Law 199 (December 17, 1943) not to exclude
people with "Chinese blood" as being eligible for citizenship or
permanent entry to the U.S., individuals with "Japanese blood"
were conspicuously omitted:

> Aliens, in order to be eligible for citizenship, must have a
> preponderance of white, African or Chinese blood, or of the
> three. An alien having as much as one half of other than white,
> African or Chinese blood, or of the three, is considered to be
> a person ineligible for citizenship.[18]

Permission to marry a Japanese woman, "a person ineligible
for citizenship," would not be granted unless the law was further
amended to include the Japanese or eliminate the racial barriers.

Would it be feasible to continue to uphold racially biased laws
such as the Oriental Exclusion Act after racial restrictions for other
countries had been denounced as incompatible with American demo-
cratic ideals and subsequently repealed? Franklin Roosevelt said an
enlightened policy of racial tolerance would be necessary to rebuild
the postwar world. In his fourth inaugural address, in 1945, he
stated:

> We have learned that we cannot live alone, at peace; that
> our own well-being is dependent on the well-being of other
> nations far away. We have learned to be citizens of the world,
> members of the human community.[19]

Military authorities continued to cite logistical reasons for not
authorizing marriages between Americans and Asians, since many
states did not recognize interracial marriages:

> Sanction of such a marriage places upon the Department
> of the Army a difficult determination as to assignment and
> scheduling of necessary travel involved in changes of station.
> The value of the soldier to the service is correspondingly
> reduced.[20]

Even if a couple hoped for reforms in the future which would
allow them to marry in a ceremony recognized by U.S. authorities
and to enter the U.S. together, there would always be the question
of whether or not they would find acceptance in the neighborhoods
they wished to live in back in the U.S. Interracial couples in states

where miscegenation was illegal risked harassment and even jail terms. Despite these deterrents, many GIs decided to marry their Japanese fiancées: since military permission was out of the question, they married in traditional Japanese ceremonies.

Duane Hennessy, an Associated Press correspondent, reported from Tokyo on a ceremonial wedding between an American soldier and a Japanese woman in March 1946:

> Names of the couple were not given. It was believed to be the first wedding between a Japanese girl and an American Caucasian serviceman since the occupation began.
>
> The two met at a dance hall and fell in love. A little later, they decided to marry. Her parents didn't object. In fact, her father performed the ceremony.
>
> The legality of the marriage remains a puzzle. The occupation army's legal department has ruled that a Japanese marriage will not hold up in an American court. It consists merely of a ritual and the changing of the wife's name to that of her husband on the books of her ward. Before the war, the American consul could give legal certification, but such a document has not been approved since the surrender.
>
> But that didn't stop the marine.
>
> Only the family and a few friends were there. The girl's father poured the ceremonial sake into three lacquer cups in turn.
>
> That sealed the marriage. That, and a kiss—Western style.[21]

Frank Pfeiffer, who landed at Atsugi Airfield near Yokohama in September 1945, met his future bride, Sachiko Sekiya, two months later while driving a jeep near Yuraku-sho railroad station in Tokyo. She was wearing huge canvas pants and sneakers and, although she weighed only ninety-four pounds herself, she was carrying a sixty-pound sack of rice. He was impressed by the fact that she was smiling, even under her burden. "I watched her struggling with the sack of rice. . . . she sprained her ankle." They dated, although she spoke no English and he didn't understand Japanese. Frank proposed in January 1946 by pointing to Sachiko's heart and then to his own. The wedding ceremony followed. In the presence of the elders of her family, the couple drank three tiny cups of hot sake wine. "Everybody said a lot of Japanese, which didn't mean anything to me, but it was pretty clear that we were married. That night I moved in." [22] Their wedding ceremony took place two months earlier than the reputed "first marriage" reported by the AP correspondent.

A commanding officer who learned of a soldier's intention to go through a Japanese wedding ceremony could retaliate by transferring him to Korea or ordering his redeployment to the U.S. Kyo Wittrock and her future husband considered themselves very lucky not to have been separated by an angry commander's threat to send him to Korea after they announced their intention to wed. "Army pretty tough to marry," Kyo said.

> Hospital commanding officer didn't like him to marry Japanese girl. Almost sent him to Korea. But friend took over his place so he didn't have to go. But husband very lucky, commanding officer real tough.

In any case, a harsh reprimand could be expected, similar to General Gruver's in James A. Michener's novel, *Sayonara,* when he learned of his son Lloyd's romantic interest in a Japanese woman:

> Suppose you do marry this yellow girl. I'm on the selection board and your name comes up. I'd pass you by and if I wasn't on the board I'd advise the others to pass you by. We don't want officers with yellow wives. And where would you live in America? None of our friends will want you hanging around with a yellow wife. What about your children? Y' can't send half-Jap boys to the Point. [23]

Col. C. G. Blakeney of the Legislative and Liaison Division responded to Senator Claude Pepper's letter on behalf of a soldier who wanted to marry his Japanese fiancée by telling the Senator outright that he believed it to be

> inappropriate to discuss this problem from the viewpoint of passage of legislation which would solve this particular man's problem. Whereas this may appear to be discriminatory to Mr. Smith at the moment, I believe that in the long run such action is eminently wise. Should Mr. Smith marry a Japanese and bring her into this country, I visualize much unhappiness for him. Because of the fact that his wife would not be accepted, she then would lack the social contacts which Japanese people

need. For Mr. Smith to think of abandoning his citizenship under these circumstances would be a most unwise thing to do. Apparently, Mr. Smith is a soldier inasmuch as he has mentioned he is waiting for reassignment. In my opinion, the best thing for him to do is to accept his new assignment and make as much of it as possible so that he will develop a new and more interesting life.[24]

Government files reveal that many soldiers contemplated giving up their American citizenship in order to remain with their Japanese fiancées and brides. In another letter, to Senator Kenneth Wherry (who also wrote on behalf of a GI who wanted to marry his Japanese fiancée even if it meant loss of citizenship), Col. Blakeney wrote condescendingly:

It is indeed unfortunate that a young man in a foreign country, who has had a difficult life to lead from his school days on, should fall back on the sympathetic treatment given him by foreigners, particularly those who were former enemies and who, by law, may not enter the U.S. I agree with you that to renounce his American citizenship would in later years cause him more heartbreak and difficulty than any possible course of action he could take. The means of effecting such an action is not within the province of the Department of the Army, and I, therefore, hesitate to suggest a way to undertake this action, in case he should go to this extreme.[25]

James A. Michener, who was stationed in occupied Japan, had met a number of soldiers who were willing to stay in Japan with their Japanese wives:

My work in Tokyo took me repeatedly to the Provost Marshall's office, and I was never there without seeing at least four GIs with their Japanese girls applying for marriage licenses. I asked several of them what they were going to do when their wives had to go back to America to live and they said, "We aren't planning to go back. We intend to live here." [26]

Walter Gentile knew several Americans who gave up their citizenship despite all the warnings and abuse from military authorities. Among them was a captain who married a Japanese dentist, changed his name, became a naturalized Japanese citizen, and opened up a chain of restaurants. Another acquaintance, a navy man, settled in the Roppongi area with his Japanese wife and also opened up a restaurant.

Just how many soldiers had married Japanese women with no intention of honoring their vows when the time came to go back home to the U.S. is uncertain. Possibly as many as 100,000 "Madama Butterflies" were left behind like the ill-fated Cio-Cio San in Puccini's opera, deserted by Lieutenant Pinkerton, who considered his Japanese marriage merely a temporary convenience. Even if a soldier's intentions were honorable, time and public opinion were against him, and the pressure to leave his Japanese love behind was enormous.

Chapter 14

Irrespective of Race

---

*The key words in the Soldier Brides Act [July 22, 1947] were
"irrespective of race." They signaled significant progress in Congress
and the nation at large.*
—Wilson and Hosokawa in East to America

Up until mid 1947, marriage did not seem a likely possibility for
couples like Bill and Hertha Rogers who wanted to marry in a
ceremony recognized by the American authorities. Although Hertha
was Eurasian, having had a German father, her mother was full-
blooded Japanese, which made it unlawful under the Oriental Exclusion Act for her to obtain a permanent visa to the United States.
Then President Truman signed the Alien Wife Bill, resulting in
the Soldier Brides Act (Public Law 213), which provided that

> The alien spouse of an American citizen by marriage occur-
> ring before 30 days after the enactment of this Act [July 22,
> 1947], shall not be considered as inadmissible because of race,
> if otherwise admissible under this Act.[1]

Between 1,500 and 2,500 couples were expected to apply under
this provision. However, as Representative Frank Fellows (R.
Maine), one of the bill's sponsors, pointed out, the thirty-day temporary legislation did not give occupation soldiers much time to fulfill
the preliminary requirements:

There's a lot of red tape to go through to arrange the details. The girls have to be "screened" over there, and soldiers have to get their commanding officer's consent to the marriage.

Fellows said that this law was intended to correct an injustice to Americans of oriental ancestry, but would also permit American soldiers of nonoriental ancestry to marry Japanese brides and bring them to the U.S.[2]

Although this was a landmark piece of legislation since it eliminated race as a discriminating factor, its temporary status dealt superficially with a long-range situation:

The key words were "irrespective of race." They signaled significant progress in Congress and the nation at large on racial attitudes. The changing attitudes were further underscored by the report of Truman's Presidential Committee on Civil Rights, released October 20, 1947.[3]

This report, which urged states to repeal discriminatory laws, served as the basis of President Truman's civil rights program recommended to Congress in 1948.

Mr. Mike Masaoka, national legislative director of the Japanese-American Citizens League Anti-Discrimination Committee in Washington, D.C., wrote to the assistant secretary of war regarding his concern over the temporary nature of the Soldier Brides Act. The response, from Col. F. P. Munson, executive officer in the office of the assistant secretary of war, reflected a lack of support for the basic concept of the bill:

In the Far East Command, General MacArthur has been faced with the inadmissibility of certain races under the prevailing immigration laws. His prohibition of marriage between military personnel and racially inadmissible persons except under unusual circumstances reflected the existing law and intended the safeguarding of the interests of military personnel and the Japanese and Korean peoples alike. I am sure that you will agree that unrestricted marriages involving an eventual choice between wife and country would be bound to have adverse effects upon the sanctity of marriage and the home as well as the dignity of woman. . . . Subordinate commanders were also advised that it was not intended nor desired that the usual standards under which the desirability of marriage is determined prior to granting be relaxed.[4]

In a memo to General Paul dated August 26, 1947, Lt. Col. H. K. Whalen, chief, Morale and Welfare Branch, issued a caution to commanders not to relax the usual standards for determining desirability of a marriage prior to granting approval:

> This decision is believed sound; difficulties will arise from rejected applications (if any) and from personnel who wish to marry Japanese at a later date. These difficulties will be the direct results of the piecemeal nature of the legislation which is an exaggerated form of private legislation designed to take care of the few known marriages and some 150 personnel believed to have been contemplating such marriages. It made no provision for the soldier who had a Japanese fiancée and who had departed the command, nor did it indicate any consideration for future arrivals who would likewise be exposed to desire based on propinquity.[5]

For those couples who worked to make the deadline, minutes ticked away like a time bomb: not only did they have to fill out multitudes of forms, the Japanese bride had to pass an investigation and the soldier had to obtain permission to marry from his commanding officer—a difficult task to say the least. Hertha Rogers remembered that she and Bill spent one entire weekend preparing their application for permission to marry:

> Upon completing this application, Bill requested the permission of his commanding officer to hand carry the documents through channels to obtain all required signatures to insure that it would not be pigeon-holed in somebody's in or out basket for the duration. Being in the Counter Intelligence Corps, Bill had to obtain not only his commanding officer's permission, but also the permission of the commanding officer of the First Regional Counter Intelligence Corps Detachment, and also permission from General MacArthur's office.

> Bill handcarried our application to Tokyo and reached the last step, which was permission from General MacArthur's staff. One of the General's aides accused Bill of being disloyal and reprimanded him for even entertaining the thought of mar-

rying a former enemy national and threatened that he would do everything in his power to see that Bill would be transferred out of Japan forthwith. There was always Korea, which was considered a less desirable post than Japan. Not withstanding the threat of the aide, Bill received General Starr's signature approving our marriage.

I was never more happy than to see Bill returning from that trip clutching that envelope with all the required signatures. We had the necessary permission! We were married by civil ceremony at the American Consulate in Kobe on August 5, 1947, but our real wedding was on August 10th, performed by the Reverend William A. McIlwayne, an American missionary who was a friend of both our families you might say. Reverend McIlwayne was a Presbyterian missionary to Japan prior to World War II, and had lived in Kobe for a time, and my family had known him then. Mr. McIlwayne's mother had attended a school for young girls with my husband's aunt prior to the turn of the century.

Our wedding was held at the Kokusai Hotel outside of Kobe. The Kokusai Hotel had been built for the 1940 Olympics, which never took place. It was not a large hotel, but very modern and equipped even with a self-service elevator, which was quite modern back in 1940. It is situated in the hills overlooking the city of Kobe—a very lovely place. The Kokusai Hotel had been appropriated by the occupation forces for housing for the Counter Intelligence Corps Unit, and that is how we were able to have our wedding there.

I had two attendants, two sisters who were also Eurasians like me. I borrowed their sister's wedding dress which she had worn only a few years before. I was lacking a veil and appropriate material was almost impossible to buy in Japan in those days. The day before our wedding, I went along with Bill to Himeji, where he had business. There he asked the Chief of Police about some thin white material. Almost magically, before long somebody appeared with a yard of white Georgette. So, the night before our wedding, I was sewing while Bill had his bachelor's party.

My mother did not necessarily disapprove of our marriage. She had several concerns, however: One, that I was very young—I turned eighteen four days after our wedding, and Bill was twenty-six at the time. Another of her concerns was that I would be leaving Japan and that she would not be able to come with us, nor did she want to at that time, and that we would be separated for some years. We spoke Japanese at home, but our household was predominantly German. And, having raised me as a German, I think my mother knew all along that I would not make Japan my home when I grew up. But knowing that, nevertheless, when the time comes to leave, it comes too soon. I don't believe she had any apprehensions for me as I contemplated making a life for myself in the U.S.

Hertha and Bill requested that he be retained for duty in the CIC notwithstanding their marriage. An exception was made after a thorough investigation. The report included the following comments:

Mrs. Rogers is an intelligent and attractive lady. She is fluent in German, English, and Japanese, and is a capable stenographer, efficient in both shorthand and typing. While working in Kobe she gained respect of many members of the Occupation Forces, and was often a guest in dependent homes in this area. The files of this office show nothing derogatory about her or any member of her family, and casual interrogation with members of the Occupation Forces and old residents of Kobe has revealed nothing derogatory. While employed she cooperated to the fullest extent with this unit, and her observation was often of notable interest.

Members of this unit have on several occasions been queried regarding the possibility of Mrs. Rogers being a security risk. Regardless of her alien status, the general expressed opinion is that she is a quiet, unassuming, well-mannered young lady who has never displayed any marked effort to show undue interest in the work of her husband or other members of this unit.

Since their marriage, Lt. and Mrs. Rogers have been under

observation. This marriage appears in every way to have the identifying qualities which one would expect to find in the average normal successful American union. At no time has there been any question of possible risk to security, nor has the efficiency of this officer been impaired. Further, the establishment of their own home has contributed to the well-being of both.

Frank and Sachiko Pfeiffer also applied to marry under the provision of the Soldier Brides Act, eighteen months after their Japanese marriage. After attaining permission, they were married at the American consulate in Yokohama. Frank got his orders to return to the U.S. and they were scheduled to arrive in Chicago on Christmas Day 1948. The Pfeiffers and their baby daughter planned to live at first with his mother. Unfortunately, Sachiko still didn't speak English; Frank had become so proficient in Japanese it hadn't seemed necessary in Japan to learn English. However, they were reassured about a happy reception when they arrived in the States after receiving a letter from his mother saying, "She looks like an adorable little doll. I was always afraid you might marry that girl on the North Side, so if Sachiko is as good a wife as you say, you're well off." [6]

Couples who could not obtain the necessary permission within the allotted time could only wait it out and hope for a change of policy. In the meantime, soldiers continued to write to their congressmen who wrote in turn to military authorities regarding soldiers' requests for new legislation which would enable them to marry their Japanese fiancées and bring them back with them to the States. Despite pressures at home in the U.S. to repeal racially discriminatory laws and the gradual reduction in the number of states with laws against miscegenation (at least twenty-eight states enforced laws against racially mixed marriages in 1943; by 1948 the number had been reduced to fifteen), a response from Col. C. G. Blakeney to Senator John C. Stennis on October 11, 1949, stressed how remote the possibility of obtaining permission to marry a Japanese fiancée still seemed at that time:

The authorities in the Far East Command charged with the administration of the regulations governing marriages in overseas areas have consistently held that to grant permission to marry when the wife cannot enter the United States would be to flaunt the sanctity of the marriage ceremony. The Commanding General of the Far East Command has made an occasional exception [Public Law 213] where he considered that very unusual circumstances were involved. For example, a Nisei, an American citizen of Japanese extraction whose residence was in Hawaii, was given permission to marry a Japanese girl. The circumstances were so unusual that it was deemed to be in the best interest of the soldier and the country as a whole to approve the marriage. The fact that a baby may be involved is considered not to be sufficiently unusual to warrant approval of the marriage.[7]

In 1950, when the war broke out in Korea, most combat soldiers were transferred there to fight, leaving thousands of Japanese fiancées behind. Then, in August 1950, passage of Public Law 717 allowed soldiers once more to apply for permission to marry Japanese women, but only until February 1951, when this temporary law expired (it was later extended to March 1952). Even if a soldier stationed in Korea had managed to get an application approved, he couldn't always get leave from duty to marry. Others had been wounded and were sent straight home to the U.S.[8]

If a soldier who married prior to being sent to Korea got killed in action, the petition he filed to allow his wife to enter the U.S. was revoked. Some brides were left alone in Japan, many with Amerasian children, disowned by their families and shunned by society. Julie Grant feared the worst when her GI returned to the U.S.:

> I received no letters, not even answers to my own. The money he had left me would not last much longer, and I was pregnant. I wanted to believe he would really come back, but I heard many stories about Japanese girls left stranded by American soldiers. Should I have an abortion? I wanted his baby, but I did not want to face raising an American child as an unwed mother in Japan. I knew what that would mean for me and the child. Still, I delayed until further delay was impossible. Taking the little money I had left, I entered a hospital and had the operation performed. It was one of the most heartbreaking experiences of my life.

Then the telegram came: "Arrived Yokosuka. Come at once."
Julie was deliriously happy.

My mother secretly hid my clothes—everything to shoes
and underwear—to prevent my joining my fiancé. But even
this stratagem did not stop me. Taking advantage of my mother's brief absence, on the next day, I located my clothing, borrowed train fare from her purse, and hurried to Yokosuka.
We had been apart only six months, but it seemed like ten or
fifteen years. Hot tears scalded my cheeks as we embraced.
He was perplexed when I told him that the letters and money
had never reached me. He fell suddenly, sadly silent when I
told him about the baby.[9]

They were married in 1951 and Julie gave birth to their son,
Richard, a year later.

Those who missed the March 1952 expiration date gave up or
waited for another law to be passed that would allow them to marry.
In the meantime, fiancées asked to join the ranks of brides attending
bride schools established by American Red Cross volunteers. By
1952, 8,000 Japanese women had graduated from these classes with
both practical and negligible information about childcare and their
future homeland:

- Always hold the baby's head while bathing him.
- All dancing in American is not jitterbugging.
- Expect friendliness and animosity in America.
- Do less bowing.
- One cent is a copper coin called a penny.
- You can whip cream with chopsticks if you wish, but it's
  easier with a beater.
- Salad is served before the meat course on the West Coast,
  with it in the Middle West, and afterward in the East.[10]

Finally, on June 27, 1952, the Immigration and Nationality
(McCarran-Walter) Act repealed the Oriental Exclusion Act of 1924
and gave all Asian nations a token immigration quota, eliminating
race as a barrier to naturalization.[11] Fewer than 900 Japanese war
brides had been recorded as having been admitted to the U.S. prior
to 1952, the figure for that year alone reaching 4,220. Another 2,000
brides would enter the U.S. the following year.

By far the majority of Asian war brides were Japanese; however, it is difficult to estimate the actual number of brides if Japanese ceremonies are included. The American Consul General reported 10,217 Japanese brides by December 1952, with over 75 percent married to Caucasian Americans.[12] Military estimates for marriages in the Far East are as high as 50,000 to 100,000.[13] Immigration statistics can be misleading, since many war brides did not enter the U.S. for years after their marriage, sometimes not until the late 1950s.

Asian brides travelled to the U.S. with high hopes, most of them aware that acceptance might not be immediately forthcoming. A reporter for the *Saturday Evening Post* recorded a Japanese mother's pledge to her child during their voyage to the U.S. in January 1952. Taking her child's hand in hers, she said:

I know everything is going to be harder and I'm expecting it. I'd be afraid to go to America thinking that everything was going to be wonderful because it may not be. But I'm going to try as hard as I can.[14]

Kyo Wittrock remembered the advice a minister gave her before she left aboard a ship bound for San Francisco, "You have to accept living American style. You have to get along with them." When she arrived in the U.S., her husband sped up her assimilation with a method of his own: "He never take me store, just drop me in front of store and say that way you learn English." They made their first home in a small town in Wisconsin where she found the people to be similar to the townspeople in her native Tono, Japan, "same people, all honest, no locked doors."

Although many Asian brides left their personal belongings behind and tried to "Americanize" as soon as possible, others brought traditional kimonos and household objects. Aiko Anderson, a former nurse from Niigata, Japan, decided to bring two hand-wrought bronze statues with her, one of the Japanese god of fishermen and the other of the god of plenty—two of the best-loved seven household gods. Aiko and her husband Orin found that they could blend cultures and traditions and still maintain harmony. With the help of their Japanese-American dictionary and Aiko's coaching, Orin had learned to speak a respectable amount of Japanese and strived to master the 6,000 characters of the official Japanese language.

Japanese women who'd married Nisei (second generation Japanese-Americans) were often surprised to learn that there were still some Japanese in America who clung to feudal traditions. A bride, hoping for a more independent existence in America, could be sorely disappointed to be greeted by such a family on her arrival. As Ryuko Ozawa put it, "girls who have tasted freedom would never go back to the old ways." [15]

Carrie (Roa) and Don Schaller on their wedding day in Manila, Philippines, June 9, 1946. (Carrie Roa Schaller Carmona)

Chinese war brides attend English class at Westminster Church in Minneapolis, Minn. (Jane Wilson collection; photo from *Chinese Women of America* by Judy Yung.)

Gloria and Capt. Mel Montesclaros at their wedding at the Archbishop's Palace in Tayuman, Philippines. February 3, 1946. (Gloria Pablo Montesclaros)

Japanese war brides and husbands at a Seattle, Washington, restaurant. Aiko and Orin Anderson second couple from left. (Aiko Kowahara Anderson)

Hertha and Bill Rogers were married in a civil ceremony at the American consulate in Kobe, Japan. August 5, 1947.

The religious ceremony followed. The bride, Hertha (Wolf) Rogers, with her mother and bridal party. August 10, 1947. (Hertha Wolf Rogers)

War brides who formed a "kaffeekranzchen" in Fort Lewis, Washington. 1950.
(Connie Eckart McGrath)

British brides club, Milwaukee, Wisconsin 1949

Into the Melting Pot

Part Four

Christiane Sielicki of Tucquegnieux, France, is among the brides from various countries who squeezed into fourth-grade seats to begin English lessons at Irving School in Detroit, 1946.

CHRISTIANE OLESKA SIELICKI

Chapter 15

Do You Like It Here?

My husband told me, "Why don't you look and behave like the American girls?" After I had been here a few years, it was "Where is the little English girl I married?"
—*Joyce Beatrice Moore, Catford, London County*

War brides who made the long journey across the ocean to the "land of plenty" were shocked to learn on arrival that there was an acute housing shortage; it would take months or years before they could move into an apartment or house of their own. "I found no home for myself," recalls Filomena Ruggiero of Naples, Italy, who arrived in New York on February 22, 1946. "My husband and I lived in one room in his sister's house." All across America newlyweds, not only war brides and grooms, had a hard time finding places of their own. Social workers blamed a high increase in the divorce rate among American couples in 1946 partly on the increased pressure of starting married life under the same roof with in-laws.[1]

In the New York region, 19,000 servicemen and veterans had filed applications with the Federal Public Housing Authority between August and November 1945 for occupancy of war housing units that might become available. By January 1946, only 3,900 had been accommodated, leaving over 15,000 still waiting for housing. A poll by the Veterans Administration revealed that 60 percent of the married GIs discharged in the Northeast and North Central states in December 1945 were still without a home or apartment three to four months later. Forty percent of those seeking living quarters were living with relatives or friends and 20 percent were living in quarters that were overcrowded or in poor condition.[2]

Lya Cutcher of Frankfurt am Main, Germany, found living with her husband's large family intolerable:

> They resented it, I didn't like it. The family decided I should go to work immediately and didn't like my sending food packages home with most of my paychecks. I felt a stranger in that house full of people (there were 10 of us) and demanded a place of my own after my father-in-law called me a Nazi.

Finding a place of one's own wasn't easy, and war brides found it hard to understand that a housing shortage could exist in a country that had suffered no bomb damage. However, the U.S. had experienced a massive shift in population to urban areas that offered well-paying jobs in the defense industry during the war. At the same time, industrial output had been channeled to the war effort, so building materials were in very short supply after the war. One veteran who was able to purchase a lot was told it would take two years before construction of a house could be completed. Soldiers who had seen barracks and airfields constructed practically overnight during the war found such delays in housing construction intolerable.[3]

War brides made their first homes in all types of dwellings, from trailers to railroad boxcars. In April, 1946, Helen Eyles of England and her husband were able to borrow just enough money to buy a homemade trailer in Kansas:

> It was about twenty feet long and so homemade the windows wouldn't open. Arthur and his brother Dan worked on them so we could open them, but they leaked and we put tin cans out to catch the drips. We had no icebox and only a two burner Kerosene stove, no running water and of course no bathroom.

Arthur reenlisted in the army and the young couple found themselves moving frequently, eventually having to give up their trailer to return temporarily to his parents. They ended up in Kearney, Nebraska, in 1948, with two babies, a Model A Ford, and an old house in which they were permitted to live rent-free in return for doing badly needed repair work on the house. A real estate agent told them of a tiny house he thought they could buy:

> We had no money, but Arthur had sold the Model A for a better car—no money involved—and over the months this had gone on two or three more times and we finally had a car worth the $350.00 we needed for a down payment on the house. The house cost $3,500.00!

> We had no furniture and sat on orange crates for months. But Arthur bought various bits and pieces at an auction and we were able to buy a wringer-type washer too.

Santo DiNaro and his English wife Vicky decided to build their own house after living with his parents in Bellport, Long Island, with their twin sons for four years. When the bank manager told them that Santo did not earn enough to qualify for the loan, Vicky burst into tears right there in his office. Sympathizing with them, he told Vicky about a house cleaning job that was available. She immediately accepted the job and the banker announced that now they qualified for a mortgage. For the next few years, Vicky loaded the twins into a wagon each weekend and pulled them to the building site, where she and Santo worked side-by-side hammering nails and building much of their new house themselves while the twins played nearby.

It was especially difficult for couples with children to find housing. As the biggest baby-boom in history was taking place in the U.S., many landlords were refusing to rent to couples with children. Parisienne Simone McGrath thought Massachusetts was a cold, unfriendly place in March 1947 when her husband lost his job and they were evicted from their apartment in the same month she gave birth to their first child. A friend offered the McGraths temporary shelter, but because of the prevalent "no children" rule, they ended up staying for five years.

For interracial couples, finding a place to live presented even more complications. When Gina Parenti, of Pisa, Italy, married black Sgt. Cadillac Harris in 1947, she had no idea they would face racial prejudice in the United States. Shortly after her arrival, the Harris family had to travel to Mississippi. Because that state still enforced miscegenation laws, Gina was told she could not go along. When the young bride insisted, her husband relented, but the two had to travel alone, separate from the rest of the family. Although the journey was accomplished without incident, it was quite a risk to take in 1947. After living temporarily with his relatives in Chicago, Gina and Cadillac moved to Mount Holly, near Ft. Dix, New Jersey, where Cadillac got a job at Walson Army Hospital. The Holly Hill apartment project where they lived was condescendingly referred to as "the league of nations" because so many interracial couples lived there.[4]

A war bride's inability to speak English made a difficult situation even more tenuous. Frank Pfeiffer's mother initially welcomed his Japanese wife, Sachiko, when they moved into her small apartment in Chicago with their daughter Penny on Christmas Day, 1948, but in time disagreements about cooking, money matters, and discipline of little Penny arose between the two women. Because they could not speak each other's language, the problems could not be discussed or resolved. When Sachiko brought home a Japanese war bride who had been abandoned by her husband, along with their baby, the small apartment was strained beyond the limits of her mother-in-law's tolerance. Frank and Sachiko left after his mother said, "I never want to hear another word of Japanese in this house."

The Pfeiffers moved into an apartment but found they were unwelcome in that neighborhood; people still harbored a "patriotic hatred" for "enemy nationals." When a woman began calling Sachiko "that dirty little Jap," the Pfeiffers decided to move again. They found a builder with a unique solution to the U.S. housing shortage, the "shell house," which consisted of a quickly constructed exterior, sewage system, running water, subflooring, and a skeleton kitchen. The buyer was to finish the construction himself. The Pfeiffers wanted to buy one of the three dozen shell houses that were built along 24th Avenue in the Melrose Park suburb of Chicago.

The builder decided to make sure other buyers would accept the idea of having a Japanese neighbor and invited several potential neighbors to the real estate office to meet Sachiko. The first to arrive was an Italian-American woman whose husband had fought the Japanese with MacArthur in the Philippines, yet this woman was immediately drawn to Sachiko because she looked as if she needed a friend. Throwing her arms around Sachiko she said, "We want the house right next to her."

The other neighbor was an air force pilot who had fought the Japanese for twenty-three months and had witnessed atrocities committed against captured Americans. Despite his experiences, he had intervened when crewmen on his plane were beating a Japanese prisoner and had made it clear that no prisoners were to be mistreated on his plane. He had mentioned the incident to his wife only once and they had never discussed it again. Although his Irish-American wife harbored a hatred for Germans because the Nazis had killed her younger brother, she too was immediately drawn to Sachiko when she met her in the real estate office. The three couples became close friends and the husbands shared tools and worked together as a team to finish their three houses.[5]

The Pfeiffers became reconciled with his mother a few years later, but for some other families a permanent rift was caused by the way in-laws treated their foreign daughters-in-law. When Velina Hasu Houston's father left his Japanese wife and their two daughters with his family in New York in 1955 while he went to Washington to receive orders from the army, the Houstons locked his wife and daughters in their attic while he was away. "They didn't want their neighbors to think they were harboring a 'Jap,' " Velina remembers. When her father returned and found out how his wife and daughters had been treated, he severed contact with his family permanently.

German and Japanese war brides were sometimes baited as "Nazis" and "Japs" by their neighbors or when they went shopping. Asking for help in a store could be a risky business, for when a heavy accent revealed a war bride's origins, she was likely to get a cold shoulder or an insult instead of assistance. Hollywood movies and newspaper stories about wartime atrocities stirred up hatred for anything German or Japanese; the war brides were convenient scapegoats, even though most of them had been children during the war.

Although the war had been over for eleven years by the time Julie Grant and her husband arrived in Illinois, shadows of the war marred Julie's acceptance by her new community:

There were few foreigners of any kind in the town where we lived. Short and conspicuous, I had to work up courage to go shopping alone. Once, in a store, an elderly woman accosted me and asked where I came from. When she learned that I was Japanese, she called me fresh and asked how I had dared come to the United States. I was hurt but understood better later when I found out that she had lost her only grandson in the Korean war and was somehow confused about all oriental peoples. I could not help feeling faint relief that the grandson had not been killed in the Pacific area during World War II.[6] German women sometimes claimed to be Swiss, to avoid harassment; Japanese women said they were Chinese for the same reason.

Another major trial for war brides and their husbands was the postwar unemployment crisis. On February 21, 1946, Gen. Omar N. Bradley, administrator of veterans affairs, said that unemployment among veterans was three times as high as among civilians and 1,500,000 discharged veterans not yet seeking work were not included in those statistics.[7] Massachusetts alone had more than 67,000 unemployed veterans in March 1946, up from 15,000 the previous November.[8]

"Had my husband not unfortunately become unemployed in 1948, we should probably have still been together," admits Audrey Bartron, who returned to Peterborough, England, when her husband was sent to Korea after reenlisting against her wishes. Upon his release from the army, William Bartron joined his wife in England because he was still unable to find work in the U.S. He found a job in England, but homesickness made him decide to return to the U.S., where he failed again to find employment. When they decided to divorce, two of their children remained American citizens and two British.

As the U.S. converted from wartime production to a peacetime economy, almost every major industry was plagued with disputes between labor and management and thousands of workers were on strike. Even war heroes found themselves unable to get civilian jobs. Many soldiers came to the conclusion that reenlisting was their only alternative. One twenty-nine-year-old major, out of the army only six weeks, signed up as a staff sergeant, not because he couldn't get a job, but because after social security and taxes were deducted from his civilian pay, he wasn't as well off as he'd been in the army.[9]

In the U.S., prices of goods and services had begun an upward spiral, and many couples found themselves in difficult financial straits. "We were poor at the beginning," recalls Hildegard Gibbs of Munich, Germany, who lived in a housing project in Richmond, California, when she first came to the U.S.:

> It was very hard to be poor in America with everything around you. In Germany my family had enough money but couldn't buy anything—here we could buy *anything* but had not enough money.

Veterans going to college under the GI Bill found it hard to get by on the monthly allowance of $65.00 for a single man and $90.00 for married vets, but many war brides encouraged their husbands to complete their education in spite of financial difficulties and personal inconvenience.[10]

One veteran wanted to reenlist because he knew his German bride was miserable living with his mother, but his wife, who came from an educated family, insisted her husband finish college. She was willing to make the sacrifice of staying with his family so that their children could have a better life.

Many war brides went to work so their husbands could complete their education under the GI Bill. In spite of the struggle to make ends meet during the years the husbands attended college, these couples found their life-styles and economic situations much improved eventually. Although she had never sewn before, Sachiko Pfeiffer worked in a garment factory for two years so her husband could study photography.[11] Joan M. Stevens of Blackpool, England, worked as an administrative secretary while her husband attended law school at the University of Michigan at Ann Arbor. Joan describes the "veteran's village" near Willow Run, Michigan, where she and her husband lived for two years:

> The area consisted of rows of barrack-like buildings with paper thin walls, the barest of furnishings, pot-bellied stove for heat, and horror of horrors—a coal stove for cooking. The stove and I remained enemies throughout our stay. Both it and the heating stove had a voracious appetite—to be fed from a coal bin outside of the apartment. I almost lost my husband

one night when he jumped inside to push out more coal during a blizzard and the lid blew down on him.

The village was occupied partly by students and the rest by workers at the Willow Run Auto Plant in Detroit. Our neighbors were mostly auto-workers from many different parts of the country and through the thin walls, the ups and downs of their lifestyles were quite public affairs, ranging from knife fights to a worn Kentucky grandmother's cry of "Junior, get out of that ice-box!"

A young bride across the street settled her disagreements with her groom by throwing dishes out of the open door and since we were 100 percent pedestrian walking home from the bus stop could be quite an experience in itself.

Through my job (and leaving the village each day was a life-saver even when the bus was skidding through the icy streets) I met some wonderful people.

Lisa Slaughter found life in Tennessee almost worse than it had been in her native Hamburg, Germany, after the bombing raids. She and her husband lived in an unfinished house that had no electricity, no running water, and no plumbing. Determined to improve their situation, she took a full-time job, encouraged her husband to finish high school and some college, and helped him learn "proper" English.

A husband's decision not to pursue an education was a great disappointment for some brides. Nelly Hunt, who had been a model in Bern, Switzerland, had hoped to lead a somewhat cosmopolitan life in the U.S. and was dismayed to end up on a farm in Iowa:

I knew Virgil's parents lived on a farm, but I had no idea, nor desire to wind up on one myself. Virgil had me think he would spend some time for further education. But after getting his discharge from the army, he wanted to have a go at farming. I felt handicapped and miserable. I missed all the good things from home. Art museums, theaters, concerts and small cafes with pastries. Cold cuts and *good bread*. Sometimes we went to a movie, but such pleasures were rare, we just did not have the money. I learned to do chicken chores and wash milking utensils. Eggs and cream we sold was the only income. There were no jobs to get in town, especially not for someone who did not speak fluent English.

In December '48 Suzanne was born, she was a sweet baby. Karin by then 2 years old, loved her little sister very much. Now I was stuck, how could I take those two little girls away from their Father. He seemed to love us and need us, he was convinced what he was doing would be for our good eventually. The farm did prosper in time, and Nelly remained happily married. Other women were less fortunate.

Some war brides faced a difficult life in America because their husbands were alcoholics. Heavy drinking was so common among soldiers overseas that a woman sometimes did not realize until after she arrived in the U.S. that her husband's drinking habit was extreme.

One German woman had this sort of rude awakening upon arriving with her husband and baby in November 1948. While staying at an army transit camp, her seemingly solicitous husband sent her into town to buy a pair of shoes, since it had been impossible to purchase shoes in Germany. When she returned, she discovered that all of her jewelry had been stolen. Eventually she learned that her husband had sold it, as he was to do with almost everything they had shipped over from Germany.

After his discharge in California, he drank most of the night and then failed to get up in the morning to look for a job. He reenlisted without telling her, but then found a job and decided not to report for active duty. When the FBI came looking for him as a deserter, the war bride was pregnant with her second child and knew she was in trouble. She wanted to return to Germany, but could find no way to do so. Her family was unable to help her financially, and her husband, aware she wanted to leave him, threatened to have her deported and to keep their child.

War brides who were unhappy with their husbands, especially those whose husbands were abusive, were afraid their children would be taken away from them if they attempted to leave their husbands or return to their home countries. One woman in an abusive situation was told by her husband

> that I had no rights in this country because the "stupid Krauts have lost the war." I was told that if I would ever go to court, I would get no help and no judge would believe me because quote, "I am an American and do you think anyone would believe the words of a stupid Kraut."

The Red Cross found it difficult to help war brides in distress because of international involvements and lack of specific laws and information. There were few facilities to transport war brides who wanted to return to their native country. In some instances transportation was available for the bride, but not for her children if the children had dual citizenship. According to the Red Cross Home Service, other groups were reluctant to assist war brides, especially those divorced from American servicemen or veterans. A divorced woman who was a quota immigrant could be deported as a public charge if she had no funds to support herself.[12]

A combination of personal strength and help from many sources helped the German war bride whose husband was sought by the FBI in California to get out of her failed marriage. Four weeks after giving birth to her second child, she was in the hospital with kidney stones and a rapidly growing tumor on her ovaries. Receiving no answer when she called home at 10 P.M., she borrowed fifty cents and a bathrobe to go home. She found her baby lying in a pool of urine in the crib and her two-year-old on the floor where he had cried himself to sleep. Her husband had gone out to a bar. When the doctor discovered she had left the hospital, and why, he arranged for the welfare department to take charge of the children while she returned to the hospital for surgery.

Neighbors helped when she came home from the hospital, and her husband promised to stop drinking, but two months later he disappeared, leaving her with the rent and gas bill overdue. The kind landlord let her stay rent free.

Friends of her husband sent her busfare after he ended up at their home when he sobered up. This family took the war bride and her children in, but told her husband he was no longer welcome in their home. Another friend sent trainfare for her and the children to come to their ranch at the Canadian border for the summer, where she could rest and recuperate in peace. "I regained my strength fast. I could even help working in the silo and make myself useful to repay these dear people."

At the end of summer, the war bride returned to California and got a small apartment in a housing project. She recalls how difficult it was to live alone at first:

I was scared to be alone at night in a strange neighborhood and I can remember being in bed with both children and moving the bed in front of the bedroom door so that nobody could come in. The heat during the summer was stifling but I was afraid to open a window.

I had not realized before how much anti-German sentiment existed in the business world. Every day I went to look for work, and often it was quite noticeable that it was anti-German sentiment that kept the people from giving me work. One person even went as far as to ask me if I had been a Nazi. Finally I found a job.

My children meanwhile were taken care of by the nuns in the Grace Day Home. The nuns took only a small fee for babysitting based on the amount of money I earned. The people I worked with helped me get to the nursery, bring the children home when it rained, sometimes they brought my lunch.

Neighbors avoided this war bride at first because the police and men from collection agencies had come to her door several times looking for her husband, who had cashed stolen checks and had not paid bills for things he had charged and then sold at the nearest bar.

Eventually, I got it all straightened out with the retailers credit association. Since I had not signed for any of the merchandise, I told them I could not pay for it and they would force me to go on welfare if they would attach my wages as they had planned to do. On the advice of the Lutheran welfare I found an attorney who started my divorce. They felt it was very urgent to get it so that I would not be liable for any more debts that my husband might make anywhere.

The attorney, also a Lutheran, was willing to undertake the divorce at his own expense, with repayment at the rate of $10.00 per month. Eventually things settled down to normal, and the war bride got to know her neighbors and made friends.

We didn't have any money left over at the end of the month, but neither were we hungry. I could take some overtime at work, and it became quite a source of content for me that I could support myself and two children.

Women whose husbands remained in the military found it even more difficult to get out of an abusive situation, for frequent transfers prevented them from establishing a network of friends who could help. When alcoholism or wife-beating resulted in intervention by the military authorities, their solution was often to detain the husband on base until he sobered up, and then ship him and his family off to another base. If the abuse occurred overseas, the soldier was transferred back to the U.S., perhaps on the theory that he could cope with his problems better in his own environment. If the abuse occurred in the U.S., sometimes the soldier was transferred back overseas, perhaps with the idea that the wife could cope with her problems better in her native land. However, these wives usually kept their problems from their families at all cost, not wanting to hear "I told you so."

Unwilling to admit that the marriage they had been permitted to enter into after so much difficulty was a mistake after all, and afraid to seek help from strangers, some women remained with abusive husbands. The common public reaction in the 1940s and 50s was to assume that an abused woman was guilty of something and deserved the treatment she got. Wives were not unaware of this sentiment and were therefore reluctant and even ashamed to seek help. Wife abuse was more tolerated in the 1940s than it is today, and it was not uncommon for it to be treated as a subject of humor. "A Yank Dopey Drama" described in the September 24, 1944, issue of *Yank,* a weekly magazine "by the men, for the men in the service," includes a description of Colonel Amnesia, who was having such a bad day that "he wishes he was at home so he could beat his wife." [13] Even in the 1980s, a veterans' reunion newsletter included among other jokes and anecdotes a quip about "the fellow who was fined $1.10 for beating up his wife. The ten cents was for Federal Amusement tax." [14]

Thirty or forty years ago, a battered bride who had no family to turn to had few options. There were no shelters for abused women, and those with small children often saw no way to survive financially on their own, so many stayed with their husbands in spite of abuse. A Japanese woman who turned to the legal officer on base for help in getting a divorce from her abusive husband was told that when her husband left the army, there would be no way to guarantee he would support their children. Having had difficulty finding employment in the U.S., this woman thought her only alternative would be "to go to little Tokyo, work for tips, something I didn't have to do in Japan." She chose to stay with her husband.

The Korean conflict also caused disappointment and heartache for war brides whose husbands reenlisted or were called back to active duty from the reserves. Women who had been in America only a short time were suddenly left alone when their husbands were sent to Korea. It was a bitter pill to swallow for women who had looked upon America as the land of peace.

Some marriages were not strong enough to survive the extended separation caused by the Korean War. Gisela Blake, who had already discovered in the scant year she had been in the U.S. that she and her husband had little in common, returned to Germany for a long visit while he was in Korea. When they both returned to the U.S. their differences seemed insurmountable and Gisela filed for divorce, retaining custody of her son.

Anneliese Uhlig Tucker, who had looked upon America as a haven safe from war, also found herself alone when her husband was sent to Korea. Having been both an actress and a journalist in Germany, she decided to move to Hollywood while her husband was away. Hollywood offered her opportunity as a foreign correspondent, because people overseas were eager to forget their drab postwar existence while reading articles about American film stars. Mrs. Tucker's parting words to her husband had been "keep down," advice that was impossible for a 6'3" soldier to follow. Wounded during an ambush shortly after his arrival at the front, Lt. Tucker remained separated from his family during a lengthy recuperation period.[15]

Some husbands were killed in Korea, leaving their war brides to cope with life in America alone. Andrée Davis, who had been decorated for her work in the French resistance and who had looked forward to a peaceful life in America, found that "Happiness was short. Colonel Davis left for the Korean conflict 14 months after marriage, leaving me with a 5-week-old son, not to return. He died in October 1951."

War brides who were widowed or deserted had to become independent in their adopted land quickly and seek employment on their own. Louise Bartley Chytka, a former ballet dancer from Würzburg, Germany, went to work in an Oregon lumber mill after her divorce in 1952, when her husband failed to provide support for their two small sons.

Many of the war brides who divorced list "standing on their own two feet" as their most important accomplishment in the U.S. Italian Dina Underwood is proud that she was able to raise her two children independently when her marriage ended after thirteen years, and that her job as a meat wrapper in a supermarket enabled her to buy and furnish an apartment and buy a new car without assistance from anyone. Divorced after twenty years, Regina Shelton from Germany raised five children and worked her way up from various office jobs to a career in the library of a university. She lists her book *To Lose a War* and working her way up to her original social level among her most important accomplishments.

Even war brides who had husbands with steady jobs entered the job market sometimes. Alice Dent, who was born and reared by British parents in Shanghai, China, found herself job hunting shortly after her arrival in 1948, after a shopping spree at Joske's, a large department store in San Antonio, Texas:

> Not understanding the principle of "$5.00 down and so much a month," I proceeded to hand the salesman in each department a "small down" for: a washing machine, a hand-rubbed mahogany console TV and radio combination, six suits for my husband, an 11-cu.ft. refrigerator, a baby bed and a collapsible playpen—returning home with $15.00. It never occurred to me to ask what "so much a month" would be, or exactly how much the total was. When "tomorrow" came and deliveries were made, my husband asked me how much I had spent and how I planned to pay for those purchases. Naively I answered, "I paid money already on them and in a few days I will get 'coupons' which I am to tear out and pay 'so much a month.'" A cursory glance told him that "so much a month" could conceivably exceed his total take home pay. When I suggested sending them all back, he said that it would not do; he would not have his credit rating marred; and that my only recourse was to "go to work," since it was my obligation

and mine alone. No amount of welled tears and pleadings swayed him, so that afternoon I went job hunting.

Finding little available on the local job market, Alice returned to Joske's and explained her predicament to the personnel manager, who said she had no job to offer her and suggested she return the merchandise delivered that morning.

I said I could not as I was more afraid of my husband than I was of Joske's; that I would camp outside her office until she found a job for me; that I was in this predicament only because I was too gullible to recognize the wiles of their salesmen and that I wish someone would explain to me what "credit" truly meant. Closing time came and I was still there. Out of desperation more so than pity, the personnel manager told me to come back the next morning when she would place me "somewhere."

Alice started work as a typist the next morning, earning $35.00 a week (increased to $75.00 a week by the time she left the job eighteen months later). She kept $5.00 a week to pay the landlady for babysitting and the rest was applied toward her $2,500.00 spending spree. When going to work became too uncomfortable during the eighth month of her second pregnancy, Alice did typing at home for the store. When her husband was transferred four weeks after the baby was born, she asked Joske's to put a hold on her payment schedule until she found work in their new location. Instead, Joske's sent her a notice that she'd earned a "meritorious bonus for continued loyalty, expertise and devotion." The bonus was for the same amount as her remaining debt to the store, which was returned marked "paid in full."

Most homemakers found themselves emulating independent American women as well. "They had a lot more freedom than the English women did," thought Eloise Howell of Watford, England. "I was surprised when my friends told me I didn't have to ask my husband's permission to buy a new dress. But I learned fast!"

War brides rarely mention initial grooming differences, such as American women shaving their legs while most war brides did not, as adjustment problems. Clothing and hairstyles were easy to adapt, and visible differences between American and European women disappeared quickly. An Austrian woman says, "After the first shopping trip in New York I fit right in—until I opened my mouth!" But Japanese war bride Kyo Wittrock says, "No matter how you look at it, Japanese face can't change."

Joyce Beatrice Moore of Catford, London County, remembers her husband saying, "Why don't you look and behave like the American girls?" "After I had been here a few years, it was, 'Where is the little English girl I married?' "

American humor was sometimes problematical. A Japanese war bride says it disturbed her husband that she never laughed with him when he tried to joke. "I didn't understand. If people were laughing I never could understand what was so funny. I was always sad. That was hard for him. It was hard on both sides." The American habit of teasing was also disconcerting. "I have never insulted anyone and then said I was 'teasing,' " says Luisa Spitler of Italy.

Too often, a foreign bride felt the joke was entirely on her. But a social gaffe was rarely repeated twice. A German woman was terribly embarrassed when her husband brought his buddies home for lunch and they broke into hilarious laughter as she opened a box of napkins to pass out at the table. She discovered that the box with the pretty white rose on it contained feminine sanitary napkins.

While some war brides found it hard to get used to American social informality, others were eager to adapt the more casual attitudes of Americans. Many were surprised to find that the casual invitation, "Come on over sometime," was not meant to be taken seriously. When Gertrude Reichenbach wanted to visit new acquaintances in Philadelphia, her husband tried to talk her out of dropping in on them on a Sunday afternoon without a specific invitation. "But they said we should come on over sometime," insisted Gertie, who missed the Sunday afternoon visits with friends that were typical in her native Holland. But the people were painting their house when Gertie and Rik arrived, and the short visit was awkward for all concerned. "We never did that again!" says Gertie.

Often, neighbors and family friends were curious about a war bride's reaction to the United States and the circumstances she had left behind. The new immigrants were questioned about their impressions of the U.S. before they had been here long enough to form an opinion. Apprehensive war brides sometimes found these often well-meant questions to be offensive. Bertha Brandstatter of Passau, Germany, who met most of her husband's friends and family at a funeral home the day after her arrival, found their behavior incomprehensible:

> Of course, this was a chance for everybody to meet the "German girl" and it seemed like everybody asked the same questions: "is it true Hitler did not let you go to church," "is it true the bombings were bad and civilians got killed," "is it true you had nothing to eat"—dumb and silly! I believe I was not very friendly but disgusted. The corpse did not look "dead" at all, but was heavily made up with cosmetics—something I had never seen before and found very strange. The people conversed loud and laughed and showed very little respect for the dead man.

American customs were sometimes bewildering to the war brides and holidays were often celebrated much differently than they were overseas. Halloween, for example, was celebrated as All Souls' Day in Europe when families attended a holy mass and visited the graves of their loved ones. Halloween, as celebrated in America, evolved from this tradition, but "trick or treat" was unknown in most European countries and presented a rather shocking innovation to the newcomer. Throwing rice at weddings seemed a terrible waste of food to women very much aware that people overseas suffered from hunger. "Or how could anyone think it funny," asked Bertha, "when pies were thrown on TV shows?!"

Homesickness was a war bride's worst enemy. "I felt so sick in my heart that I thought I would have a heart attack so young," said an Italian woman who went to Indian Gulch, Pennsylvania. When her husband was transferred to Kentucky, she felt as if she'd gone back to pioneer days when she saw an old woman in a bonnet sitting in a rocking chair on the porch of an old farmhouse. Looking for a place to live, they stopped at another old farmhouse which had been divided into small apartments. Hearing the war bride's accent, the landlady asked where she was from and then said, "You should meet the lady upstairs. She's Italian, too." "I don't need to see the apartment," was her excited reply. "Just show me the lady upstairs!" The apartment was rented sight unseen and the two Italian women became fast friends.

Other war brides "were like my family, and still are," says Joy Baase of Australia. Unlike immigrants who arrived in family groups or settled in neighborhoods of earlier immigrants from their own countries, a war bride often started out feeling like the only foreigner in her new family or neighborhood. No matter how kind or helpful husbands and in-laws were, many war brides felt isolated and alone when there was no one from their country with whom they could discuss their homesickness.

It was essential for war brides to have contact with each other during their early years in the U.S., and consequently they flocked to the clubs formed by the YWCA and the Red Cross, and to classes sponsored by local businesses, civic associations, and churches. Although they received helpful instruction in the English language and tips on child care, shopping, and household economics, the primary benefit of these clubs and classes was the contact with other women from overseas. "We had one sure thing in common," said Renata Chiaro of Italy, recalling the meetings at the YWCA in Chicago in 1946, where war brides of many different nationalities discussed their impressions of American life through interpreters: "We were all homesick."

Brenda Hasty of Liverpool, England, remembers that when the Overseas Women's Club was founded in Jacksonville, Florida, it was originally intended for British women only:

Into our midst came some very lonely Germans, a Polish, and some Oriental brides. A meeting was hurriedly held and we decided to let bygones be bygones and to welcome them as we apparently were all in the same boat and not on different sides.

The Sunday school at the Westminster Presbyterian Church in Minneapolis became a meeting place for Chinese brides who attended English classes given by Jane Wilson, who recalled:

One Sunday afternoon in the fall of 1948 we looked up and there were *fourteen* Chinese brides without one word of English. We must have had twenty brides that first year, and the next year twenty babies, so the Sunday School was in business for another ten years.

When there was no church, YWCA, or Red Cross chapter to start a club or school, the war brides found each other via the mailman, the milkman, the telephone man. An Italian woman recalls trying to get rid of a pesky Fuller Brush man until he happened to mention that he had just sold a brush to another Italian war bride who lived nearby; the cost of a brush was a small price to pay for finding a compatriot. It wasn't until these early clubs were formed "that we really felt we had friends who grew up with similar backgrounds. In each other's company we could let our hair down and discuss the days of growing up and times no American could be expected to know," recalls Marjorie Schiappa of Australia.

Anticipating the needs of daughters who had gone to the U.S., George Higgins, the father of war bride Elizabeth Roberts, contacted parents of some of the war brides in the Forty-Eight Club in Oxford, England, and formed CANUSPA, the Canadian and U.S. Parents' Association, in May 1946. The organization had ninety members on January 21, 1947, and sent a newsletter to daughters in the U.S., with addresses to help them make contact with each other. In the early days, the association worked through the Salvation Army, the Red Cross, and the British consulate to assist brides who were having problems in the U.S., giving financial aid to help them get back to England if that appeared to be the best solution. Special fund raisers were held for this purpose. CANUSPA also worked to arrange affordable transport for parents who wanted to visit their daughters in America.

Some clubs, like the Trans-Atlantic Brides and Parents Association (TBPA), were formed specifically to organize charter flights to join war brides and their parents overseas. Still active, TBPA publishes a regular newsletter called *Together Again*. Some of the TBPA groups evolved out of YWCA overseas wives clubs.

In 1949, Betty Arrieta, president of the Britannia Club, formerly the British Brides Club, in Oakland, California, organized a large enough group to charter a Transocean Company DC-4 to fly club members overseas for a reunion with their parents. The cost for what they called "Operation Grandchildren Showoff" was $500.00 per person, round trip. Special seats were installed on the plane so the women could sit five abreast, and basinettes were hung from the plane's ceiling. Although the normal commercial load was forty-four adult passengers, this flight transported forty-four war brides, sixteen children, and twelve babies. It was the largest single planeload of persons ever to take off at New York's Idlewild (now Kennedy) Airport. Two of the brides were returning home for good, and Thomas Bell of Berkeley, California, and his wife Ruth Ivy had decided to emigrate to her native England. Three French war brides were included in the group.

A "Grannies' Express" flew sixty-eight Australian mothers of war brides to the U.S. in 1957. The reunion was organized by Mrs. G. A. H. McTiernan Watson, J.P., of New Farm, founder and vice president of the U.S. and Canadian War Brides, Parents, and Relatives Association in Queensland. Mrs. Watson was looking forward to a reunion with her daughter, whom she hadn't seen since their tearful farewell fifteen years earlier.

While women of most nationalities seemed to form clubs whenever a group of them lived in one town or neighborhood, German women showed a noticeable reluctance to form clubs, even though a few individual Germans sometimes joined organizations that had an international membership. Some German and Austrian women did meet in informal "kaffeeklatsch" groups, but, unlike women of other nationalities, these groups did not seek community recognition or publicity. Irma Bremer of Nürnberg expressed this opinion:

German war brides in general are not as proud of their heritage as war brides from other nations. Somehow, the German war bride assimilates to a point where she almost loses her identity. Of course, when one war bride meets another, they acknowledge to where they came from, but to really try to get together and recognize and publicize that they are unique in their experiences on a larger scale, most of them apparently have not had the interest.

Another German war bride feels similarly and says this is her greatest regret about her life in America:

I lost my own German identity in my struggle of adjustment and submerging into the American melting pot. Unlike other immigrants that came in family groups, I was always very much on my own. No one in my family is here to share memories with. I have never been "back home," had no German friends here and except for writing letters back home, reading German books and papers, have had no chance to use my mother language.

Many Germans and Austrians tended to assimilate into the general American culture as quickly as possible rather than seeking each other out to form mutual support groups. They felt pressured to disassociate themselves from the country held responsible for the war. Others felt less burdened by postwar resentments and joined German clubs established by earlier immigrants before the war, or enjoyed traditions from home by joining folk dance and entertainment groups. It was perhaps not until 1963, when President John F. Kennedy proclaimed, "Ich bin ein Berliner," that the study of the German language and culture became popular again. West Germany was no longer identified as an enemy or defeated nation, but as an ally.

Interracial couples also began to gain acceptance in the 1960s as the civil rights program gained force. Some of these couples had chosen to remain in the service because there were more couples like them in the military community, hence less notoriety, and because President Truman's Executive Order 9981 of July 26, 1948, had promised "equality of treatment and opportunity for all persons in the armed services without regard to race, color, religion, or national origin." [16] When the U.S. Supreme Court ruled against antimiscegenation laws in 1967, growing numbers of interracial couples could finally live legally anywhere in the U.S.

Chapter 16

Home at Last

For a number of years it was easy to blame America for any problems I had. This farm and this town are where I belong now. I have no regrets.
—*Phyllis E. Totman, London, England*

Once established in the U.S., the war bride had to consider whether or not she would become a naturalized citizen. Since 1922, an alien woman marrying an American citizen did not automatically acquire American citizenship through her marriage.[1] For war brides, however, the five-year residency requirement prior to filing first papers to petition for U.S. citizenship was waived. War brides and grooms could begin the naturalization process by filing second papers after only two years of residency in the U.S. as the spouse of an American citizen.[2]

"It's your country—forget yesterday, live in today, believe in tomorrow," British Consul Capt. H. Cotton Minchin advised the 140 British war brides who arrived in Kansas City in the spring of 1946. A stranger is expected to assume the habits and customs of the new land as quickly as possible, Minchin advised:

> The Briton, the Slav, the Norseman, the Italian who settles on these shores is being formed into an American; he has become a citizen of a new country and a citizen if he is wise, with no strings attached.

So let it be with all of you who have made the choice of your hearts . . . you may have memories infinitely dear of other people and of other places, but your choice is set and those memories are better kept close to your hearts and distant from your tongues.[3]

That was easier said than done, for many war brides felt torn between loyalty for their former homelands and love for their adopted land. "We are drawn from one side to the other, warmly defending equally France or the United States, depending on which is being attacked," said Pierette Goldberg of France.

British Consul Minchin advised war brides to accept the inevitable inner conflict with a sense of humor:

You can sing with fervor *The Star Spangled Banner*—few know beyond the first verse anyhow—and some of you can get satisfaction out of knowing that you sing it to an old English drinking song melody and, most assuredly, an echo of previously learned words will come to you when you join in *My Country 'Tis of Thee*.[4]

Most of the war brides interviewed for this book have become U.S. citizens, and many of them did so as soon as they had met the two-year residency requirement. Only a few have not become citizens, not due to any lack of loyalty to this country, where they have lived over forty years now, but because they have been unable to "absolutely and entirely renounce and abjure all allegiance and fidelity" to their former homeland, as required by the Oath of Allegiance.[5] One woman states:

Even though I have spent the past 40 years watching a small town grow into a large one and being involved to a small degree in some of the development, I am still an Australian citizen and would not relinquish my own nationality for anyone. My family over there are all fiercely proud of their homeland and I could never turn my back on them.

For another Australian, Stella Frey, the decision to become a U.S. citizen was based on fear of separation from her American children: "I was planning a trip home to see an ailing mother and was told if war broke out that my children would be brought back but that I could be left."

Phyllis Totman of London became a U.S. citizen in 1951 after much hesitancy:

In 1949 when we came to the farm, a whole new life started for me. I was a city girl. In civilian life I had done office work with weekends off. I soon found that on a farm you work when there is work to be done and for us that meant every day of the week, from dawn to dark. It was good work and I enjoyed the animals once I got over being afraid of them. But we got tired, bone tired with no break in sight. I often thought how much easier life would have been in England even with its postwar limitations.

I became an American citizen in 1951. I was very hesitant. I had no bad feelings about England, I had had a good life there and was proud of my Britishness. On the other hand it was more than likely that I would be staying here. I was interested in local and state politics and could not vote. After much thought and a lot of guilt feelings I went ahead. I just hope that in my lifetime the two countries never get on opposite sides in a conflict.

By 1953 we were beginning to feel we could keep our heads above water. We got along well with our neighbors and the children were getting big enough to help with the farm work. In July, just after we had finished getting in the hay for the winter, our barn burnt down. I can never say enough for the neighborhood people who spent hours and weeks helping to build the new barn. My life has been almost totally concerned with my husband and children and the farm. I have nothing remarkable to report about myself, a million others could tell a similar story. It wasn't easy adjusting to living away from all my relatives and not going home for 25 years. I have no way of knowing whether my life would have been better if I'd stayed in England. It's hard to imagine it. This farm and this town are where I belong now. I have no regrets.

Although Anna Gonzales still longs for her native Italy, she is proud that she passed her citizenship exam on her own. When her husband, John, worked the night shift she had a friend drive her to classes and then studied on the front porch while John slept in the afternoon. "I wrote all my questions in Italian and then I answered myself in English. I passed and got my paper right away. He said it was very good—even if I didn't speak too good. I still don't!" Anna says, laughing at her strong Italian accent.

Elsbeth Maginn of Switzerland took citizenship courses at the University of California but lacked the confidence to take the exam. "I was afraid I would flunk it," she says. When she finally became naturalized in 1953, she told the reporter from her local newspaper, "I don't know whether to laugh or cry in my coffee. I'm giving up a swell country—one which gave me a good education and many opportunities." [6]

German women had little choice in the matter of citizenship, for a German woman who married a citizen of any other country prior to May 24, 1949, lost her German citizenship. [7] Since marriage to an American did not automatically confer U.S. citizenship on foreign brides, German women were rendered stateless by such a marriage. Their choice was to remain stateless or become U.S. citizens. If they wanted to travel overseas, they could not remain stateless, as Lya Cutcher discovered on a trip to Germany in 1951, when she was almost not permitted to reenter the U.S.:

> My salvation was knowing all of the Immigration officers at the New York airport as I was a Pan Am employee at that time. They knew me, knew I had a job and an apartment in New York and didn't request my departure to Ellis Island on arrival. Had the U.S. deported me under the McCarthy witch-hunt, Germany would not have been responsible for taking me in. I suppose I would have been an eternal stewardess, never setting foot on any land again.

Lya had entered the U.S. in 1947, but because she separated from her husband before the two years of required residency had passed, she hesitated to apply for U.S. citizenship, thinking she might return to Germany. Once divorced, she found she had to wait five years to apply for citizenship. She finally got her U.S. citizenship in February 1952 because, as a stewardess for Pan Am, she was limited to the Puerto Rico or Bermuda flights without a U.S. passport.

A day trip to Juarez, Mexico, turned into a nightmare for German war bride Else Smith when she was arrested by the Mexican border authorities when she tried to return to El Paso, Texas, with her husband and his family. Americans could cross the border quite easily, merely having to state they were U.S. citizens, but because of her accent, Else was asked to show her passport. She did not have one, so she was detained in a Juarez jail overnight, while her husband and in-laws returned to El Paso to sort out the bureaucratic muddle. Becoming a naturalized U.S. citizen became a priority for Else after she was released the next day.

A number of war brides, including Gertrude Reichenbach of The Netherlands and Elly Rogers of Hungary, became citizens in 1952 because they wanted to vote for Eisenhower. Like many European war brides, they felt loyalty and gratitude toward the general who had released their homelands from the yoke of Nazi oppression. Mrs. Rogers was one of the many war brides who became active in politics. She was president of the Republican Women's Club and travelled throughout the western U.S. as a speaker at various Republican events, winning many awards for her speeches. Mrs. Rogers often speaks out against communism, for she, like many of the war brides whose former homelands came under communist rule after World War II, is a staunch supporter of democracy in government. Following in her mother's footsteps, Mrs. Rogers' eldest daughter Ann served a term as mayor of Sausalito, California. British war bride Doris L. Whittaker served as an appointed officer on the county board of elections in Hopatcong, New Jersey.

Elisabeth Honey, who had been imprisoned by the new leftist government in her native Czechoslovakia, avoided politics in the United States. "Even here I was always afraid that if I spoke out someone would come and get me," she says. During the 1960s, however, Mrs. Honey became concerned about the protests against the U.S. government:

> I think the protests were a facade, with the communists behind it. People here just don't understand it at all. I was through it—I know. It frustrates me. American people don't know what freedom means, they only know when they lose it, then it is too late. I love this country. It's the greatest country.

Italian war bride Enza Andreatta is among the many who feel similarly. Mrs. Andreatta considers her work in a factory "for the defense of America" her most important contribution to this country.

For many women, becoming a U.S. citizen was one of the most satisfying events of their lives. Joan Cater of England remembered her naturalization ceremony with pride:

In October 1952 I stood in Room Courthouse with two hundred other would-be citizens from many countries. After the Pledge of Allegiance the judge gave a wonderful speech. He welcomed us as new citizens and said the United States of America asked of us that we not forget our country, to bring the best of its traditions to be incorporated into the United States.

Most of the war brides felt that the aspect of American life they have cherished most was personal freedom. While leaving much that they valued behind, they also gained many opportunities they would not have had in their native countries. In America, women had more professional choices than in most other countries. Once their families were grown, many entered the work force in a variety of capacities. Others went back to college, another privilege many could not have enjoyed in their native countries.

Yolande Dauphin, who was nicknamed "le bébé" because at age fifteen she was the youngest war bride aboard her 1946 voyage of the *Brazil,* took night classes to get a high school diploma. While raising five children, Yolande earned both B.A. and M.A. degrees at the University of Michigan, and has been teaching French in the Flint School System for over fifteen years.

Some war brides found that academic credentials from overseas were not accepted in the United States. Lydia Clifton, who hadn't expected to have to start her education all over again, found that her Abitur degree from Germany was meaningless on the U.S. job market, so she went to business college in Tacoma, Washington. "But I had to start my career in the U.S. from the bottom up," she said. "I picked strawberries to survive, beans, then became a manager, administrative assistant, auditor, and business owner."

Christiane Buchanan, who met her husband near Paris when she served on a French welcoming committee after the liberation, was asked to teach in her Appalachian community when the principal learned that she had been a teacher in France. The profound impact she had on her students is reflected in these excerpts from a speech given by the Honorable Lamar Gudger of North Carolina in the House of Representatives on August 1, 1979:

> Over the years, she touched the lives of thousands of students, providing a bridge of communication and understanding between the country of her birth and her adopted land. No nation has made stronger contributions to music, the arts, and letters than France and this leadership is reflected in the role of the French language as a leader in Civilized dialog between nations and among individuals in the international community.
>
> Madame Buchanan's love and command for her native tongue, her singular ability to inspire her students to share this love, have made her an unusually effective teacher. As an educator, she served as an unofficial goodwill ambassador for her native country, infusing her western North Carolina students and neighbors with an understanding of France that went far beyond mere language.[8]

Adele Weaver of Vienna, Austria, formed the Austrian American Society of Delaware with a friend. This group works to further cultural exchange between Austria and America and sends a music student to the prestigious Mozarteum in Salzburg each summer.

A resolution passed in the California Senate honored Ina Lathrop, originally from Berlin, Germany, for her work during the Winter Olympics in Squaw Valley in 1960, when she was in charge of 210 interpreters speaking twenty-one languages. While raising her two children to be fully bilingual, Mrs. Lathrop worked as a teacher from fifth grade to college and assisted in writing three books.

Dutch-American relations have been strengthened by Gertrude Reichenbach, who earned her M.S. degree at the University of Utrecht and taught English in The Netherlands prior to her marriage. After raising five children, Mrs. Reichenbach founded and still directs the Dutch Studies Program at the University of Pennsylvania, where she lectures in Dutch studies and Germanic languages and literature. Through her efforts, the Dutch Studies Program, one of only a few in the U.S., is funded jointly by the university and the Dutch government. Mrs. Reichenbach is coeditor of *Two Hundred Years of Netherlands-American Interaction,* a collection of essays from the Dutch Studies Lecture Series, published in 1985.

Italian Cesi Kellinger, who is a buyer and seller of rare books, taught Italian at Syracuse University and the Eastman School of Music, among other schools, and was director of the language lab at Wilson College.

Because of their own experiences as immigrants, war brides were quick to volunteer to help others. Brunhild Voss, who was an interpreter during her husband's army career and later taught German at a private college in Wisconsin, heard a plea on the radio for volunteers to teach English to Vietnamese refugees and to help them adjust to life in the U.S. "I could identify with the problems these people were facing, so I volunteered," recalls Brunhild, who was hired by the school system after the first semester to keep working with the Vietnamese until 1978. Another German war bride, Gia Hawthorne, who was a medical lab technician and worked with Head Start children and retarded citizens, also taught English to Vietnamese boat people as a volunteer.

When her husband was stationed in Japan, Ingrid Hardy of Czechoslovakia volunteered to teach Japanese war brides:

> Many GIs stationed in Japan were marrying Japanese girls, and knowing the adjustment they had before them our wives club decided to help those girls. Each club member was assigned girls, three to me. They would visit once a week at my apartment and I would teach them American-style cooking, showing them our appliances and how they worked. In turn I also learned how to do Japanese dishes, learned Japanese words, and was given hints where shopping was best.[9]

A number of war brides made a career with the Red Cross, both as volunteers and as salaried employees, perhaps remembering the many services the Red Cross had provided to war brides from overseas. Ursula Hunter of Germany was asked to volunteer twice a year with the Red Cross bloodmobile, "and before I knew it I was knee deep into it. We provide shelter, food banks, help military families." Ursula has been employed by the Middlesex County Chapter of the Red Cross in Connecticut for nearly twenty years.

Other organizations also benefitted from the many volunteer hours contributed by war brides. Tomi Hamelin of Japan has served for more than twenty years as a volunteer at St. Vincent's Hospital in Worcester, Massachusetts. English war bride Marcella Turner, who has been volunteer hospital president for several years in Colorado City, Texas, feels her most important accomplishment was "gaining respect and trust from my many American friends, and being a good neighbor and parent."

Many war brides found themselves thrust into a multitude of civic and political activities due to their husbands' professions. For Australian Lillian Cherry, her husband's position as mayor of Hazlet, New Jersey, and president of the fire department required her to support him in many civic functions. Soon she was organizing and serving on committees in her own right, in addition to being involved in PTA, cub scouts, boy scouts, and girl scouts with their two children. After she headed the fundraising effort to build a community hospital, Lillian was appointed director of volunteers when the hospital opened in 1972. For twelve years she coordinated the efforts of 250 volunteers.

Monica Dickens Stratton, the great-granddaughter of Charles Dickens, continued her career as a writer after coming to the U.S. as a war bride. Among her many books is a novel called *No More Meadows,* about an English war bride. *An Open Book* tells about Mrs. Stratton's own experiences, which include starting a branch of the British organization, The Samaritans, in Boston. Samaritan volunteers staff a hot-line for potential suicides; the Boston branch received more than 200,000 calls and visits in the first four years of operation.[10]

After a long and varied career as actress, journalist, and author, Anneliese Uhlig Tucker did extensive research on German immigrants in California and was active in the German-American tricentennial celebration of 1983. She lectured on a variety of topics, including "The Dilemma of the Artist in a Totalitarian Society." In her autobiography, *Rosenkavaliers Kind,* published in Germany in 1977, Mrs. Tucker describes her experiences as a war bride from Germany.[11] *Einladung Nach Kalifornien* (1981) is a well-researched declaration of affection for her new home on the West Coast.[12] Concerned with the life of the American Indian, she and her husband are sponsors of a Zuni girl in the nonprofit, nondenominational education program *Futures for Children*.

A number of war brides and their husbands expressed their concern about children orphaned by war by adopting some of them. Maria and Lloyd Hixon, who met in Austria when Maria was still a child, adopted two Korean-American orphans through the U.N. Steve Condur and his Swedish wife Karin adopted two German orphans in 1956. Joan (Penny) K. Wood, whose parents were killed during the Blitz in London, adopted two children in the U.S.

In order to visit their families overseas more often, many war brides chose to work in the travel industry. Kay and Daniel Militello, who married without permission in Germany in 1946, own a successful travel agency in New York, which enables them to visit Germany often. June Harris, transport organizer of Trans Atlantic Brides and Parents in Texas, is also a travel agent who enjoys frequent trips to her native England. Catherine M. Roberts-Swauger, who married a GI in England while serving in the WAAF, worked for American Airlines in Boston for thirty years. Now she serves as director of the USO at Boston's Logan Airport, a job she says she enjoys very much because, "Seeing these young men and women of the military services brings back many happy memories of my own military life in Great Britain 40 years ago."

Directors of American firms who have to entertain foreign clients frequently call upon bilingual war brides to act as interpreters. Terry Grimes, who was born to Russian immigrants in Japan, has found herself in the role of goodwill ambassador on the job in an aerospace firm in Dallas, Texas, whenever the company has Japanese visitors:

I was invited to escort them around, have dinner with them, and make them feel at ease. One man in particular has been very considerate, and every year since I met him, has mailed me a gorgeous Japanese greeting card at Christmastime. Some of them knew a little English, but had a hard time understanding the Texas brogue. One time, I was being introduced and one of the fellows kept trying to read my name on the badge that I wore. He kept bowing, and finally said, "Ahhh, Mrs. Materials," (yes, you guessed I work in the Materials Dept.). I really had a wonderful visit with those eleven—one of them even said that I spoke beautiful Japanese, but with a "Texas accent."

Being able to cook with a French accent brought Denise Khaitman Schorr an audience on television. She had begun her culinary career by giving classes on French cooking in her home, and has published a cookbook, *My French Kitchen*.

While war brides in general were gaining acceptance in their communities and in the work force, some encountered unexpected difficulties at home, for sometimes a son or daughter tried to disassociate from a foreign-born mother perceived as "different" at a stage when children want most to fit in and be "just like one of the gang." Children sometimes teased mothers about their foreign accents. A mother's sense of her child's shame was acutely painful for war brides who wanted more than anything to be good wives, mothers, and citizens.

The experience of children of war brides was different from that of children in families in which both parents were immigrants and shared a cultural unity in the home. First-born children in particular tended to identify with their mothers, often speaking her native language and acting as a go-between when mother had difficulty with shopping or communication. "I was my mother's *confidante*," said a Belgian war bride's daughter, who felt burdened by the responsibility but now feels fortunate to be bilingual and to have a dual cultural heritage. Bertha Brandstatter recalled the conflict faced by one of her children:

When my oldest son was in 6th grade he was quite upset about what he learned in history—as a matter of fact he thought everything bad had started with the Germans—Karl Marx, Luther, Hitler—and to top it off he had a German mother! The nun [his teacher] was very helpful and this was shortlived.

As interest in foreign cultures grew, many sons and daughters of war brides started coming home with letters inviting mother to speak to the class at school about her native country. Being "different" became an asset and many children took new pride in mother.

Molly Ingersoll of England reflected on her attempts to assimilate and on how her origins affected her children:

> As children are often sensitive when their parents have a different accent, I worked hard at acquiring an American accent. Now they are grown they are pleased with their heritage. However, my oldest daughter told me recently that she never asked me to help her with her English homework because she thought I wouldn't understand because I was a foreigner. We laughed for hours.

Author Lois Battle travelled from Australia with her mother as a child. Memories of the experiences of her mother and her mother's war bride friends inspired Lois to write the poignant novel *War Brides,* which was published in 1982.

Children born to interracial parents tended to have special identity conflicts, but many were also inspired by their multiplicity and the example of their war bride mother's courage. Concert pianist André Watts, the son of a black American and a Hungarian war bride, praised his mother during an interview after a masterful performance of Gershwin in Cupertino, California in 1984. His mother's fortitude and perseverance were inspiration while he was growing up. She had endured much during and after the war, yet she was able to set goals and meet them; he knew he too could accomplish anything once he set his mind to it. André said his mother had always told him:

> When you see a situation and you want to be there, to get involved in it, you can't worry about how difficult it is. You can't say to yourself, "I can't because I am this or I am not that, or they are this." You can't complain about it. You just have to do what you want to do. My mother had many difficulties, and she did just that, whatever she had to do.

Franco Harris, star running back for the Pittsburgh Steelers for twelve years, is one of the nine children born to Cadillac Harris and his Italian wife Gina, who made the perilous journey to Mississippi in 1947 as an interracial couple. Although Franco remembers his mother crying sometimes and wanting to go back to Italy during the early years, he considers his family pretty lucky: "There were really no traumatic experiences for us kids." [13]

Playwright Velina Hasu Houston, whose GI father was black and Native American Indian and whose mother was a Japanese war bride, found inspiration for her work in her background:

In America, I exist as a cultural oddity because I am not Japanese American in the Caucasian definition of what that means, neither am I black American or Native American Indian. An Asian Hybrid with an immigrant mother, I cannot and do not care to be infused with any of those categories. I am not much for conventional definitions.

I remain a misfit, both a foreigner and at home in Japan and America. I find something to love and something to hate about being Japanese, about being American, and about being black and Indian. Every August especially, I am painfully, pointedly absorbed with thoughts of the war that created me.

As soon as I could speak, my parents said I became obsessed with color and would ask them, "Papa, why are you chocolate and why is Mami vanilla?" My parents were unprepared for my interrogation; they had thought it would come later. But my father thought of a way to make their point about being proud of being mixed and not letting anyone push me into a racial category. For I was something new. Something that looked new and thought new, and they wanted that to sustain and persevere. He went to the grocery store and came back with neapolitan ice cream.

"You see this vanilla stripe?" he said, I nodded, challenging him. "Well, that's your mother," he said. "You see this chocolate stripe and the strawberry one? That's me; half Indian and half black. You following me, Pumpkin?" I nodded as he lovingly pinched my cheek. I feared that pinch. My face was already round enough thanks to my Japanese heritage. I watched as my father took a teaspoonful out of each color of ice cream and stirred it together in a bowl. Soon, the colors melted into a soft, even brown tone. "You see that?" I nodded. "That's you," he said. "Now Pumpkin. Think about this. Can you

take this blend and separate it back into three colors?" "No,"
I said, looking at him as if he was being silly. "You can't
take them apart." He had made his point and the worried look
in my mother's eyes disappeared, giving way to relief and love
that she could only convey with her eyes and not with words.
"Okay, Pumpkin," Papa said. "That's how we want you to
live your life. Don't try to take the colors apart and don't let
anybody try to do it for you. Because it can't be done and
you'd only waste a lot of time."

Papa was right.[14]

Another daughter of a Japanese war bride and a Caucasian
GI experienced a difficult identity crisis in her early teens. As the
only half-oriental in her school, Elena Creef was persecuted and
taunted by the other students. The racial mix at her southern
California school gave Elena an opportunity to hide her Japanese
heritage:

I pretended to be Mexican. My long black hair and sun
darkened skin helped add to the effect. Plus, my name mispro-
nounced sounded curiously Hispanic. For the next two years
I obsessively hid my Japanese background and roots, and consequently also tried to hide my mother. I wouldn't let her answer
the phone if I could help it. I sabotaged the school's P.T.A.'s
efforts to get her to attend their monthly meetings, and I conve-
niently got dates mixed up with the "Open House" invita-
tions. Once I even pointed to a passing car with a Hispanic-
looking woman inside and told friends that "that was my
mother." [15]

Elena's mother was busy working to supplement her husband's
income and remained unaware of her daughter's problem. But Elena's
pride in her mother and her heritage was restored by a visit to
Japan for her mother's high school reunion, when she learned that
her mother had graduated with highest honors as the leader of her
class of 1944.

Ceth and Ursula Hunter's sons were proud of their German
mother and military father. From the time he was six years old,
Michael Hunter said that he wanted to be a soldier like his dad.
Ceth, who had become an officer when the army gradually began

to fulfill Truman's promise of opportunity for blacks, told him, "That's fine, son, but you do it the right way by going to West Point. Don't work your way up from the bottom like I did." Two of the Hunters' sons did graduate from West Point; one is a major in the army and the other served five years and then became a lawyer, while a third son pursued a career in dance.

A school teacher commented that she had originally expected the children of war brides to feel rootless and insecure because of a divided loyalty between a foreign mother's native country and America. In fact, she observed that students whose mothers were war brides seemed to have a more worldly outlook and acceptance of diverse cultures. Many of these children had travelled overseas with their mothers and some were born overseas and spent part of their early childhood in their mothers' native countries; some became so fluent in their mother's language that they decided to teach it. Both sons of Germaine and Emery Delongchamp, who had married in Paris, teach French in high schools in Massachusetts. Most children of war brides feel they have benefitted from having a dual cultural heritage.

How happy have the war brides themselves been? It is difficult to say, comments Jane Wilson, affectionately called Aunt Jane by her Chinese war bride students, whose progress Jane has followed over the past forty years:

Who knows how happy *any* marriages are, when the doors are closed and the shades down. All I know is that the women have worked hard right beside their husbands. They appear together at parties. Their clothes are very smart, and as fortunes improve, they wear more jewelry and drive better cars, indicating that their husbands shower them with the more obvious reflections of their own success. Naturally they take great pride in their children and whenever possible (which isn't much) they try to get their sons to go back to China to find a wife. My guess is that the marriages are about as successful as the American average.

Kazu Unbehaun, who challenged a negative article about the plight of Japanese war brides in the U.S., found that according to her own study of thirty-two Japanese women, thirty-one have made a positive adjustment. Some had their own businesses, others worked in beauty salons and at various occupations:

> Thirty-one of the war brides believe that they made the right decisions to marry American soldiers and never plan to go back to Japan. Japanese public and their own relatives criticized them to marry American soldiers, but war brides had foreseen their hope and happiness in the United States. Japan had no name such as "war bride" before. To Japanese, the name of war bride is an insulting language. They believed that war brides deserted Japan just for sweet taste of candies, therefore, war bride would never be happy in the United States. War brides are strong enough to build new lives in this country because they are strong enough to forsake their own motherland. War brides wish people in Japan to understand that they are living comfortably in the United States and still love their homeland.[16]

Because of their individual strengths, these women have adapted to life in America in spite of many difficulties. Without the support of their overseas families, and without lasting organizations for mutual support, the war brides have survived the challenge of adjusting to life in a new country. As wives, mothers, and part of the work force, they have given much to their adopted country, but their contributions have gone largely unrecognized.

Unlike veterans of World War II, who had a tradition of getting together at formal reunions, war brides in America didn't have the opportunity to enjoy the camaraderie and recognition that the GIs shared, because they never organized on a statewide or national basis. Although grouped together briefly in transit camps overseas and on voyages to the U.S., the war brides came from different countries and went to various destinations, each to cope on her own with life in America. The support groups of early clubs and associations quickly dissolved as the women began to assimilate and got busy with day-to-day tasks of raising children, pursuing careers, and meeting family responsibilities. But so many of the war brides we contacted during the research for this book longed to meet with other war brides, perhaps to find someone from their own locality with whom they could talk over old times and their present lives, or to make new friends with whom they had a common background, that we decided to arrange the first nationwide reunion for war brides in the U.S.

The event took place on the *Queen Mary* in Long Beach, California, on April 12, 13, and 14, 1985. Permanently docked and converted to a Wrather Hotel, the *Queen Mary* is the only survivor of the more than thirty ships that carried war brides to America. The grand old ship served as a symbol for the fleet that plied the seas during the postwar "Operation Diaper Run." Nearly 300 war brides and grooms from fifteen countries gathered from all over the U.S. to celebrate the successful accomplishment of the difficult task they had undertaken when they said "I do" over forty years ago.

In the *Queen Mary*'s Grand Ball Room, the war brides watched a slide presentation of "the way they were" that left hardly a dry eye in the house. Capt. John Gregory greeted Karin Trenina Yount, who wore the same boots, hat, and rabbit fur coat she had worn on her flight from Bamberg, Germany, to New York on December 29, 1947. In the same cardboard suitcase she had carried on that trip, Karin carried the now yellowed documents she had needed to immigrate as a fiancée. The captain welcomed the war brides back to the ship on which many of them had travelled, and extended hearty wishes to a dozen couples celebrating their fortieth wedding anniversaries. In the evening, one would have thought they were newlyweds again as they jitterbugged across the floor to the 1940s music of the Lou Dokken Band. The women who made the trip to Long Beach without husbands danced with each other, just as they did during the war, when there weren't enough men to go around. One war groom also made the trip to the *Queen Mary*; Jørgen Nielsen of Denmark came with his American wife Virginia, whom he had met in Germany in 1946. Jørgen was presented with a T-shirt announcing his status as the only "Male War Bride" in the group.

The event was recognized by dignitaries in the United States and abroad, who sent greetings and congratulations to the war brides. President Ronald Reagan acknowledged the many contributions war brides have made to this country:

THE WHITE HOUSE

WASHINGTON

April 5, 1985

I am delighted to send warm greetings to all those
gathered for the World War II War Bride Reunion
aboard the historic Queen Mary in Long Beach,
California.

The approximately one million European women
who married American servicemen and came to the
United States after the Second World War have
played a significant role in the life and history of
our nation.   They have contributed to many fields
and developments since that time and made a great
impact on their adopted homeland.   America has
indeed been fortunate to have had the benefit of
the strength and ability of these citizens and I
proudly join with so many others in saluting their
impact and their continuing gift to this great land.

Nancy joins me in sending best wishes for this
occasion and for the future.   God bless you.

Ronald Reagan

Geraldine A. Ferraro, the first female candidate for vice president
and herself the daughter of immigrants, congratulated the war brides
on their accomplishments:

Experiencing the ravages of war first hand, you arrived
in this country eager to assume special responsibilities to
uphold liberty. We are thankful not only for the significant con-

tributions you have made to American life, but for your inspiration and leadership in preserving the freedoms we cherish.

From the embassies of their former homelands came letters acknowledging the role war brides played in the peace and reconstruction of new relationships between countries. Richard H. Fein, ambassador from The Netherlands, wrote:

You are the symbol and visible signs of the process of renewal and rebirth which has brought our nations back to a normal existence. You are also bridge builders, creators of undying ties across the seas, each of whom, in however modest a way, has brought a bit of the old world to the new and thereby helped a new generation to remember what must never be lost from view: we are all members of one family who wish each other peace and happiness.

German women, one of whom had asked, "Are enemies invited?" when she heard about the reunion, were pleased that Dieter Koepke, Deputy Consul General of the Federal Republic of Germany, was one of the speakers at the reunion. Recognizing the difficulties these women had had due to their loss of citizenship and uncertain status as "enemy aliens" when they first arrived in the U.S., Mr. Koepke said:

We in the Heimat sometimes did not realize to what extent these War Brides contributed to the healing process of the wounds, which World War II and the Nazi-Regime had afflicted on the people on both sides of the Atlantic.

The Consul General of Austria, Dr. Paul A. Eisler, sent this gracious message to be read at the reunion:

Austria's loss is the United States' gain! Even though Austria is sorry to have lost some of the most beautiful women as war brides to members of foreign military and civilian personnel, nevertheless, Austria rejoices in knowing of the success that the ladies have registered in their adopted countries.

Sir Oliver Wright, the British ambassador to the United States, had a personal reason to congratulate the war brides, for he had been able to observe their arrival in the U.S. firsthand:

MESSAGE FROM SIR OLIVER WRIGHT, BRITISH AMBASSADOR TO THE UNITED STATES

I am delighted to send greetings to the British War Brides and those from other nations reunited at Longbeach this weekend to celebrate the 40th Anniversary of the end of the Second World War.

I do so with particular pleasure since my first assignment in the British Diplomatic Service was as Vice-Consul in New York City from 1946-7 and so I was able to observe at first hand the remarkable wave of fresh blood coming to the United States and to share in the successes and failures, but overwhelmingly the successes, of these new pioneers. You deserve congratulations on many scores for yours have been a unique set of challenges, and a fascinating record of experiences which deserve to be told and celebrated.

Congratulations also on the work which many of you have done over the years to further international understanding and the welfare of your fellow citizens.

Finally, congratulations to you and the organisers of the War Brides Revisited on bringing about this imaginative gathering. This 40th Anniversary provides a fitting occasion for us all to remember the sacrifice of those who died for our liberty, as well as to give thanks for the reconciliation and prosperity which the post-war years have brought.

I am sure this will be a heart-warming occasion for everybody, and I send you my very best wishes.

A year and a half later, on September 25, 1986, war brides were reunited in Southampton, England, the port from which many had departed in 1946. Two Italian war brides and a French woman joined the 250 British women who attended this reunion. The four-day event included a visit to Tidworth, the camp where so many British brides had been processed for the journey to the U.S., including a stop at the Garrison Theatre, infamous in the memories of many war brides because of the humiliating medical examinations they had endured there. This time, however, the British army, long since in charge again at Tidworth, served a delicious cup of English tea and welcomed the returning brides, who laughed as they reminisced together and searched in vain for the quonset huts they had once occupied. The Carleton Hotel in Bournemouth, where large numbers of brides with babies were processed, also welcomed the brides back. During high tea at the Carleton, Vicky Candelaria, who was processed there with her baby daughter prior to boarding the *Queen Mary* on February 5, 1946, was awarded a long overdue medal for her wartime service with the Women's Royal Navy Service.

The reunion came to a close with Dame Vera Lynn singing *We'll meet again,* a promise echoed by many of the women as they departed for home. Home . . . which is now in America.

Yolande Dauphin with four of her five children on the day she received her Master's Degree. 1976. (Yolande Dauphin)

Gertrude Consten Reichenbach heads the Dutch Studies Program she founded at the University of Pennsylvania. (Chris Scibetta)

Pauline R. Julius from St. Johann im Pongau, Austria, working now as a Certified Operating Room Technologist. (Pauline Julius)

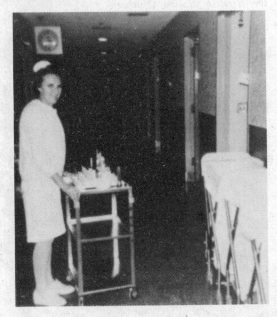

Mary Berthiaume from Bad Mitterndorff, Austria, working as a nurse in Massachusetts. (Mary Grill Berthiaume)

Velina Hasu Houston's mother is among a large group of Japanese and European war brides taking the oath of citizenship in Junction City, near Fort Riley, Kansas. (Velina Hasu Houston).

Annaliese Uhlig Tucker, actress, journalist, and author, in her home in Santa Cruz, California, came as a war bride from Germany in 1948.

Hostesses for Queen Mary *reunion, April 1985: Talvikki Manninen, Finland; Else Smith, Germany; Thelma Gailey, England; Penny Wood, England; Barbara Brisbin, England; Helen Thompson Colony, American Red Cross; Moyra Lindstrom, England; and Eloise Howell, England (seated).*

Tidworth Army Camp. As part of the GI brides reunion, war brides search in vain for the Quonset huts they lived in in 1946. September 1986. (Barbara Scibetta)

Appendix A

Locations from which World War II War Brides Originated

Africa
Albania
Algeria
Armenia
Australia
Austria
Belgium
Bulgaria
Burma
Canada
Central America
China
Czechoslovakia
Denmark
Egypt
England
Estonia
Finland
France
French Possessions in
   Africa

Germany, East and West
Greece
Hawaii
Hungary
Iceland
India
Iran
Iraq
Ireland
Italy
Japan
Latvia
Libya
Lithuania
Luxembourg
Mexico
Morocco
Netherlands
Newfoundland
New Zealand
Northern Ireland

Norway
Palestine
Papua/New Guinea
Philippines
Poland
Portugal
Puerto Rico
Rumania
Russia
Scotland
South Africa
South America
Spain
Sweden
Switzerland
Syria
Turkey
Wales
West Indies
Yugoslavia

Appendix B

Public Law 271: The War Brides Act

[CHAPTER 591]

AN ACT

December 28, 1945
[H. R. 4857]
[Public Law 271]

To expedite the admission to the United States of alien spouses and alien minor children of citizen members of the United States armed forces.

Be it enacted by the Senate and House of Representatives of the United States of America in Congress assembled, That notwithstanding any of the several clauses of section 3 of the Act of February 5, 1917, excluding physically and mentally defective aliens, and notwithstanding the documentary requirements of any of the immigration laws or regulations, Executive orders, or Presidential proclamations issued thereunder, alien spouses or alien children of United States citizens serving in, or having an honorable discharge certificate from the armed forces of the United States during the Second World War shall, if otherwise admissible under the immigration laws and if application for admission is made within three years of the effective date of this Act, be admitted to the United States: *Provided,* That every alien of the foregoing description shall be medically examined at the time of arrival in accordance with the provisions of section 16 of the Act of February 5, 1917, and if found suffering from any disability which would be the basis for a ground of exclusion except for the provision of this Act, the Immigration and Naturalization Service shall forthwith notify the appropriate public medical officer of the local community to which the alien is destined: *Provided further,* That the provisions of this Act shall not affect the duties of the United States Public Health Service so far as they relate to quarantinable diseases.

Sec. 2. Regardless of section 9 of the Immigration Act of 1924, any alien admitted under section 1 of this Act shall be deemed to be a nonquota immigrant as defined in section 4 (a) of the Immigration Act of 1924.

Sec. 3. Any alien admitted under section 1 of this Act who at any time returns to the United States after a temporary absence abroad shall not be excluded because of the disability or disabilities that existed at the time of that admission.

Sec. 4. No fine or penalty shall be imposed under the Act of February 5, 1917, except those arising under section 14, because of the transportation to the United States of any alien admitted under this Act.

Sec. 5. For the purpose of this Act, the Second World War shall be deemed to have commenced on December 7, 1941, and to have ceased upon the termination of hostilities as declared by the President or by a joint resolution of Congress.

Approved December 28, 1945.

Side notes:
Admission of certain aliens.
39 Stat. 875.
8 U. S. C. § 136; Supp. IV, § 136.

Medical examination on arrival.
39 Stat. 885.
8 U. S. C., Supp. IV, § 152.

Quarantinable diseases.

43 Stat. 157.
8 U. S. C. § 209.

43 Stat. 155.
8 U. S. C. § 204.

Readmission after temporary absence abroad.

Fines and penalties.
39 Stat. 884.
8 U. S. C. § 150.

Appendix C

Public Law 471: The Fiancées Act

[CHAPTER 520]

AN ACT

To facilitate the admission into the United States of the alien fiancées or fiancés of members of the armed forces of the United States.

June 29, 1946
[S. 2122]

[Public Law 471]

Be it enacted by the Senate and House of Representatives of the United States of America in Congress assembled, That on or before July 1, 1947, the alien fiancée or fiancé of a citizen of the United States who is serving in, or who has been honorably discharged from, the armed forces of the United States during World War II may be admitted into the United States with a passport visa as a nonimmigrant temporary visitor for a period of three months (unless in exceptional circumstances such period is extended by the Attorney General) under the provisions of subdivision 2 of section 3 of the Immigration Act approved May 26, 1924, as amended (43 Stat. 154; 8 U. S. C. 203) : *Provided,* That—

Alien fiancées or fiancés.
Admission into U. S.

8 U. S. C., Supp. V, § 203(2).
Conditions.

    (a) the alien is not subject to exclusion from the United States under the immigration laws;

    (b) the nonpreference portion of the quota to which the alien would be chargeable is exhausted at the time the alien applies for a visa;

    (c) the administrative authorities find that the alien is coming to the United States with a bona fide intention of being married to a citizen of the United States who is serving in, or who has been honorably discharged from, the armed forces of the United States during World War II ; and

    (d) the administrative authorities find that the parties to the proposed marriage are able and intend to contract a valid marriage within the period for which the alien is admitted.

SEC. 2. In the event the marriage does not occur within the period for which the alien was admitted, the alien shall be required to depart from the United States and upon failure to do so shall be deported at any time after entry in accordance with the provisions of sections 19 and 20 of the Immigration Act of February 5, 1917, as amended (39 Stat. 889-890; 54 Stat. 671-673; 56 Stat. 1044; 8 U. S. C. 155; 39 Stat. 890-891; 57 Stat. 511; 8 U. S. C. 156).

Deportation of alien.

57 Stat. 553.
8 U. S. C., Supp. V, §§ 155, 156.

SEC. 3. The Secretary of State shall have authority to prescribe regulations for the administration of the provisions of this Act which relate to the performance of functions by diplomatic or consular officers of the United States and he shall include in such regulations a requirement that the parties to a proposed marriage shall furnish satisfactory evidence to the American consular officer concerned, including sworn statements corroborated by other appropriate evidence showing that the parties have entered into a valid agreement to marry and are legally able and actually willing to conclude a valid marriage in the United States within a period of three months after the alien's arrival, or within such period as may be extended by the Attorney General.

Authority of Secretary of State.

Authority of Attorney General.

Sec. 4. The Attorney General shall have authority to prescribe regulations for the administration by the Immigration and Naturalization Service of the provisions of this Act in connection with the arrival of the aliens concerned at ports of entry in the United States, and he shall include in such regulations a requirement that the prospective American citizen spouse of an alien covered by the provisions of this Act shall furnish to the Commissioner of Immigration and Naturalization a suitable bond, which shall be in an amount sufficient to cover the cost of the deportation of the alien concerned, and which shall be forfeited to the United States if and when the alien becomes deportable, or shall be cancelled by the Commissioner upon receipt of satisfactory evidence that a valid marriage has been concluded, or that the alien has left the United States without expense to the said United States.

Period of World War II.

Sec. 5. For the purposes of this Act the period of World War II shall be considered as having started on September 1, 1939, and to have ended upon the formal conclusion thereof by a treaty of peace, or by the passage of a joint resolution of Congress, or by a proclamation by the President declaring an end to hostilities.

Approved June 29, 1946.

[CHAPTER 521]

June 29, 1946
[S. 2219]
[Public Law 472]

AN ACT

To extend for the period of one year the provisions of the District of Columbia Emergency Rent Act, approved December 2, 1941, as amended.

55 Stat. 788.
D. C. Code, Supp.
V, § 45-1601 (b).

Be it enacted by the Senate and House of Representatives of the United States of America in Congress assembled, That the Act entitled "An Act to regulate rents in the District of Columbia, and for other purposes", approved December 2, 1941, as amended, is further amended by striking out in section 1 (b) thereof the figure "1946" and inserting in lieu thereof "1947".

Approved June 29, 1946.

Appendix D

Contributors

Special thanks to all the war brides and grooms, both those listed below and those who requested anonymity, for participating in our study.

ALGERIA

Brown, Paulette
Carpenter, Francine
Lang, Nadia
Sotnik, Alichka

AUSTRALIA

Amestoy, Joan
Baase, Joyce
Battle, Doreen
Calvetti, Veronica
Cherry, Lillian
Dixon, Nydia
Dlugosinski, Molly
Fletcher, Beryl
Foltz, Dorothy
Frey, Stella
Gardner, Norma
Greer, Aileen
Heely, Isobel
Hexom, Jane
Hyde, Helen

Indelicato, Yvonne
Kiefer, Madge
Klaren, Peggy
Lagala, Norma
Miller, Beryl
Minahan, Mavis
McClellan, Joy
McIntire, Betty
Neumann, Joanne
Perucci, Irene
Pine, Shirley
Preder, Grace
Raum, Shirley
Rourke, Edna
Rycyk, Barbara

Schiappa, Marjorie
Schommer, Mollie
Selby, June
Stern, Grace
Stone, Joyce
Tronic, Shirley
Udelhofen, Alice
Valee, Muriel
Walsh, Sheila
Yescavage, Gert
Young, Norma
Zenchyk, Lorraine

AUSTRIA

Berthiaume, Margarete
Berthiaume, Mary
Braeske, Hilde M.
Conner, Gisela
Conner, Katherine
Cycyk, Margarete
Dvorshock, Gertrude
Fitzell, Margarethe

Fox, Charlotte
Guidry, Ingrid
Hixon, Maria
Jensen, Elisabeth
Julius, Pauline
Knight, Maria
Rafferty, Julie
Robichaud, Hilde

Siebert, Ingeborg
Simmons, Lucia
Simpson, Elfriede
Swift, Maria
VanSciver, Elizabeth
Wall, Madeleine
Weaver, Adele
Webb, Ella

BELGIUM

Baker, Georgette
Bustillos, Jacqueline
Choat, Clemence
Gardner, Sylvia
Gumina, Elsa

Howland, Simone
Kergis, Carmen
Sinclair, Josette
Smyth, Anna
Stefaniak, Esther

Thompson, Julia
Turney, Georgette
Wilken, Angele

CANADA
Barker, Lillian   Bullock, Alice

CHINA
Dent, Alice   Weed, Joan

CZECHOSLOVAKIA
Avery, Mary   Lucas, Ann   Watson, Liba
Korda, Ingrid (Hardy)   St. Perry, Ernestine
Honey, Elisabeth   Twardowski, Gertrude

DENMARK
Nielsen, Jørgen

EIRE
Lancaster, Phyllis   Munger, Esther

ENGLAND

Allenson, Betty	Browning, Madge	Dammling, May Ann
Amundson, Julia	Burgess, Millicent	Davis, Betty
Anstey, Rose	Burke, Brenda	Degnan, Olive
Arrieta, Betty	Burkett, Mary	Deuink, Monica
Arthur, Barbara	Burlew, Iris	Dieckerhoff, Gwen
Armstrong, Kathleen	Burwell, Doreen	DiFalco, Helga
Astrella, Mary	Cain, Ann	DiNaro, Vicky
Bachman, Betty	Candelaria, Vicky	Doak, Evelyn
Bargout, Marjorie	Capek, Marion	Draper, Phyllis
Bartron, Audrey	Care, Dorothy	Dunn, Sheila
Beaver, Sylvia	Carter, Olive	Dyer, Joan
Berdo, Rosemary	Cater, Joan	Eason, Veronica
Biggs, Jean N.	Chaffee, Mary	Eberly, Vicky
Bivens, Nora	Clark, Josephine	Edler, Norma
Blanchard, Lilian	Coffman, Mary	Eeles, Betty
Blashaw, Nita	Cohen, Pearl	Ellis, Roy
Boren, Louise	Colao, Edna	Evans, Emily
Bradley, Dorothy	Coleman, Vera	Eyles, Helen
Bradshaw, Mary	Collins, Edna	Faraglia, Mary
Brandmarker, Beryl	Coppinger, Lalli	Farley, Iris
Bray, Joan	Cornwell, Jean	Farmer, Edna
Breaux, Grace	Cornwell, Marion	Fehn, Irene
Brekke, Rosemary	Cottone, Margaret	Ferus, Pat
Brock, Barbara	Cox, Jeanne	Finlayson, Mary
Brown, Ann	Cress, Kathleen	Fitch, Ruth
Brown, Margaret	Cye, Hilda	Fitzpatrick, Eileen
Brown, May	Dahler, Jean	Flynn, Elsie

Folmar, Ivy
Franklin, Theresa
Fritsch, Violet
Furones, Beryl
Gailey, Thelma
Gerber, Mary
Gerdus, Margaret
Gier, Vera
Gillam, Grace
Ginnis, Muriel
Giuffre, Olive
Glasser, Ellen
Goldberg, Leonie
Gordon, Edna
Gradisher, Agnes
Graham, Stella
Griggers, Betty
Grissom, Betty
Gross, Constance
Grove, Doreen
Hafner, Joan
Hagan, Rose
Hall, Ellen
Hamrick, Peggy
Harisiades, Coline
Harrah, Peggy
Harrington, Nancy
Harris, June
Harris, Sylvia
Hart, Brenda
Hasty, Brenda
Hatzinger, Crystal
Hedrick, Pauline
Hegele, Alwyn
Herman, Florence
Hersey, Lilian
Hettinga, Connie
Heyn, Beryl
Hill, Wynn
Himebauch, Ursula
Hittle, Ivy
Hobbs, Pat
Hockman, Doris
Hogeland, Edith
Horban, Heather
Houran, Enid
Howard, Iris
Howell, Eloise
Huck, Miriam

Hurtado, Jeanne
Huster, Audrey
Hutchinson, Doris
Ice, Joan
Ingersoll, Molly
Ital, Erica
Iverson, Gladys
Johnson, Marguerite
Johnson, Mary
Johnson, Nora
Johnston, Mona
Jones, Irene
Jones, Pamela
Jordan, Joyce
Judson, Doreen
Kaufman, Naida
Kennedy, Thelma
Kern, Joyce
Kerns, Vera
Kiernan, Christine
King, Elsie
King, Violet
Kirby, Linda
Knapp, Antonie
Koerting, Ellen
Krzyzaniak, Pam
Law, Kathleen
Legon, Rita
Leighty, Betty
Leroy, Iris
Lewis, Dilys
Lind, Dorothy
Lindevig, Doris
Lindstrom, Moyra
Lockshin, Hannah
Long, Vera
Lundy, Irene
MacDonald, Hilda
Maio, Irene
Malloy, Marjorie
Marble, Joan
Marshall, Christina
Martin, Kathleen
Matherne, Ruth
McChesney, Pat
McGibbon, Jean
McKinney, Lena
Meade, Sylvia
Meredith, Frances

Meyers, Lillian
Michel, Barbara
Michelsen, Lilian
Miller, Hannah
Moore, Jean
Moore, Joyce B.
Moore, Joyce R.
Morris, Elsie
Mountford, Eileen
Mueller, Audrey
Muller, Maureen
Mulloy, Yvonne
Myers, Lillian
Myers, Mary
Navolio, Joyce
Newman, Jean
Newman, Jennie
Nichols, Mary
Norway, Cynthia
Ochocki, Sheila
Ogozalek, Joan
Orton, Eileen
Ozsvath, Fran
Palermo, Irene
Parker, Ruby
Patterson, Pearl
Payne, Frances
Peattie, Joyce
Perez, Rose Anne
Peters, Betty
Pfleuger, Agnes
Plym, Ellen
Porter, Joyce
Porterfield, Joan
Powell, Joan
Rayner, Donald
Rendell, Margaret
Rich, Lily
Richards, Gloria
Roberts, Elizabeth
Roberts, Sybil
Roe, Eileen
Rojas, Mary
Romano, June
Roop, Irene
Ross, Cecilia
Roth, Maureen
Sahlin, Ann
Schepers, Margaret

Schoenstein, Moira
Schommer, Mollie
Selhorst, Joan
Sell, Evelyn
Showers, Pauline
Siddons, Irene
Silverman, Miriam
Simper, Mary
Simpson, Mollie
Sky, Anastasia
Sleik, Kathleen
Smith, Audrey
Smith, Barbara
Smoker, Kathleen
Snow, Jean
Snyder, Terry
Sostak, Alice
Spinner, Mary
Sprinkle, Mary
Stanizzi, Elsie
Steeby, Gladys
Steel, Dorothy
Steinbach, Audrey
Steinke, Winifred

Stenehjem, Edna
Stettler, Mary
Stevens, Joan
Stievo, Betty
Stiner, Margaret
Stratton, Monica
Straub, Winifred
Sturm, Cecilia
Suesz, Audrey
Sullivan, Jean
Summers, Margaret
Szymonik, Frances
Taylor, Eileen
Tegg, Ann
Thomas, Kathleen
Thompson, Elena
Thorn, Josephine
Toeppen, Elizabeth
Totman, Phyllis
Tricinella, Iris
Truluck, Irene
Tubman, Betty
Tune, Margaret
Turner, Marcella

Upchurch, Eunice
Varilly, Betty
Varney, Violet
Vogts, Mary
Wade, Anne
Wagner, Beryl
Wakefield, Marion
Walker, Gladys
Watkins, May
Weir, Bertha
Whitcomb, Audrey
White, Marie
Whitlatch, Irene
Whittaker, Doris
Williams, Rosemary
Wilson, Eileen
Winer, Cissie
Wolforth, Alice
Wood, Joan
Wurm, Betty
Yeater, Barbara
Zabrowski, Edith
Zobkin, Freda
Zweig, Nancy

FINLAND
Manninen, Talvikki

FRANCE
Bernar, Monique
Bollens, Colette
Brenton, Lucette
Brock, Lisette
Brozak, Alice
Buchanan, Christiane
Buckley, Suzanne
Byham, Olga
Calviello, Madeleine
Campbell, Jacqueline
Coghlan, Huguette
Cormier, Gilberte
Dauphin, Yolande
Davis, Andrée
Delongchamp, Germaine
DiNardo, Christiane
Elholm, Françoise
Garrett, Madeleine

Gillikin, Eliane
Goldberg, Pierrette
Hines, Simone
Howard, Miquette
Hufford, Denise
Inman, Marie
Kammert, Janine
Knapton, Antoinette
Koehler, Raymonde
Labermeier, Yvette
Leboeuf, Janine
Loeffler, Suzanne
Lovett, Henriette
Malenfant, Yvette
Markus, Simone
Mautone, Josette
Migden, Simonne
Molina, Andrée

Muller, C.
McGrath, Simone
Pazik, Victoria
Plamondon, Rachel
Post, Gabrielle
Reeves, Josiane
Savage, Madeleine
Schorr, Denise
Sielicki, Christiane
Smith, Renée
Studey, Huguette
Theodore, Yvonne
Trunzo, Olga
Wadas, Irene
Walden, Jacqueline
Wohlschlegel, Liliane
Wszalek, Leonie

GERMANY

Allen, Ilse Eva
Anastos, Ingeborg
Bals, Goldie
Beckner, Elfriede
Biskup, Herta
Blake, Gisela
Blaze, Ilse
Bohling, Margarete
Bouchard, Margot
Brahm, Irmgard
Brandstatter, Bertha
Breckenridge, Lore
Bremer, Irma H.
Brooks, Helga
Chytka, Louise
Clark, Anneliese
Clements, Doris
Clifton, Lydia
Curatolo, Isolde
Curtis, Lieselotte
Cutcher, Lya
Ditzler, Marie
Dodson, Dorothea
Donahue, Lily
Drexler, Anne
Duchatel, Burgunde
Galbraith, Christine
Galvez, Elizabeth
Gibbs, Hilda

Gosler, Anne Marie
Graham, Paula
Grant, Paula
Gribas, Therese
Hawthorne, Gisela
Herman, Erika
Higgs, Maria
Holden, Eva
Horton, Jutta
Hunter, Brigitte
Hunter, Ursula
Iobst, Margot
Johnstone, Herma
Kreitl, Elisabeth
Krempl, Franziska
Lane, Henriette
Lathrop, Ina
Ludwig, Sonny
Mack, Ruth
Militello, Katharina
Mills, Helga
McGrath, Connie
Parker, Lia
Parkin, Karola
Pike, Irene
Prefontaine, Elfriede
Rahmer, Eugenie
Randall, Annie
Reed, Maria

Relation, Helga
Retzer, Irene
Schroeder, Margarete
Scott, Anna Barbara
Shelton, Regina
Shiffrar, Rosemarie
Slaughter, Lisa
Smith, Brigitta
Smith, Else H.
Stone, Liselotte
Sussel, Siri
Swanson, Hildegard
Tannenbaum, Hanneliese
Tappan, Gerda H.
Tetlow, Hildegard
Thomas, Hildegard
Torrealday, Elizabeth
Turner, Henriette
Tyson, Elizabeth
Tucker, Anneliese Uhlig
Voss, Brunhild
Wahl, Gitta
Williams, Margot
Williamson, Judith
Wolffram, Elfriede
Wooster, Emma
Yount, Karin
Zombek, Liane

HUNGARY

Fisher, Ilonka

Rogers, Elly

Zamiar, Kitty

ITALY

Andreatta, Enza
Andreottola, Tina
Billo, Diana
Brixner, Maria
Chiaro, Renata
Conicella, Romilda
D'Angelo, Ines
Fields, Mirella
Gioseffi, Maria

Gonzales, Anna
Goudy, Elda
Guarino, Bruna
Herrera, Costanza
Kellinger, Cesi
Knutson, Armida
Losee, Sirena
Lucatorto, Rosalia
McMullin, Iolanda

O'Dell, Liliana
Pieron, Brigitte
Rando, Bruna
Riggs, Iole
Ruggiero, Filomena
Spinoso, Maria
Spitler, Luisa
Underwood, Dina
Wheeler, Mary

JAPAN

Anderson, Aiko
Gentile, Cheiko
Grimes, Terry
Hamelin, Tomoko
McKnight, Veronica
Rogers, Hertha
Wittrock, Kyo

LATVIA

te Groen, Illona

MOROCCO

Tonkin, Eliane

NETHERLANDS

Allen, Carla M.
Goode, Elisabeth
Reichenbach, Gertrude
Stephens, Jeanne G.

NEW GUINEA

Liptak, Lydia

NEW ZEALAND

Asher, Ingeborg
Ashmead, Fran
Channel, Dawn
Kelley, Annie May
Miller, Marjory
Noble, Nancy
Pearson, Florence
Sansom, Nena

NORTHERN IRELAND

Carlson, Marion
Corda, Jean
Frantz, Betty

PHILIPPINES

Carmona, Carrie
Montesclaros, Gloria

POLAND

Applebaum, Ruth
Balicki, Barbara
Collins, Sonja L.
Morgan, Margot

RUSSIA

Carpenter, Vera
Ritter, Mania
White, Rosa

SCOTLAND

Barrie, Chris
Brisbin, Barbara
Cortner, Chris
Dolleman, Mary
O'Brien, Evelyn
Oldendorph, Maisie
Schoonmaker, Beverley
Walker, Agnes

SWEDEN

Condur, Karin

SWITZERLAND

Critser, Verena
Edgar, Madeleine
  (Crighton)
Hunt, Nelly
Maginn, Elsbeth
Pavlich, Jeannette

WALES

Allen, Beryl
Chushcoff, Gwen
Donelson, Yvonne
Dulaney, Eve
Hinze, Joyce

Janise, Mona
Lanier, Hazel
Morrison, Gwyneth
Pierce, Freda

Pillman, Mary
Roberts-Swauger, Catherine
Voyvodich, Doreen

Notes

Chapter 1

1. See introduction regarding war bride estimates. Department of the Army, the Chief of Military History and the Center of Military History, Washington, D.C., cites Longmate's estimates for Great Britain: 30,000 wartime transports, 70,000 postwar. *History of the USAF in the Far East 1943–1945,* Gen. Hq. Far East Command, Military Intelligence Section General Staff, 8-5.1 AAC1 2305, Appendix X, gives estimate of 6,000 American-Australian marriages up to the end of 1944, while E. D. Potts and A. Potts, *Yanks Down Under 1941–45,* p. 362, estimate 12,000 marriages, noting that possibly one in five wives elected to stay in Australia, at least temporarily. Memo to the War Department, dated February 27, 1945, from CG, USAF, Pacific Ocean Areas, Ft. Shafter, TH, Nr. R53519 notes "potential total demand of 1061 wives and 155 children" for transportation from New Zealand.
2. *The New York Times,* April 27, 1944.
3. *Newsweek,* May 1, 1944.
4. Norman Longmate, *The G.I.'s: The Americans in Britain 1942–1945* (London: Hutchinson & Co., Ltd., 1975), p. 284.
5. Ibid., p. 284.
6. Ibid., p. 117.
7. John Hammond Moore, *Over-Sexed, Over-Paid, and Over Here: Americans in Australia 1941–1945* (St. Lucia, Queensland: University of Queensland Press, 1981), p. 212.
8. Longmate, p. 237.

Chapter 2

1. *Newsweek,* May 1, 1944, p. 30.
2. *Newsweek,* April 6, 1942, p. 22.
3. *The New York Times,* March 10, 1946, p. 9.
4. Cir. #20, Hq USAFFE, July 28, 1942.
5. AAC1 2305, *History of the USAF in the Far East 1943–1945,* Appendix X.
6. *The New York Times,* November 26, 1944, p. 20.
7. AG 291.1, September 11, 1943, OB-S-SPGAL-M, November 24, 1943, Major Gen. J. A. Ulio, The Adjutant General.
8. Cir. #31, Hq USAFFE, 1944, AG USAFFE 291.1.
9. *The New York Times,* January 26, 1944, p. 5.

10. *Newsweek,* May 1, 1944, p. 30.
11. Longmate, p. 340.
12. FO 371/61021, AN509. *Reynolds News,* February 9, 1947.
13. FO AN668/13/45, Hector McNeil, M.P., Foreign Office, to David Gammans, M.P., April 30, 1947.
14. *The New York Times,* March 10, 1946, p. 15.
15. *The New York Times,* May 24, 1946, p. 20.
16. AGO 291.12, June 28, 1942.
17. AGO 291, February 23, 1946.
18. *The Oxford Mail,* March 29, 1946.
19. *Newsweek,* September 18, 1944, p. 92.

Chapter 3
1. *Newsweek,* October 22, 1945, p. 58.
2. Unidentified U.S. news article, October 14, 1945.
3. *Life,* November 19, 1945, pp. 45–48.
4. *Newsweek,* October 22, 1945, p. 56.
5. *The New York Times,* December 22, 1944, p. 10.
6. Unidentified, undated Australian news articled entitled "GI Wives Make Call," from Mrs. Norma Lagala, who was among the demonstrators.
7. AG 291.1, letter to Senator Morse from Mr. David W. Keys, dated February 25, 1946.
8. OSW 510, letter to the Hon. Robert P. Patterson from William R. Thom, Representative in Congress, 18th District, November 9, 1945.
9. Longmate, p. 345.
10. Voyage report, Fred Stindt, Chief Purser, S.S. *Lurline,* September 1945.
11. Chester Wardlow, *The Transportation Corps: Movements, Training, and Supply* (Washington, D.C.: Office of the Chief of Military History, Dept. of the Army, 1956), Vol. 6, Pt. 5, C. 2, p. 233.
12. AN 564, FO 51617, summary of report for American Ambassador after meeting between General Betts, U.S. Army and Mr. Stebbins, U.S. Embassy, called by Sir Frank Newsam, British Home Office, regarding divorces initiated by GIs against British wives, March 19, 1946.
13. AN 782, telegram No. 444 from Lord Halifax to the Washington Foreign Office, sent January 19, 1946, in answer to FO telegrams, Nos. 58 AN3793/7/45 and 70 AN34/345.
14. Wardlow, p. 232.
15. Ibid., p. 233.
16. Ibid., p. 233.
17. NND 740112, SPTOM 513.4DF, to Operations Div., WDGS, from

Movements Div., OCT., March 24, 1945, Donald E. Fare, Colonel, Transportation Corps, Chief, Movements Division.

18. FO 371/51621, September 24, 1948, to H. McNeil, Esq., M.P., London, from Michael Stewart, FO, Washington, D.C.; and FO 371/51622, October 28, 1946, letter to D. A. Logan, FO, London, from W. J. Ford, American Vice Consul, American Embassy, London.

19. Memorandum for the Assistant Secretary of War from W. D. Styer, Major General, USA, Commanding, attached to AG 291.1, September 1943, OB-S-SPGAL-M, KLS/gc-2B-939-Pentagon, dated November 24, 1943.

20. FO 371/68048, letter to Foreign Office from W. C. Duncan, ex-S.Ldr., R.A.F., D.F.C., undated.

21. FO 371/68048 (attached to above letter).

22. Ibid.

23. AN57-51617, *Daily Mail*, January 2, 1946.

24. FO 371/51621, "L.A. Vet Blames British Camp in Deaths of Babies," *Los Angeles Herald*, May 27, 1946.

25. Rose I. Daniels, *Journal of Social Casework*, Vol. 28, July 1947, pp. 243–249.

26. War Department press release, January 18, 1946, ARC files: *American Red Cross World War II War Bride Activities*.

Chapter 4

1. The first official voyages of the *Argentina* and the *Queen Mary* received a great deal of publicity and were well documented. Personal recollections were mainly from the war brides interviewed, while statistical information was taken from these public sources and documents: *The Transportation Corps: Operations Overseas,* Joseph Bykofsky and Harold Larson, Office of the Chief of Military History, Dept. of the Army, Washington, D.C., AR M-A, OCMH WAR-10, p. 374; "The Immigration of G.I. Brides," Ernest E. Salisbury, *Monthly Review*, May 1946, p. 305–308; "Pilgrims of 1946," Lt. O'Donald Mays, *Army Transportation Journal*, May 1946, p. 2–3 and 36; "Adapting Casework to the Needs of War Brides in England," Rose I. Daniels, *Journal of Social Casework*, Vol. 28, July 1947, p. 243–249; *The New York Times,* January 17 and 27, 1946, February 2, 3, 4, 5, 11, 1946; *Life,* Vol. 20, No. 7, February 18, 1946, p. 27–31; *Newsweek,* January 23 and 27, 1946, and February 18, 1946, p. 2–4; *The Stars and Stripes,* January 24 and 26, 1946, and February 2 and 5, 1946. Magazines and newspapers in Great Britain: *Picture Post*, Vol. 30, No. 7, February 16, p. 7–11; *The Illustrated Sunday News,* Vol. 208, February 16, 1946, p. 115; *Herald,* January

23, 24, 25, 1946, and February 5, 1946; *Daily Mail,* January 23 and 24, 1946; *Chronicle,* January 25, 1946; *Sunday Graphic,* January 27, 1946; and ship newsletters.

2. *The New York Times,* March 16, 1946, p. 17.

3. *Belfast Telegraph,* February 3, 1946, March 1 and 6, 1946; *Irish Independent,* March 5, 1946; *Northern Whig,* March 5, 1946.

4. FO 61017, Letter from Mrs. W. Henry France, National Hq. English-Speaking Union of the U.S., January 20, 1947, to B.E.F. Gage, Esq., Foreign Office, London.

5. *San Francisco Chronicle,* March 4 and 7, 1946.

6. Voyage report, Fred Stindt, Chief Purser, S.S. *Lurline,* March 22, 1946, war bride transport.

7. Letter of commendation from Mrs. Isabelle Wade forwarded to Mr. H. Gallagher, Vice President, Matson Navigation Company, by Fred Stindt, Chief Purser, on June 17, 1945, regarding S.S. *Lurline,* voyage 231.

8. *San Francisco Chronicle,* March 4, 1946, p. 3.

9. FN Hq ASF, Office of the Judge Advocate General, Washington, D.C., October 22, 1945, SPJGA 1945/10408, Memorandum for the Chief of Transportation from J. W. Huyssoon, Col., JAGD, Chief of Military Affairs Division; SPJGA 1942/5718, 291.1, December 4, 1942, Memorandum for the Director of Military Personnel, S.O.S., from Myron C. Cramer, Major Gen., The Judge Advocate General.

10. *The New York Times,* July 5, 1946, p. 5.

11. *The New York Times,* November 11, 1946, p. 18.

12. *The New York Times,* January 22, 1946, p. 7.

13. Unidentified news article from Mrs. Christine Kiernan, who was a passenger aboard the flight.

Chapter 5

1. *The Oxford Mail,* April 12, 1946.

2. "A Short Guide to the United States, an American Red Cross Introduction for War Brides," part of a war bride talk series, undated.

Chapter 6

1. Alistair Cooke's comments as recorded in *Wives Aweigh,* a newsletter for war brides aboard the *Queen Mary,* February 28, 1946.

Chapter 7

1. Norman Lewis, *Naples '44* (New York: Pantheon Books, a Division of Random House, Inc., 1978), p. 30.

2. Anna Gonzales did sponsor two of her brothers when they immigrated to the U.S. later, but her parents never joined her here.

3. Margaret Bourke-White, *They Called It "Purple Heart Valley": A Combat Chronicle of the War in Italy* (New York: Simon and Schuster, 1944), p. 106.

4. H. Stuart Hughes, *The United States and Italy*, 3rd ed. (Cambridge, MA: Harvard University Press, 1979), p. 12.

5. Giuseppe Mammarella, *Italy After Fascism: A Political History, 1943–1965* (Notre Dame, IN: University of Notre Dame Press, 1966), p. 120.

6. Lewis, p. 115.

7. Robert M. Hill and Elizabeth Craig Hill, *In the Wake of War* (University, Alabama: The University of Alabama Press, 1982), p. 99.

8. Lewis, p. 193.

9. John Horne Burns, *The Gallery* (New York: Harper & Brothers Publishers, 1947), pp. 266–267.

10. *War Brides and Their Shipment to the United States* (Occupation Forces in Europe Series, 1945–46, Office of the Chief Historian, European Command), p. 3.

11. AG-330.14, November 8, 1945, Chief of Staff Directive.

12. John Hammond Moore, "Italian POWs in America: War is Not Always Hell," *Prologue,* Vol. 8, Fall 1976, p. 141.

13. Moore, p. 149.

14. Moore, p. 149.

15. Ralph A. Buxco and Douglas D. Adler, "German and Italian Prisoners of War in Utah and Idaho," *Utah Historical Quarterly,* Vol. 39, 1971, p. 64.

Chapter 8

1. A. J. Liebling, *Liebling Abroad* (New York: Playboy Press, 1981), p. 400–401.

2. Ibid., p. 405.

3. Ibid., p. 563.

4. *France-Amérique,* March 9, 1947, p. 4.

5. *Life,* April 19, 1945.

6. *Libération Soir,* December 10, 1944, p. 1.

7. *The New York Times,* February 11, 1946.

8. *Life,* April 22, 1946.

9. Theodore H. White, *In Search of History—A Personal Adventure* (New York: Warner Books, 1978), pp. 264–265.

10. Edwin R. W. Hale and John Frayne Turner, *The Yanks Are Coming* (New York: Hippocrene Books, Inc., 1983), p. 137.
11. *The New York Times,* May 28, 1946.
12. DOS File #811-22/4-2645, from George Platt Waller, Chargé d'Affaires ad interim, Luxembourg, to Secretary of State, Washington, D.C., letter No. 151, April 26, 1945.
13. *The New York Times,* January 19, 1946, p. 19.
14. Ibid., March 1, 1946, p. 6.
15. Ibid., March 7, 1946, p. 15.
16. Ibid., June 11, 1946, p. 25.

Chapter 9
 1. Richard Fawkes, *Fighting for a Laugh* (London: Macdonald and Jane's, 1978), p. 180.
 2. Carl J. Friedrich and Associates, *American Experiences in Military Government in World War II* (New York: Rinehart and Company, Inc., Publishers, 1948), p. 384.
 3. Douglas Botting et al., *The Aftermath: Europe* (Alexandria, VA: Time-Life Books, Inc., 1983), p. 51–52.
 4. Hans Habe, *Our Love Affair with Germany* (New York: G. P. Putnam's Sons, 1953), p. 10.
 5. Maria Higgs, *Maria* (Badger Press, Inc., 1981), p. 5–6.
 6. Regina Maria Shelton, *To Lose a War* (Carbondale, IL: Southern Illinois University Press, 1982), p. 45.
 7. Marc Hillel, *Die Invasion der Be-Freier, Die GIs in Europa 1942–1947* (Hamburg: Ernst Kabel Verlag, 1983), p. 129.
 8. *The Stars and Stripes,* May 11, 1948, p. 5.
 9. *The New York Times,* September 21, 1945.
10. *The New York Times,* March 4, 1946.
11. *The New York Times,* March 16, 1946.
12. Habe, p. 10.
13. AG 291.1 GAP-AGP, Subject: Nonmarriage Policy, Military History Branch, National Archives. Letters: October 16, 1945, Brig. Gen. R. B. Lovett to Adjutant General, Washington, DC; June 29, 1944 Maj. Gen. J. A. Ulio, Adjutant General, to Commanding Generals, Overseas Commands; January 25, 1946, Col. C. E. Hixon, Director Military Personnel Division; October 23 1945, Brigadier General L. H. Sims to Adjutant General Farle P. Butles.
14. *The Stars and Stripes,* May 16, 1948, p. 1 & 5.
15. *Life,* June 17, 1946, p. 12.
16. *The New York Times,* June 3, 9, 17, and 22, 1946.

17. *The New York Times,* June 13, 1946.
18. *The Stars and Stripes,* May 5, 1948.
19. Habe, p. 11.

Chapter 10

1. AG 291.1. September 5, 1946, restricted letter from General McNarney to War Department.
2. *The New York Times,* January 23, 1946, p. 2.
3. *The New York Times,* January 18, 1946, p. 8.
4. AG 291.1. November 4, 1946, memorandum for Judge Advocate General, prepared by J. W. Hayssoon, Col. JAGD, Chief, Military Affairs Group.
5. AG 291.1. November 26, 1946, Personal for McNarney from Eisenhower.
6. AG 291.1. December 5, 1946, Personal for Eisenhower from McNarney.
7. AG 291.1. December 5, 1946, Personal for McNarney from Eisenhower.
8. *The New York Times,* December 11, 1946.
9. AG 291.1. September 12, 1945, letter to Senator W. Lee O'Daniel.
10. AG 291.1. October 11, 1945, Maj. Gen. Edward F. Witsell, Acting Adjutant General, to Senator W. Lee O'Daniel.
11. AG 291.1. February 5, 1947, Maj. Gen. Edward F. Witsell, Adjutant General, to Mr. Harry Kennedy.
12. Maria Higgs, *Maria* (Badger Press, Inc., 1981), p. 17.
13. *The New York Times,* February 27, 1947.
14. Douglas Botting et al., *The Aftermath: Europe* (Alexandria, VA: Time-Life Books, Inc., 1983), p. 52.
15. Although other countries had similar laws revoking a woman's citizenship when she married a foreign national, only German women consistently mentioned this as a major problem.
16. Anneliese Uhlig, *Rosenkavaliers Kind: Eine Frau und Drei Karrieren* (Munich: F. A. Herbig, 1977), p. 249–250.
17. Higgs, p. 19.
18. Uhlig, pp. 252–253.
19. *The Stars and Stripes,* January 3, 1948, p. 3.

Chapter 11

1. Jeff Jordan, "She Escaped Nazis, Russians," *Sunday World Herald,* June 20, 1982, p. 1.

2. OPD 291.1, July 21, 1945, memo recapping State Department correspondence, subject: Treatment of Soviet-born Wives of Liberated POWs.
3. *The New York Times,* March 22, 1947, p. 4.
4. "Displaced Persons," *Life,* May 14, 1945, p. 88A.
5. Joseph B. Schechtman, *Postwar Population Transfers in Europe 1945–1955* (Philadelphia: University of Pennsylvania Press, 1962), p. 195.
6. Schechtman, p. 37.
7. Ingrid Hardy, *Plucky Lady: Memoirs of a Czech War Bride,* unpublished manuscript, p. 23.
8. Hardy, p. 24.
9. Hardy, p. 26–28.
10. Hardy, p. 29.
11. Hardy, p. 38.
12. Hardy, p. 40–42.
13. Talvikki Manninen, *Refuge Under the Boot* (New York: Vantage Press, 1985), p. 178.
14. Manninen, p. 189–191.
15. Manninen, p. 201.
16. Manninen, p. 210.
17. Manninen, p. 223.
18. Manninen, p. 228–230.
19. Jean R. Komaiko, "A War Bride Looks at America," *Family Living,* June 5, 1955, p. 35.

Chapter 12

1. Masataka Kosaka, *A History of Postwar Japan* (New York: Kodansha International, Ltd., 1982), pp. 28–29, 35.
2. James A. Michener, *Voice of Asia* (New York: Random House, 1951), p. 20.
3. Edwin O. Reischauer, *The United States and Japan* (Cambridge, MA: Harvard University Press, 1965), p. 221.
4. Kosaka, p. 35.
5. *San Francisco Chronicle,* September 22, 1945, p. 2.
6. *The New York Times,* June 3, 1946, p. 5.
7. *The New York Times,* January 2, 1946, p. 1.
8. *Life,* Vol. 19, No. 12, September 17, 1945, p. 115.
9. Lindesay Parrott, *The New York Times Magazine,* "Now a Japanese Woman Can Be a Cop," June 2, 1946, p. 18.
10. Michener, *Voice of Asia,* p. 20.

11. *Peace is Our Duty—Accounts of What War Can Do to Man,* compiled by the Youth Division of Soka Gakkai (Tokyo: *The Japan Times,* 1977), translated by Richard L. Gage, 1982, p. 220.
12. *The New York Times,* April 3, 1946, p. 14.
13. *Chicago Daily News* article reprinted in *San Francisco Chronicle,* September 1945.
14. Kosaka, p. 36.
15. *The New York Times,* July 25, 1946, p. 4.
16. *Life,* December 3, 1945, p. 109.
17. *The New York Times,* July 12, 1946, p. 9.
18. *Peace is Our Duty,* p. 221.
19. *Life,* December 3, 1945, p. 109.
20. Ernest J. Sternglass, *Secret Fallout* (New York: McGraw-Hill, 1981), p. 161.
21. *San Francisco Chronicle,* February 2, 1977, p. 14.

Chapter 13
 1. Jack Chen, *The Chinese of America* (San Francisco: Harper & Row, 1982), p. 161.
 2. Ibid., p. 202–203.
 3. Daniel Kubat with Ursula Merklander and Ernst Gehmacker, *The Politics of Migration Policies* (New York: Center for Migration Studies, 1979), p. 53.
 4. Chen, p. 205.
 5. Ibid., p. 206.
 6. *The New York Times,* April 12, 1946, p. 29.
 7. Judy Yung, *Chinese Women of America: A Pictorial History* (Seattle, WA: University of Washington Press, 1986), p. 81–85.
 8. Chen, p. 212.
 9. Louis Chu, *Eat a Bowl of Tea* (Seattle, WA: University of Washington Press, 1979).
10. Anna Chennault, *A Thousand Springs* (New York: Paul S. Eriksson, Inc. 1962).
11. U.S. Dept. of Justice, Immigration and Naturalization Service, Table 9A, *Chinese War Brides Admitted under the War Brides Act of December 28, 1945.*
12. Bruno Lasker, *Asia on the Move* (New York: Henry Holt & Co., 1945), p. 70.
13. Gorel A. Gruner, *The Philippines and the U.S.* (Norman, Oklahoma: University of Oklahoma Press, 1951), p. 261.

14. Ibid., p. 271.
15. Bok-Lim C. Kim, Amy Izuno Okamura, Naomi Ozawa, and Virginia Forrest, *Women in Shadows* (La Jolla, CA: National Committee Concerned with Asian Wives of U.S. Servicemen, 1981), p. 28.
16. DeWitt MacKenzie, *The Associated Press News Annual 1946, Vol. II* (New York: Rinehart & Co., Inc., 1947), p. 488.
17. Unidentified article entitled "Not 'Hanggang Pier' Only," dated September 22, 1946, from Carrie Carmona.
18. Circular No. 57, signed by Brig. Gen. D. L. Weart, GSC, Deputy Chief of Staff, Rear Echelon Hq. U.S. Forces, China Theater, April 28, 1945.
19. Chen, p. 205.
20. AG 291.1, ref. CSLLD 014.33-27, letter to Senator Kenneth S. Wherry from Col. C. G. Blakeney, GSC, October 10, 1949.
21. MacKenzie, *The Associated Press Annual 1946,* pp. 164–165.
22. James A. Michener, "Pursuit of Happiness by a GI and a Japanese," *Life,* February 21, 1955, p. 124.
23. James A. Michener, *Sayonara* (New York: Fawcett Crest Books, 1954), p. 139.
24. AG 291.1, ref. CSLLD 014.36-155, letter to Senator Claude Pepper from Col. C. G. Blakeney, GSC, August 29, 1949.
25. AG 291.1, ref. CSLLD 014.22-17, letter to Senator Kenneth S. Wherry from Col. C. G. Blakeney, GSC, October 10, 1949.
26. James A. Michener, "Japan," *The Voice of Asia* (New York: Random House, 1951), p. 17–18.

Chapter 14

1. AG 291.1, letter to the Honorable Oren Harris, House of Representatives, from Lt. Col. Lyle J. Robertson, GSC, Office of the Chief of Legislative Liaison, August 14, 1950.
2. Unidentified, undated news article entitled, "Truman Signing Alien Marriage Law Verified," from Hertha Rogers.
3. Robert A. Wilson and Bill Hosokawa, *East to America—A History of the Japanese in the United States* (New York: Quill, 1982), p. 259.
4. AG291.1, WDGPA/72403, ref. WDGPA 080, letter to Mike Masaoka from Col. F. P. Munson, Exec. Officer, Office of the Assistant Secretary of War, June 30, 1947.
5. WDGPA 291.1, memo to General Paul from Lt. Col. H. K. Whalen, Chief, Morale and Welfare Branch, War Department, Washington, D.C., August 25, 1947.

6. James A. Michener, "Pursuit of Happiness by a GI and a Japanese," *Life,* February 21, 1955, p. 126.
7. AG 291.1, ref. CSLLD 014.36-161, letter to Senator John C. Stennis from Col. C. G. Blakeney, GSC, October 11, 1949.
8. Janet Wentworth Smith and William L. Worden, "They're Bringing Home Japanese Wives," *Saturday Evening Post,* January 19, 1952, p. 27 and 79.
9. *Peace is Our Duty—Accounts of What War Can Do to Man,* compiled by the Youth Division of Soka Gakkai (Tokyo: *The Japan Times,* 1977), translated by Richard L. Gage, 1982, p. 221–222.
10. *Saturday Evening Post,* January 19, 1952, p. 79.
11. Jack Chen, *The Chinese in America,* (San Francisco: Harper & Row, 1982), p. 213.
12. Anselm L. Strauss, "Strain and Harmony in American-Japanese War-Bride Marriages," *Marriage and Family Living,* Vol. 16, No. 2, May 1954, p. 99.
13. Charles C. Moskos, Jr., Office of the Chief of Military History, General Reference Branch, *The American Enlisted Man,* (New York: Russell Sage Foundation, 1970), p. 95.
14. *Saturday Evening Post,* January 19, 1952, p. 79.
15. James A. Michener, *The Voice of Asia,* (New York: Random House, 1951), p. 23.

Chapter 15

1. Richard L. Neuberger, "This Is a World I Never Fought For," *New York Times Magazine,* July 23, 1946, p. 33.
2. *The New York Times,* June 9, 1946, p. 35.
3. Neuberger, p. 33.
4. Stephen Hall, "The Reluctant Superstar," *Attenzione,* November, 1980, p. 54.
5. James A. Michener, "Pursuit of Happiness by a GI and a Japanese," *Life,* February 21, 1955.
6. *Peace is Our Duty—Accounts of What War Can Do to Man,* compiled by the Youth Division of Soka Gakkai (Tokyo: *The Japan Times,* 1977), translated by Richard L. Gage, 1982, p. 223.
7. *The New York Times,* February 21, 1946, p. 11.
8. *The New York Times,* March 10, 1946, p. 6E.
9. *The New York Times,* January 13, 1946, p. 17.
10. *The New York Times,* July 24, 1946, p. 21.
11. Michener, "Pursuit of Happiness," p. 125.

12. Ruth Walrad, "The History of Home Service 1916–1947," in *The History of the American Red Cross*, Vol. 9, pp. 314–315. (ARC Archives)

13. Pfc. James M. Warren, "T/O Trouble: A Yank Dopey Drama," *Yank*, Vol. I, No. 9, September 24, 1944, p. 11.

14. Unidentified newsletter from private papers of a World War II veteran.

15. Anneliese Uhlig, *Rosenkavaliers Kind: Eine Frau und Drei Karrieren* (Munich: F. A. Herbig, 1977), p. 182.

16. Phillip McGuire, *Taps for a Jim Crow Army* (Santa Barbara, CA: ABC-Clio, Inc., 1983), p. 250.

Chapter 16

1. AG 291.12. April 30, 1942, letter from Maj. Gen. H. C. Pratt, Commanding General Caribbean Defense Command to Adjutant General, Washington, D.C.

2. "Becoming a Citizen," part of a lecture series entitled *A War Bride Talk* given by American Red Cross workers on the *Queen Mary* enroute to the U.S. in 1946. From private papers of Helen Thompson Colony.

3. Captain H. Cotton Minchin, "It's Your Country—Forget Yesterday, Live in Today, Believe in Tomorrow," speech reprinted in *The Kansas City Star*, August 1, 1946.

4. Ibid.

5. Oath of allegiance reprinted in "Becoming a Citizen," *A War Bride Talk*, ARC.

6. *Iowa News*, October 1, 1953.

7. May 18, 1984, letter from Dr. Jellinck, Bundesminister des Innern, West Germany, to Barbara Smith Scibetta (Ref. No. V II 5-124 406 II Smith Scibetta), translated by Ernst Knolle.

8. *Congressional Record*, Extension of Remarks, August 2, 1979.

9. Ingrid Hardy, *Plucky Lady: Memoirs of a Czech War Bride*, unpublished manuscript, p. 119.

10. Monica Dickens, *An Open Book* (New York: Mayflower Books/Heinemann, 1978), p. 191.

11. Anneliese Uhlig, *Rosenkavaliers Kind: Eine Frau und Drei Karrieren* (Munich: F. A. Herbig, 1977).

12. Anneliese Uhlig, *Einladung Nach Kalifornia* (Munich: Langen Muller, 1981).

13. Stephen Hall, "The Reluctant Superstar," *Attenzione*, November, 1980, p. 54.

14. Velina Hasu Houston, "On Being Mixed Japanese in Modern Times," *Pacific Citizen*, December 20–27, 1985, p. B1–3.

15. Elena J. Creef, *My Mother Was a Japanese War-Bride,* unpublished manu-
    script.
16. Kazu M. Unbehan, "Japanese War Brides in the United States," unpub-
    lished manuscript, Chapman College, Orange, California, December
    1983.

Selected Bibliography

ARCHIVES

American Red Cross
British Foreign Office/United States Correspondence Files 1946–1948, Jonsson Library of Government Documents, Stanford University
Center for Military History, National Archives, Washington, D.C.
Hoover Institute on War, Revolution and Peace, Stanford University
Library of Congress
U.S. Immigration and Naturalization Service

NONFICTION

Badoglio, Pietro. *Italy in the Second World War*. Trans. Muriel Currey. London: Oxford University Press, 1948.

Barnet, Richard J. *The Alliance: America—Europe—Japan, Makers of the Postwar World*. New York: Simon and Schuster, 1983.

Bourke-White, Margaret. *They Called It "Purple Heart Valley": A Combat Chronicle of the War in Italy*. New York: Simon and Schuster, 1944.

Chen, Jack. *The Chinese of America*. San Francisco: Harper & Row, 1982.

Chennault, Anna. *A Thousand Springs*. New York: Paul S. Eriksson, Inc., 1962.

Coles, Harry L., and Albert K. Weinberg. *Civil Affairs: Soldiers Become Governors*, United States Army in World War II, Special Studies. Washington, D.C.: Office of the Chief of Military History, Department of the Army, 1964.

Davis, Franklin M., Jr. *Come as a Conqueror: The United States Army's Occupation of Germany 1945–1949*. New York: The Macmillan Company, 1967.

De Conde, Alexander. *Half Bitter, Half Sweet: An Excursion into Italian-American History*. New York: Charles Scribner's Sons, 1971.

DeWitt, MacKenzie. *The Associated Press Annual 1946, Volume II*. New York: Rinehart & Co., Inc., 1947.

Dickens, Monica. *An Open Book*. New York: Mayflower Books/Heinemann, 1978.

Editors of Time-Life Books. *The Aftermath: Asia; The Aftermath: Europe; The Fall of Japan; The Home Front: Germany; The Italian Campaign;*

Italy at War; Liberation; Prisoners of War; Return to the Philippines; The Second Front. Alexandria, Virginia: Time-Life Books, 1981–1983.

Fawkes, Richard. *Fighting for a Laugh: Entertaining British and American Armed Forces 1939–1946.* London: Macdonald and Jane's, 1978.

Friedrich, Carl J. and Associates. *American Experiences in Military Government in World War II.* New York: Rinehart & Company, Inc., 1948.

Gimbel, John. *The American Occupation of Germany: Politics and the Military, 1945–1949.* Stanford, California: Stanford University Press, 1968.

Gorel, A. Gruner. *The Philippines and the United States.* Norman, Oklahoma: University of Oklahoma Press, 1951.

Habe, Hans. *Our Love Affair with Germany.* New York: G. P. Putnam's Sons, 1953.

Hale, Edwin R. W. and John Frayn Turner. *The Yanks Are Coming.* New York: Hippocrene Books, Inc., 1983.

Hibbert, Joyce. *The War Brides.* Toronto, Canada: PMA Books, 1978.

Higgs, Maria. *Maria.* Badger Press, Inc., 1981.

Hill, Robert M., and Elizabeth Craig Hill. *In the Wake of War.* University, Alabama: The University of Alabama Press, 1982.

Hillel, Marc. *Die Invasion der Be-Freier: Die GIs in Europa 1942–1947.* Hamburg: Ernst Kabel Verlag, 1983.

Hughes, H. Stuart. *The United States and Italy.* 3rd edition, enlarged. Cambridge, Massachusetts: Harvard University Press, 1979 (original edition published 1953).

Hunter, Brigitte. *Kitty.* Frankfurt am Main: Stroemfeld/Roter Stern, 1981.

Kim, Bok-Lim C. et al. *Women in Shadows: A Handbook for Service Providers Working with Asian Wives of U.S. Military Personnel.* La Jolla, California: National Committee Concerned with Asian Wives of U.S. Servicemen, 1981.

Kosaka, Masataka. *A History of Postwar Japan.* San Francisco: Kodansha International, Ltd., 1982.

Kubat, Daniel, et al. *The Politics of Migration Policies.* New York: Center for Migration Studies, 1979.

Lasker, Bruno. *Asia on the Move.* New York: Henry Holt & Co., 1945.

Lewis, Norman. *Naples '44.* New York: Pantheon Books, a Division of Random House, Inc., 1978.

Liebling, A. J. *Liebling Abroad.* New York: Playboy Press, 1981.

Longmate, Norman. *The G.I.'s: The Americans in Britain 1942–1945.* London: Hutchinson & Co., Ltd., 1975.

Mammarella, Giuseppe. *Italy After Fascism: A Political History, 1943–1965.* Notre Dame, Indiana: University of Notre Dame Press, 1966.

Manninen, Talvikki. *Refuge under the Boot*. New York: Vantage Press, 1985.

McGuire, Phillip. *Taps for a Jim Crow Army, Letters from Black Soldiers in World War II*. Santa Barbara, California: ABC-Clio, Inc., 1983.

Michener, James A. *The Voice of Asia*. New York: Random House, 1951.

Moore, John Hammond. *Over-Sexed, Over-Paid, & Over Here—Americans in Australia 1941–45*. St. Lucia, Queensland: University of Queensland Press, 1981.

O'Hara, Peggy. *From Romance to Reality*. Ontario, Canada: Highway Book Shop, 1983.

Origo, Iris. *War in Val D'Orcia, 1943–1944, A Diary,* intro. Denis Mack Smith. Boston: David R. Godine, Publisher, 1984.

Peace is Our Duty—Accounts of What War Can Do to Man. Compiled by the Youth Division of Soka Gakkai. Trans. Richard L. Gage. Tokyo: *The Japan Times,* 1982.

Potts, E. Daniel and Annette. *Yanks Down Under 1941–1945*. New York: Oxford University Press, 1985.

Schechtman, Joseph B. *Postwar Population Transfers in Europe 1945–1955*. Philadelphia, Pennsylvania: University of Pennsylvania Press, 1962.

Schmitt, Hans A. *U.S. Occupation in Europe After World War II*. Lawrence, Kansas: The Regents Press of Kansas, 1978.

Shelton, Regina Maria. *To Lose a War: Memories of a German Girl*. Carbondale, Illinois: Southern Illinois University Press, 1982.

Trevelyan, Raleigh. *Rome '44: The Battle for the Eternal City*. New York: The Viking Press, 1981.

Uhlig, Anneliese. *Rosenkavaliers Kind: Eine Frau und Drei Karrieren*. Munich: F. A. Herbig, 1977.

War Brides and Their Shipment to the United States, Occupation Forces in Europe Series 1945–1946. Headquarters European Command: Office of the Chief Historian European Command.

White, Theodore H. *In Search of History: A Personal Adventure*. New York: Warner Books, 1978.

Wilson, Robert A. and Bill Hosokawa. *East to America: A History of the Japanese in the United States*. New York: Quill, 1982.

Winfield, Pamela and Brenda Wilson Hasty. *Sentimental Journey*. London: Constable, 1984.

Yung, Judy. *Chinese Women in America: A Pictorial History*. Seattle, Washington: University of Washington Press, 1986.

Zink, Harold. *The United States in Germany 1944–1955*. Princeton, New Jersey: D. Van Nostrand Company, Inc., 1957.

FICTION

Battle, Lois. *War Brides*. New York: St. Martin's Press, 1982.

Burns, John Horne. *The Gallery*. New York and London: Harper & Brothers Publishers, 1947.

Chu, Louis. *Eat a Bowl of Tea*. Seattle, Washington: University of Washington Press, 1979.

Deighton, Len. *Goodbye, Mickey Mouse*. New York: Ballantine Books, 1982.

Dickens, Monica. *No More Meadows*. London: Wyman & Sons, Ltd., 1953. (Published in the U.S. as *The Nightingales are Singing*.)

Habe, Hans. *Off Limits*. Trans. Ewald Osers. New York: Frederick Fell, Inc., 1957 (originally published in German by Verlag Kurt Desch, reprinted 1985 by Langen-Muller Verlag, Munich).

————. *Walk in Darkness*. Trans. Richard Hanser. New York: G. P. Putnam's Sons, 1948 (originally published in German as *Weg ins Dunkel*, reprinted 1980 by Langen-Muller Verlag, Munich).

Ishiguro, Kazuo. *A Pale View of Hills*. New York: Penguin Books, 1983.

Michener, James A. *Sayonara*. New York: Fawcett Crest, 1954.

————. *Tales of the South Pacific*. New York: Fawcett Crest, 1954.

Morante, Elsa. *History: A Novel*, trans. William Weaver. New York: Vintage Books, 1984 (originally published in Italian as *La Storia: Romanzo*, c. 1974).

Moravia, Alberto. *Two Women*, trans. Angus Davidson. New York: Playboy Paperbacks, 1981 (originally published in 1958 in Italy).

Puzo, Mario. *The Dark Arena*. New York: Bantam Books, 1953.

UNPUBLISHED MANUSCRIPTS

Björnsdóttir, Inga Dóra. *Images of Women Who Dated American Servicemen and of the Americans in Two Icelandic Novels*. University of Arizona, Tucson, 1981.

Creef, Elena J. *My Mother Was a Japanese War Bride*.

Hardy, Ingrid. *Plucky Lady: Memoirs of a Czech War Bride*.

Houston, Velina Hasu. *Asa Ga Kimashita ("Morning Has Broken")*. [play]

————. *Tea*. [play]

Street, Betty Eulalia. *The Adjustment of Foreign War Brides*. Thesis, University of North Carolina, Chapel Hill, 1948.

Unbehan, Kazu M. *Japanese War Brides in the United States*. Orange, California: Chapman College, December 1983.

Index